Social Justice

Opposing
Viewpoints ®

Other Books of Related Interest in the Opposing Viewpoints Series:

American Values
Civil Liberties
Criminal Justice
Economics in America
The Elderly
The Homeless
Immigration
Male/Female Roles
Poverty
Violence in America
War on Drugs

Additional Books in the Opposing Viewpoints Series:

Abortion
AIDS
American Foreign Policy
American Government
America's Elections
America's Future
America's Prisons
Animal Rights
Biomedical Ethics
Censorship
Central America
Chemical Dependency
China
Constructing a Life Philosophy
Crime and Criminals
Death and Dying
The Death Penalty
Drug Abuse
Eastern Europe
The Environmental Crisis
Euthanasia
Genetic Engineering
The Health Crisis
Israel
Japan
Latin America and U.S. Foreign Policy
The Mass Media
The Middle East
Nuclear War
The Political Spectrum
Problems of Africa
Religion in America
Science & Religion
Sexual Values
The Soviet Union
The Superpowers: A New Detente
Teenage Sexuality
Terrorism
The Third World
The Vietnam War
War and Human Nature

Social Justice
Opposing
Viewpoints ®

David Bender & Bruno Leone, *Series Editors*

Carol Wekesser, *Book Editor*
Karin Swisher & Janelle Rohr, *Assistant Editors*

OPPOSING VIEWPOINTS SERIES ®

Greenhaven Press, Inc.   PO Box 289009   San Diego, CA 92198-0009

No part of this book may be reproduced or used in any form or
by any means, electrical, mechanical, or otherwise, including,
but not limited to, photocopy, recording, or any information
storage and retrieval system, without prior written permission
from the publisher.

Library of Congress Cataloging-in-Publication Data

Social justice : opposing viewpoints / Carol Wekesser and Karin
Swisher, book editors.
    p.   cm. — (Opposing viewpoints series)
Includes bibliographical references and index.
Summary: Observers present differing views on issues of
economic and social justice in the United States, focusing
especially on the question of just treatment of minorities and
women.
    ISBN 0-89908-457-5 (pap.). — ISBN 0-89908-482-6 (lib.)
    1. Civil rights—United States.   2. Minorities—Civil
rights—United States.   3. Social justice.   4. United States—
Social policy.   5. United States—Economic policy. [1. Civil
rights.   2. Minorities—Civil rights.   3. Social justice.] I.
Wekesser, Carol, 1963- . II. Swisher, Karin, 1966- . III.
Series: Opposing viewpoints series (Unnumbered)
JC599.U5S5945   1990
323'.0973—dc20   90-42855

"Congress shall make no law . . . abridging the freedom of speech, or of the press."

First Amendment to the U.S. Constitution

The basic foundation of our democracy is the first amendment guarantee of freedom of expression. The Opposing Viewpoints Series is dedicated to the concept of this basic freedom and the idea that it is more important to practice it than to enshrine it.

Contents

Chapter 5: What Policies Can Promote Social Justice?

Why Consider Opposing Viewpoints?

"It is better to debate a question without settling it than to settle a question without debating it."

Joseph Joubert (1754-1824)

The Importance of Examining Opposing Viewpoints

The purpose of the Opposing Viewpoints Series, and this book in particular, is to present balanced, and often difficult to find, opposing points of view on complex and sensitive issues.

Probably the best way to become informed is to analyze the positions of those who are regarded as experts and well studied on issues. It is important to consider every variety of opinion in an attempt to determine the truth. Opinions from the mainstream of society should be examined. But also important are opinions that are considered radical, reactionary, or minority as well as those stigmatized by some other uncomplimentary label. An important lesson of history is the eventual acceptance of many unpopular and even despised opinions. The ideas of Socrates, Jesus, and Galileo are good examples of this.

Readers will approach this book with their own opinions on the issues debated within it. However, to have a good grasp of one's own viewpoint, it is necessary to understand the arguments of those with whom one disagrees. It can be said that those who do not completely understand their adversary's point of view do not fully understand their own.

A persuasive case for considering opposing viewpoints has been presented by John Stuart Mill in his work *On Liberty*. When examining controversial issues it may be helpful to reflect on this suggestion:

9

The only way in which a human being can make some approach to knowing the whole of a subject, is by hearing what can be said about it by persons of every variety of opinion, and studying all modes in which it can be looked at by every character of mind. No wise man ever acquired his wisdom in any mode but this.

Analyzing Sources of Information

The Opposing Viewpoints Series includes diverse materials taken from magazines, journals, books, and newspapers, as well as statements and position papers from a wide range of individuals, organizations, and governments. This broad spectrum of sources helps to develop patterns of thinking which are open to the consideration of a variety of opinions.

Pitfalls to Avoid

A pitfall to avoid in considering opposing points of view is that of regarding one's own opinion as being common sense and the most rational stance, and the point of view of others as being only opinion and naturally wrong. It may be that another's opinion is correct and one's own is in error.

Another pitfall to avoid is that of closing one's mind to the opinions of those with whom one disagrees. The best way to approach a dialogue is to make one's primary purpose that of understanding the mind and arguments of the other person and not that of enlightening him or her with one's own solutions. More can be learned by listening than speaking.

It is my hope that after reading this book the reader will have a deeper understanding of the issues debated and will appreciate the complexity of even seemingly simple issues on which good and honest people disagree. This awareness is particularly important in a democratic society such as ours where people enter into public debate to determine the common good. Those with whom one disagrees should not necessarily be regarded as enemies, but perhaps simply as people who suggest different paths to a common goal.

Developing Basic Reading and Thinking Skills

In this book, carefully edited opposing viewpoints are purposely placed back to back to create a running debate; each viewpoint is preceded by a short quotation that best expresses the author's main argument. This format instantly plunges the reader into the midst of a controversial issue and greatly aids that reader in mastering the basic skill of recognizing an author's point of view.

A number of basic skills for critical thinking are practiced in the activities that appear throughout the books in the series. Some of the skills are:

Evaluating Sources of Information. The ability to choose from among alternative sources the most reliable and accurate source in relation to a given subject.

Separating Fact from Opinion. The ability to make the basic distinction between factual statements (those that can be demonstrated or verified empirically) and statements of opinion (those that are beliefs or attitudes that cannot be proved).

Identifying Stereotypes. The ability to identify oversimplified, exaggerated descriptions (favorable or unfavorable) about people and insulting statements about racial, religious, or national groups, based upon misinformation or lack of information.

Recognizing Ethnocentrism. The ability to recognize attitudes or opinions that express the view that one's own race, culture, or group is inherently superior, or those attitudes that judge another culture or group in terms of one's own.

It is important to consider opposing viewpoints and equally important to be able to critically analyze those viewpoints. The activities in this book are designed to help the reader master these thinking skills. Statements are taken from the book's viewpoints and the reader is asked to analyze them. This technique aids the reader in developing skills that not only can be applied to the viewpoints in this book, but also to situations where opinionated spokespersons comment on controversial issues. Although the activities are helpful to the solitary reader, they are most useful when the reader can benefit from the interaction of group discussion.

Using this book and others in the series should help readers develop basic reading and thinking skills. These skills should improve the reader's ability to understand what is read. Readers should be better able to separate fact from opinion, substance from rhetoric, and become better consumers of information in our media-centered culture.

This volume of the Opposing Viewpoints Series does not advocate a particular point of view. Quite the contrary! The very nature of the book leaves it to the reader to formulate the opinions he or she finds most suitable. My purpose as publisher is to see that this is made possible by offering a wide range of viewpoints that are fairly presented.

David L. Bender
Publisher

Introduction

"America, in the assembly of nations, has uniformly spoken among them the language of equal liberty, equal justice, and equal rights."

John Quincy Adams 1767-1848

The United States is just one of many countries born of the violence of revolution. Unlike many nations, however, the United States has consistently attempted to sustain the ideals chiseled from its revolutionary past. Justice, liberty, and equality remain American goals. Every schoolchild can recite Abraham Lincoln's moving words that bind equality inextricably with the goals of our nation: "Fourscore and seven years ago, our fathers brought forth on this continent a new nation, conceived in Liberty and dedicated to the proposition that all men are created equal." This idealism places America at the center of a basic dilemma: If equal justice is guaranteed to all American citizens, how can Americans allow unequal conditions to exist?

In order to eradicate unequal conditions, the U.S. government has played in the past, and continues to play, a substantial role. Social security, the New Deal, affirmative action, and the civil rights amendments are all examples of a government attempting to assure equal justice, the final aim being for America to exist both in reality, as in philosophy, as the country that places the equality of individuals above all else.

However, government attempts to remove social inequities through regulation and legislation have often proven controversial. After all, it is argued, America is the land of opportunity, and as such, individuals should be able to achieve their goals without the aid of government. In the middle of the nineteenth century, Horatio Alger's popular stories showed ordinary people succeeding in America simply by displaying industry and other allegedly positive personal qualities. Alger's "Match Stick" boy, Mark, rose above his humble beginnings by hard work, resolve, and cleverness. By becoming a self-made millionaire, Mark informed countless legions of American readers that success, acceptance, and equality could be achieved by personal, not governmental, initiative.

Not everyone agrees with Alger's optimism. Alexis de Tocqueville, for example, believed inequality to be a natural state, one that people, government, and laws are unable to alter. He wrote over a century ago in *Democracy in America*, "People will never succeed in reducing all the conditions of society to a perfect level; and even if they unhappily attained that absolute and complete equality, inequality of minds would still remain." In contrast, Abraham Lincoln believed equality should be something "constantly looked to, constantly labored for and even though never perfectly attained, constantly approximated and thereby constantly spreading." He challenged America to strive toward the perfection of equality at all times.

Social Justice: Opposing Viewpoints replaces Greenhaven Press's 1984 book of the same title. This volume contains all new viewpoints and several new topics. The authors in this anthology debate the following questions: Is the U.S. a Just Nation? Does America's Economy Promote Social Justice? Does the U.S. Provide Equal Opportunities for Minorities? What Policies Would Promote Social Justice for Women? What Policies Can Promote Social Justice? These questions reflect the deeper and broader issue of how America can live up to the ideals upon which it was founded and create a society in which all people are truly equal.

Is the U.S. a Just Nation?

Social Justice

Chapter Preface

"The freedoms flowing from [the Constitution] created a land of opportunities. Ever since then discouraged and oppressed people from every part of the world have made their way to our shores. . . . This is the meaning of our Constitution." These words by former U.S. Supreme Court chief justice Warren Burger reflect the belief many Americans have in the power of the U.S. Constitution to promote freedom and equality and to provide opportunities for all citizens. Unlike the constitutions of some other nations, the U.S. Constitution guarantees such basic rights as the freedom to worship, speak, and assemble. Many Americans would agree with these words of former U.S. Supreme Court justice David Davis: "The Constitution of the United States is a law for rulers and people . . . and covers with the shield of its protection all classes of men, at all times, and under all circumstances."

Other Americans, like political science professor Bertell Ollman, view the Constitution as flawed because it fails to guarantee the needs and rights of poor and disadvantaged Americans. The Constitution was written by wealthy white men who worked in secret to create a document that promoted their own interests, Ollman and others contend. They argue that the founders created a strong federal government, protected private property, and promoted private enterprise to provide opportunities for the wealthy and powerful while keeping many Americans poor and powerless. Rather than establishing a land of opportunity, "the founding fathers were determined to write a charter of government that would ensure control over common people by men of property," author Philip Agee writes.

The following chapter will debate the status of justice in the United States and whether justice is present in the Constitution, in the courts, and in American society itself.

"The Constitution of the United States is unusual . . . in the way that it protects the rights of the people."

The U.S. Constitution Guarantees Social Justice

Robert A. Goldwin

Robert A. Goldwin, an author known for his articles on human rights, education, politics, and the Constitution, is a resident scholar and director of constitutional studies at the American Enterprise Institute in Washington, D.C. He has edited or co-edited more than twenty books on American politics, including *How Democratic Is the Constitution?*, *How Capitalistic Is the Constitution?*, and *How Does the Constitution Protect Religious Freedom?* Goldwin believes in the U.S. Constitution, and in the following viewpoint he defends his beliefs by explaining how the Constitution promotes social justice and protects the rights of blacks, women, and Jews.

As you read, consider the following questions:

1. What evidence did Frederick Douglass give to show that the Constitution is not pro-slavery, according to Goldwin?
2. What does the author feel are the qualities of a good constitution?
3. How does the Constitution protect minority groups by not directly mentioning them, according to Goldwin?

Robert A. Goldwin, *Why Blacks, Women, and Jews Are Not Mentioned in the Constitution, and Other Unorthodox Views.* Washington, DC: AEI Press, 1990. Reprinted with permission of the American Enterprise Institute for Public Policy Research.

The bicentennial we celebrated in 1987 honored the Constitution written in 1787, that is, the original, unamended Constitution. Some well-meaning citizens denounced celebrating or even praising that Constitution. They contended that its many severe defects should be considered a matter of national shame. For example, lacking the Thirteenth Amendment, the original Constitution permitted slavery to continue; lacking the Nineteenth Amendment, it did not secure the right of women to vote; and, lacking the First Amendment, it provided no protection for religious freedom, not to mention other rights. Why, they ask, should we celebrate a constitution that treated blacks as less than human, that left women out, and that did not combat religious intolerance?

Misreading the Constitution

These charges would be distressing if true, but fortunately they are false. They stem from a misreading of the document, a misreading that comes from not appreciating the importance of knowing how to read the original Constitution on subjects it does not mention.

Why bother with subjects not mentioned? Because we have no choice. The list of unusually important subjects the Constitution does not mention is very long. The fact that they are not mentioned has not prevented cases and controversies from arising, nor has it relieved courts and legislatures of the duty of determining what is constitutional with regard to them. The words "education" and "school," for example, do not occur in the Constitution, but even so the courts have been busy for decades deciding school controversies. There is no mention of labor unions, corporations, political parties, the air force, radio and television broadcasting, telecommunications, and so on, but the courts deliberate constitutional controversies on these subjects all the time. The list of subjects not mentioned in the text of the Constitution also includes words like "abortion," "contraceptives," and "sodomy" and phrases like "right to privacy," "substantive due process," "separation of powers," and the "high wall separating church and state"—all matters on which the Supreme Court has pronounced.

The inescapable fact is that many subjects not mentioned in the Constitution must be interpreted, unavoidably, by anyone for whom the meaning of the Constitution is important. My argument is that there are valuable lessons to be learned about how we are constituted as a nation and what in the original Constitution is worth celebrating, by devoting serious attention to subjects not mentioned in it. For that purpose, I propose close attention to three such subjects—blacks, women, and Jews. . . .

In the original Constitution there is no mention of color, race, or slavery, and nowhere in it are slaves called anything but "persons."

There is nothing new in the point that the original Constitution does not mention slavery. Luther Martin, a Maryland delegate to the Constitutional Convention who opposed ratification, explained to the Maryland legislature in 1787 that the authors of the Constitution did not use the word slave because they "anxiously sought to avoid the admission of expressions which might be odious in the ears of Americans." And the great black leader and orator Frederick Douglass commented on this silence in 1852, arguing against the "slander" on the memory of the founders that the original Constitution was pro-slavery. "In that instrument," he said, "I hold there is neither warrant, license, nor sanction of the hateful thing." And a major element of his evidence is that "neither *slavery, slaveholding*, nor *slave* can anywhere be found in it. . . . Now, take the Constitution according to its plain reading, and I defy the presentation of a single pro-slavery clause in it."

The Rights of All

In our system of government, the rights of all, liberals and conservatives, people of all races and both sexes, the majority and minority groups, are accorded constitutional protection.

Mary Frances Barry, *The New York Times Magazine*, September 13, 1987.

These two very different speakers, Luther Martin and Frederick Douglass, knew this fact about the silence of the Constitution about slavery, and so did many, many others. But apparently it needed to be pointed out in their times, and it needs to be pointed out today. And especially when we recall that there is an equal silence about race, do we see the importance of reminding ourselves about this point that seems to have been forgotten or persistently ignored by most Americans. . . .

Despite the existence of slavery and the persistence of it for seventy-five years more, the founders left us with a constitutional document that has accommodated a very different order of things with regard to the place in our society of the descendants of former slaves. I do not contend that delegates foresaw the present-day consequences of emancipation, that the descendants of black slaves would become voting citizens and officeholders throughout the nation. But the founders left in their text no obstacles to the profound improvements that have come about. After the addition of the amendments abolishing slavery, the text retained no residue of racism, however much of it may remain in the society itself.

Therefore when the time came to terminate official segregation, we had to purge the racial provisions from federal regulations like those segregating the armed forces, and from state constitutions and state and local laws—but not from the Constitution of the United States. In fact, lawyers and judges were able to argue for profound changes by asserting that they were in accord with and demanded by the Constitution. We did not have to change it to fit new circumstances and times. Instead, the argument could be made, and was made, that conditions had to be changed to fit the Constitution. In that historic national effort, it made a very great difference that there was no racism in the original Constitution.

We must acknowledge that there was indeed intense and widespread racism among Americans, which helped to sustain for so long the vicious system of black slavery and its century-long aftermath of racial segregation, discrimination, persecution, and hatred. How best can we understand the meaning of this disjunction between the racism in the society and the absence of it in the written Constitution?

If a written constitution is not in close accord with the way the society itself is constituted, it will be irrelevant to the everyday life of the people. A constitution will be a failure if it is no more than a beautiful portrait of an ugly society. But it must be more than an accurate depiction of how the society is constituted. A good constitution provides guidance and structure for the improvement of the society. A good constitution is designed to make the political society better than it is and the citizens better persons. It must be enough like the institutions and the people to be relevant to the working of the society, but it should also have what might be called formative features, a capacity to make us better if we live according to its provisions and adhere to its institutional arrangements. The constitutional goal for Americans would be to develop a nation of self-governing, liberty-loving citizens in a new kind of political society where the fundamental rights of all would be secure—and that would mean a society where slavery would have no place.

A Better Society

In that formative way of thinking about the task of constitution writing, it seems entirely possible that the most foresighted and skillful of the founders sought to make a constitution that—while accepting and even protecting slavery for a time as an unavoidable evil, the price to pay for union—tried to make provisions for its ultimate extinction. They even gave thought to the constitutional preparations for a better society that would eventually be free of slavery. In that respect the original Constitution was better than the political society it constituted.

We would face a very different situation in our own time if there had been in the original Constitution any evidence of the kind of thinking ascribed to the founders by Chief Justice Taney in the *Dred Scott* case. Taney said that the founders thought that blacks were not included in the declaration that "all men are created equal," and that blacks were "so far inferior, that they had no rights which the white man was bound to respect." But Taney was wrong; there is no such racism to be found in the Constitution, then or now, not a word of it. Those who wrongly assert, however laudable their motives, that the three-fifths clause" was racist, that it somehow denied the humanity of blacks, do a disservice to the truth and also to the Constitution, to the nation, and to the cause of justice and equality for black Americans.

No Mention of Women

The fact that blacks are not mentioned in the original Constitution requires some explanation because there are several provisions obviously concerning black slavery. But no such explanation is required in the case of women. Not only are women not mentioned in the original Constitution, there is no provision anywhere that applies to women as a distinct group. To the best of my knowledge, there is no evidence that the subject of women was ever mentioned in the Constitutional Convention.

A Law for All People

The Constitution of the United States is a law for rulers and people, equally in war and in peace, and covers with the shield of its protection all classes of men, at all times, and under all circumstances.

U.S. Supreme Court Justice David Davis, *Ex Parte Milligan,* 1868.

This has led to the charge, heard frequently during the prolonged debate over the proposed Equal Rights Amendment, that "women were left out of the Constitution." The fact is, however, that women were not left out; they have always been included in all of the constitutional protections provided to all persons, fully and equally, without any basis in the text for discrimination on the basis of sex. How were they included without being mentioned? . . .

In the original Constitution, the words "man" or "male" do not occur, nor does any other noun or adjective denoting sex. By not mentioning women or men and speaking instead only of persons, the Constitution must mean that every right, privilege, and protection afforded to persons in the Constitution is afforded equally to female persons as well as male persons.

The terms used throughout the original Constitution are consistently what are now called nonsexist: for example, "electors," "citizens," "members," "inhabitants," "officers," "representatives," "persons." There are pronouns—"he," "his," and "himself"—but in the entire text of the original Constitution, as I have said, there is not a single noun or adjective that denotes sex.

There are some who think that because of these pronouns, all masculine, the founders meant that only men were to hold national office, and most certainly the presidency. But it can be shown that the text itself presents no obstacle whatever to having a woman in the office of president or any other national office, because these pronouns can clearly be read as generic or neutral or genderless—or whatever we call a pronoun capable of denoting either sex.

No Obstacles to Women

The Constitution says of the president, *"He* shall hold *his* office during the term of four years"* (the emphasis here and throughout this section is added). It says that when a bill passed by Congress is presented to the president, "if *he* approves *he* shall sign it, but if not *he* shall return it," etc. There are similar usages of the pronoun for the vice president and for members of Congress. Are those pronouns exclusively masculine and therefore a definitive indication that the offices are to be held by men only, or could they be genderless pronouns, leaving open the possibility that the antecedent is meant to be either a man or a woman? If the latter is the case, as is my contention, then there is no obstacle in the Constitution, and there never has been, to a woman's occupying any office under the Constitution of the United States, including the presidency, and every protection and every right extended to men by the Constitution is extended equally to women. . . .

We are speaking, of course, of a written document, the text of the original Constitution, which is not the same as asserting that women enjoyed political equality in practice in 1787, or for a long time thereafter. Women's suffrage in the United States seems to have begun in 1838, when women in Kentucky voted in school elections. Women voted on an equal basis with men for the first time anywhere in the United States in 1869, in the Wyoming Territory. But as late as 1914, only ten more states, in addition to the state of Wyoming, had accorded women the right to vote. It was not until the Nineteenth Amendment was ratified in 1920 that the right to vote was made secure for women. That amendment provides that: "The right of citizens of the United

States to vote shall not be denied or abridged by the United States or by any State on account of sex."

First we must observe that this addition to the Constitution, amended nothing and was intended to amend nothing in the Constitution of the United States. No provision in the text had to be changed or deleted, because there was never any provision in the Constitution limiting or denying the right of women to vote. The barriers to voting by women had always been in the state constitutions or laws.

The Logic of the Constitution

The relentless logic of a Constitution in the name of the people is that a national state exists for their sake, not the other way around. The undeviating logic of a Constitution in the name of the people is that the privilege of life under its domain is equitable, which is to say, universal. That you cannot have democracy only for yourself or your club or your class or your church or your clan or your color or your sex, for then the word doesn't mean what it says. That once you write the prophetic text for a true democracy—as our forefathers did in their draft and as our amending legislators and judiciary have continued to do in their editing of its moral self-contradictions and methodological inadequacies—that once this text is in voice, it cannot be said to be realized on earth until all the relations among the American people, legal relations, property relations, are made just.

E.L. Doctorow, *The Nation*, February 21, 1987.

It may very well be that the founders never contemplated the possibility of a woman as president, or even of women voting on an equal basis with men. Nevertheless, the text they adopted and that the American people ratified presents no obstacle whatsoever to the changes that have occurred.

Religion and the Constitution

The significance of not being mentioned in the Constitution becomes clearest when we consider the last of the three unmentioned subjects—Jews. Most of us, when we think of the Constitution and freedom of religion, think of the double security provided by the First Amendment, against "an establishment of religion" and for the "free exercise thereof." These protections were not, of course, part of the original Constitution. The original Constitution mentions religion just once, but that one provision is remarkable. Article VI, section 3, says simply that "no religious test shall ever be required as a qualification to any office or public trust under the United States.". . .

Religious toleration was amazingly prevalent in America,

given the intensity of religious conviction observable everywhere, but political equality for members of different religious groups was rare. That is, provisions for the free exercise of religion were common in the state constitutions; but political equality was a different story. The free exercise of religion happened in church or synagogue; it did not ensure the right to vote or hold office. Nevertheless, for whatever reasons, in a nation that had almost universal religious testing for state offices, the delegates proposed and the states ratified a constitution barring religious tests for holding national office.

Add to this the less easily discernible fact that Jews are not mentioned in the Constitution. As we view things now, that Jews are not mentioned is no more remarkable than that Baptists or Roman Catholics or Muslims or any others are also not mentioned. But Jews had never been treated simply as "persons," let alone "citizens," anywhere in the world for more than 1,500 years. By not mentioning them, that is, by not singling them out—the Constitution made Jews full citizens of a nation for the first time in all Diaspora history. By this silence, coupled with the prohibition of religious tests, the founders "opened a door" to Jews and to all other sects as well.

Unspoken Principles

The Constitution of the United States is unusual, and perhaps unique, among the constitutions of the world in the way that it protects the rights of the people. The unspoken principles—at least unspoken in the Constitution—are that rights are inherent in individuals, not in the groups they belong to; that we are all equal as human beings in the sense that no matter what our color, sex, national origin, or religion, we are equal in the possession of the rights that governments are instituted to protect; and that as a consequence, the only source of legitimate political power is the consent of the governed. Because these principles, all stemming from the primacy of individual rights, are the unmentioned foundation of the Constitution, it is not only unnecessary to mention race, sex, or religion, it is inconsistent and harmful.

In short, the reason no group of any sort included in the nation it founded is mentioned in the Constitution—originally and now—is that the founders designed a better way to make sure that no one was left out, and that everyone was included on a basis of equality.

To anyone who asks why we should celebrate this Constitution, let that be the answer.

"The Constitution provides us with a kind of bourgeois fairy tale in which claims to equal rights and responsibilities are substituted for the harsh realities of class domination."

The U.S. Constitution Does Not Guarantee Social Justice

Bertell Ollman

The U.S. Constitution promotes injustice because it promotes capitalism, Bertell Ollman contends in the following viewpoint. Ollman, a professor of political science at New York University, argues that the wealthy writers of the Constitution created a document that protects the interests of the wealthy and powerful. He points out that the Constitution did not protect the interests of blacks and women, who had to struggle for decades to achieve equality. Ollman is the author of several books, including *Alienation: Marx's Conception of Man in Capitalist Society* and *Class Struggle Is the Name of the Game: The Confessions of a Marxist Businessman.*

As you read, consider the following questions:

1. Why did the framers of the Constitution shroud their work in secrecy, according to Ollman?
2. What does the author see as the three levels of criticisms made against the Constitution?
3. What is the most fundamental contradiction in the Constitution, according to the author?

When Moses invented ten fundamental laws for the Jewish people, he had God write them down on stone tablets. Lycurgus, too, represented the constitution he drew up for ancient Sparta as a divine gift. According to Plato, whose book, *The Republic* offers another version of the same practice, attributing the origins of a constitution to godly intervention is the most effective way of securing the kind of support needed for it to work. Otherwise, some people are likely to remain skeptical, others passive, and still others critical of whatever biases they perceive in these basic laws and hence less inclined to follow their mandates.

Closely Guarded Secret

As learned men, the framers of the American Constitution were well aware of the advantages to be gained by enveloping their achievement in religious mystery, but most of the people for whom they labored were religious dissenters who favored a sharp separation between Church and State; and since most of the framers were deists and atheists themselves, this particular tactic could not be used. So they did the next best thing, which was to keep the whole process of their work on the Constitution a closely guarded secret. Most Americans know that the framers met for three months in closed session, but this is generally forgiven on the grounds that the then Congress of the United States had not commissioned them to write a new Constitution, and neither revolutionaries nor counterrevolutionaries can do all their work in the open. What few modern-day Americans realize, however, is that the framers did their best to insure that we would never know the details of their deliberations. All the participants in the convention were sworn to life-long secrecy, and when the debates were over, those who had taken notes were asked to hand them in to George Washington, whose final task as chairman of the convention was to get rid of the evidence. America's first President, it appears, was also its first shredder.

Fortunately, not all the participants kept their vows of silence or handed in all their notes. But it wasn't until 1840, a half century after the Constitution was put into effect, with the posthumous surfacing of James Madison's extensive notes, that the American people could finally read what had happened in those three crucial months in Philadelphia. What was revealed was neither divine nor diabolical, but simply human, an all-too-human exercise in politics. Merchants, bankers, shipowners, planters, slave traders and slave owners, land speculators, and lawyers who made their money working for these groups, voiced their interests and fears in clear, uncluttered language; and, after settling a few, relatively minor disagreements, they drew up plans for a form of government they believed would serve these interests most effectively. But the fifty years of silence had the desired myth-building effect. The human actors were transformed into "Founding Fathers," their political savvy and common sense were now seen as all-surpassing wisdom, and their concern for their own class of property owners (and, to a lesser extent, sections of the country and occupational groups) had been elevated to universal altruism (in the liberal version) or self-sacrificing patriotism (in the preferred conservative view). Nor have we been completely spared the aura of religious mystery so favored by Plato. With the passage of years and the growing religiosity of our citizenry, it has become almost commonplace to hear that the framers were also divinely inspired. . . .

Controlling the Common People

The founding fathers were determined to write a charter of government that would ensure control over common people (the majority) by men of property (a small minority) whose determination to use and accumulate more property (and power) they saw as their "natural right." Among other instruments of force, they provided in the new Constitution for a national army to put down revolt, for federal takeover of state militias, for suspension of habeas corpus and for federal control of interstate and foreign commerce. For good measure they made these "rules of the game" exceedingly hard to change.

Philip Agee, *The Guardian*, October 11, 1989.

What is in danger of being lost among all the patriotic nonsequiturs is the underside of criticism and protest that has accompanied the Constitution from its very inception. Not everyone has been satisfied to treat this product of men as if it came from God. Even before the Constitution was officially adopted, many people, known to history as Anti-Federalists, questioned whether what was good for the property-owning factions that were so well represented in Philadelphia would be as good for those who owned little or nothing. Then as subsequently, the main questions raised dealt with the limitations on suffrage, the inadequate defense of individual rights and freedoms, the acceptance and even strengthening of the institution of slavery, and the many other benefits given to men of property.

Taken at face value, the Constitution is an attempt to fix the relations between state and federal governments, and between the three branches—legislative, executive, and judiciary—of the latter. And most accounts of this document have concentrated on the mechanical arrangements that make this balancing act possible. In the process, the Constitution's basic assumptions and particularly its social and economic purposes have been grossly neglected. It is a little like learning in some detail how a car works before even knowing what kind of machine it is, what it is supposed to do, and why it was constructed in just this way. Learning the functioning of any system, whether mechanical or institutional, is not without value in determining its meaning and use, but we would do better to approach their symbiosis from the other side, to examine who needed what and how the specific structures created responded to these needs. What is really at stake in any political dispute, the real-life questions involved, and why different people take the positions they do, can never be adequately understood by focusing solely or even mainly on the legalistic forms in which the issues are presented and fought out.

Who Benefits?

In examining any political phenomena, it is always wise to ask, "Who benefits?" As regards the American constitutional system, the answer was given clearly, if somewhat crudely, by Senator Boies Penrose, a late nineteenth-century Republican from Pennsylvania, who told a business audience: "I believe in a division of labor. You send us to Congress; we pass the laws under which you make money . . . and out of your profits you further contribute to our campaign funds to send us back again to pass more laws to enable you to make more money." When, a few years later, Charles Beard suggested that the same kind of considerations may have played a role in the writing of the Constitution, he unleashed a political storm against his book that has few if any parallels in our history. Then-President Taft publicly denounced this unseemly muckraking as besmirching the reputations of our Founding Fathers. Not particularly noted for his indifference to economic gain when he became president, Warren Harding, at that time a newspaper publisher, attacked Beard's "filthy lies and rotten perversions" in an article entitled, "Scavengers, Hyena-Like, Desecrate the Graves of the Dead Patriots We Revere." And even as a growing number of professional historians came to accept Beard's interpretation, the city of Seattle banned his book.

Obviously, Beard had touched a tender nerve, but it is also obvious that economic motivations—as Beard himself recognized—are only part of the explanation for political phenomena. Other factors influence people's behavior, and some people act often and even primarily out of other kinds of motives. The problem is how to credit these necessary qualifications without unduly compromising the original insight (not really that original, since political theory has known about the importance of economic motivation from Plato on).

In an attempt to redirect attention away from the mechanical and socially uninformative details of checks and balances, criti-

28

cisms of the Constitution have proceeded on three distinct though closely related levels. The first concentrates on the people who wrote the document, on who they were and what they thought, feared, and wanted. The second deals with the classes and subclasses to which they belonged and which they more or less consciously represented, with the objective interests of these classes and what was required to satisfy them. Here what is decisive are the assumptions and ways of thinking that correspond to membership in a particular class, or the part of human understanding that comes from what we take for granted, not so much because of who we are as because of where we fit in society. Hence, for example, one might favor strong laws to protect private property not because one wants to remain wealthy (though I suspect most wealthy people do), but because one has been socialized as a member of a property-owning class to take this requirement and its connection to life, liberty, and the pursuit of happiness for granted. The third level introduces the nature of the capitalist mode of production and tries to bring out how the Constitution, together with other political institutions, function as both cause and effect within the life process of a developing capitalist society.

A Revolutionary Act Is Needed

We must accept our humanity, but to accept our humanity means that we must work to regain control of our work lives, to build communities that are not structured by market considerations, to establish a harmonious relationship with nature and to live our lives in a way that is in solidarity with the oppressed . . . to accept one's humanity means to openly reject many of the values and principles of the Constitution. And that is a revolutionary act . . . the struggle that surrounded the establishment of the Constitution is still ongoing. We have yet to have *our* revolution.

Jerry Fresia, *Toward an American Revolution: Exposing the Constitution and Other Illusions*, 1988.

From the start, most criticisms have been situated on the first and second of these levels. However, given the necessary relations between levels, a fully adequate analysis of what our Constitution means would have to devote more attention to the larger context, capitalism, in which it was produced and which it helps in no small measure to reproduce. To be sure, capitalism doesn't exist apart from the social and economic classes whose struggle over opposing interests constitutes its central drama. Nor can these classes be completely understood apart from the lives of the real individuals who compose them. But the reverse is equally true: the actions of the individual framers makes little sense—opening the way for various superficial interpretations —if viewed apart from the class interests which they sought to further; just as the nature of these classes, their specific interests, and the conditions and means available to satisfy them require a contextualization that could only come from an account of the enveloping capitalist system. It was early commercial capitalism in its free worker and slave variants that gave rise to the main property-owning classes represented at Philadelphia; that established the conditions for their alliance and made this alliance politically dominant; that led to the most pressing problems from which these classes suffered; and finally that provided both the possibilities and limits for the resolution of these problems. Unfortunately, the book that treats the Constitution as a political extension of the capitalist mode of production, as an organic function of this historically developing whole, while not losing sight of how it is also a product of a particular class alliance and of the real individuals who gathered in Philadelphia remains to be written.

A Bourgeois Fairy Tale

What still needs to be stressed—chiefly because even most critics ignore it—is that on all three levels of analysis and throughout the entire two hundred years of its history, the Constitution has been a way of understanding reality as much as it has served to shape it. And it has succeeded in ordering society in part through how it has made people think about it, just as these practical achievements have secured widespread acceptance for the intellectual modes that they embody. In sum, an important part of the Constitution's work is ideological. As ideology, the Constitution provides us with a kind of bourgeois fairy tale in which claims to equal rights and responsibilities are substituted for the harsh realities of class domination. Through the Constitution, the struggle over the legitimacy of any social act or relationship is removed from the plane of morality to that of law. Justice is no longer what is fair but what is legal, and politics itself is transformed into the technical wrangling of lawyers and judges. The Constitution organizes consent not least by its manner of organizing dissent. The fact that two thirds of the world's lawyers practice in the United States is not, as they say, a coincidence.

Unlike political theory, the Constitution not only offers us a picture of reality but through the state's monopoly on violence it forces citizens to act, or at least to speak, "as if." Acting as if the rule of law, equality of opportunity, freedom of the individual, and the neutrality of the state, all of which are inscribed in the Constitution, are more than formally true inhibits people's ability to recognize that they are all practically false, that the society set up with the help of the Constitution simply does not operate

30

in these ways. It is not a matter of reality failing to live up to a set of commendable ideals but of these ideals serving to help mask this reality through misrepresenting what is legal for what is actual, what is permissible in law for what is possible in society. When does an ideal become a barrier to the realization of what it supposedly promotes? When people are encouraged to treat the ideal as a description, however imperfect, of the real, as in the claim that ours is a society ruled by law, where whatever actually exists that goes counter to this claim is relegated to the role of a passing qualification. Viewed in this way, the dynamics of who is doing what to whom and why, together with the structural reforms needed to change things, can never be understood. . . .

Bulbul. Reprinted with permission.

Can the Constitution serve a people bent on a democratic socialist transformation of capitalist society? It has done everything a document could possibly do to forestall such an eventuality; and as the central institutional prop of our capitalist society, it continues to act in this way. And yet, despite its lopsided and deceptive form and the worst elitist intentions of its framers, the

31

changes it has undergone in the past two hundred years suggest that this possibility cannot be ruled out. Nothing, of course, came easy. Every amendment to the Constitution, just like most new interpretations by the Supreme Court (in some ways more important than new amendments), and each change of emphasis in its administration and enforcement have come about as a result of popular struggle. Neither blacks, nor women, nor unpropertied males, for example, were simply handed the right to vote. It might be said that the expansion of democracy only occurred after it became clear that the influence of party machines, public education, newspapers, churches, mass spectator sports, patriotism and especially the growth of the economic pie through capitalist development and American imperialistic adventures "abroad" (including Indian and Mexican lands west of the Mississippi) would suffice to ensure that the newly enfranchised publics would not use their power for subversive ends.

A Fundamental Contradiction

But the most fundamental contradiction in the entire Constitution cannot be dismissed so easily. This is the contradiction between political democracy and economic servitude. The framers did everything they could—consistent with winning acceptance for the document—to avoid placing the loaded gun of popular sovereignty in the hands of the people. They had no doubt as to what would happen to the grossly unequal distribution of property in our country (at present, one percent of the population own 50 percent of all wealth) should this ever occur. Well, it has occurred, and the mass of America's citizens have made little use of political democracy to obtain economic democracy. For some, therefore, the trial is over, and the verdict is in. For us, the jury is still out. Capitalism *in extremis* has many catastrophes in store for all of us. And with the stakes so high, history can afford to take its time. Meanwhile, more informed criticism of the one-sided, deceptive, and biased rules of the game by which we are all forced to play can hurry history along just that little bit, and in the process encourage thinking on the role—if any—of the Constitution in the transition to a socialist society.

"What the framers established was a process for seeking . . . justice."

America's Courts Provide Social Justice

Abram Chayes

Abram Chayes is the Felix Frankfurter Professor of Law at Harvard Law School in Cambridge, Massachusetts, and a former legal advisor at the U.S. Department of State. He is the author of many articles and books, including *The International Legal Process* and *The Cuban Missile Crisis, International Crisis and the Role of the Law*. In the following viewpoint, Chayes argues that America's judicial system promotes justice by protecting personal liberties and by ensuring that social goals, such as affirmative action, are enacted to protect the less powerful members of society.

As you read, consider the following questions:

1. How does America's judiciary differ from the judiciaries of other nations, according to Chayes?
2. What does the author see as the most important result of the judicial system's involvement in civil rights?
3. Why does Chayes believe the judicial branch is the most powerful branch of the U.S. government?

Abram Chayes, "How the Constitution Establishes Justice," in *The Constitution, the Courts, and the Quest for Justice*, edited by Robert A. Goldwin and William A. Schambra. Washington, DC: AEI Press, 1990. Reprinted with permission of the American Enterprise Institute for Public Policy Research.

What does the Constitution do "to establish justice"? Here is a deceptively simple answer: it provides for "the judicial power of the United States" to be exercised by "one Supreme Court and such other courts as Congress may ordain and establish." In the quasi-constitutional Judiciary Act of 1789, many members of the Constitutional Convention, sitting now as congressmen, rounded out the work by establishing the lower federal courts, which in one form or another have been with us ever since.

Custodian of Justice

The federal judiciary is the institutional custodian of justice in our system. I do not mean by this to denigrate the other departments of government in which the founders vested other powers of the new state. Nor do I mean to say that Congress and the executive are never or ought never to be concerned with justice. But compared with providing for the common defense or promoting the general welfare, establishing justice requires a longer view, responding to values and considerations both less tangible and more transcendent than are commonly emphasized by elected political leaders conducting the ordinary affairs of government. So the judicial department, less responsive to transient political currents and relying, as the framers said, on reason rather than will as its activating principle, is the institutional custodian of justice, just as Congress controls the purse and the president is the institutional embodiment of the nation in war and foreign affairs.

The judicial department established by the framers was unique in 1787, and to a large extent it remains unique today. The Constitution establishes the judiciary as a coequal branch of government, on the same plane as the other two and responsible jointly with them for the governance of the state. No other judicial system can make that statement.

All modern societies have judges, and an independent judiciary is a hallmark of liberal democracy. But outside the United States, judicial systems are regarded primarily as a service provided by the government, much like an educational system or a sewage system, to take care of the workaday business of disposing of the disputes that arise in the ordinary course of social and economic life. They are not partners in the governance of those societies. . . .

Judicial Action

How has the judicial branch exercised its power to govern? The usual answer focuses on the distinctive institution of judicial review, emphasizing the adversary relationship between court and legislature and calibrating the level of constraint judges have imposed on legislative bodies at a given period. . . .

In the civil rights and institutional cases, the most important result of judicial action has been to energize the Congress and state legislatures, to change legislative agendas, to force reconsideration of spending and resource allocation, to transform the terms of public debate, and to lubricate the processes of change. The judicial department does not govern by itself; it shares in the work.

No Person Is Above the Law

Throughout our history, Americans—and their leaders—have displayed a special fidelity to law and ethics. If anything, our revolution militantly rejected arbitrary government and embraced the principle that no person is above the law—or, as Roman lawmakers put it, *Fiat justitia ruat caelum* ("Let justice be done, though the heavens fall.")

Mark Green, *America's Transition: Blueprints for the 1990s,* 1989.

You will notice that I have described an active judiciary. I maintain that this institutional outcome is implicit in the decision of the framers to create the federal judicial branch as a department of government, on an equal plane with the legislative and executive, and thus to vest it with a share of the power to govern. The judicial branch has exercised this power in different ways in response to different requirements of the society at different times in its history:

- At first it created a system of federal private law.
- From the property rights and liberty of contract of nineteenth-century entrepreneurs to the right of privacy in the anonymity of a crowded contemporary urban environment, it has defined an expanding array of personal liberties and defended them against government encroachment.
- It joins with Congress and the administrative agencies in the administration of the regulatory state.
- It deploys affirmative remedial techniques in the service of positive social objectives validated by Constitution and statute.

In whatever form, the federal judiciary, throughout American history, has been an active participant in governing the country. I believe that is what the founders intended. The institutional response of the judiciary, however, has been driven more by the practical and pragmatic needs of government than by theory.

A Government of Laws

The framers said they wanted to create a government of laws and not of men, and they succeeded. We have had a good deal of soul searching in recent years about the resulting "juristocracy" of ours. By no means have all the conclusions been favorable. I have no quarrel with much of the criticism. Judges are not immune from error, as all of them who do not sit on the Supreme Court soon find out. Even about the Supreme Court, Justice Robert Jackson said, "We are not final because we are infallible; we are infallible because we are final." And the federal judiciary as an institution is, like all human institutions, radically imperfect.

There are things to be said for a "law-ridden" society, though. For one thing, when law is the social integument, there is a feedback effect. Law and justice become the concern of legislators and officials and common people, not just the courts. That does not render America proof against official lawlessness, as we have had recent occasion to observe. But I take a certain pride when European friends, with different legal or judicial systems, profess not to understand how we can make such a public fuss about it.

For another thing, law is not static. It changes and grows in a symbiotic relationship with the society. This process of change and growth merits attention. Attorney General Edwin Meese took a good deal of criticism for his statement that the Constitution was not necessarily what the Supreme Court says it is. I do not see how anyone could disagree with that, certainly not any law professor. Our most sacred professional prerogative is to be able to tell students the Supreme Court is wrong.

Challenging the Constitution

Much of the history of expanding liberty we justly celebrate was made by people who refused to accept the Constitution as the Supreme Court said it was. Jehovah's Witnesses challenged the compulsory schoolroom flag salute five times in the Supreme Court before it was declared unconstitutional. Three times the case was dismissed "for want of a substantial federal question." Then the Court after plenary consideration upheld the practice with only Justice Jackson dissenting. Finally, *West Virginia Board of Education v. Barnette* held such a requirement to be inconsistent with First Amendment freedom of religion.

Challenge to established doctrine is an engine of growth in the law, and we should not choke it off. The Jehovah's Witnesses, though, were in a different position from the U.S. government. They had to violate the law—to exercise the "right" of civil disobedience—in order to create the case or controversy that would get them into court. The executive, in my view, does not need and has no right of civil disobedience. While the government is free to challenge an existing reading of the Constitution or any other law—and it has often done so with great benefit to all—it is not free to violate the law in order to do so. Nor is it free to decide for itself what law shall govern its actions, without regard to the law on the books. It is bound until the law is changed.

36

Finally, we may ask, what is the active principle that governs change in the law? And what is the safeguard against error?

It is not the vote. The Supreme Court reads the election returns, but it is not bound by them. That would not, I think, have unduly disturbed the framers. They were by no means wholly enamored of the vote as a universal solvent. Neither the president nor the Senate, in the original plan, was chosen by direct suffrage. So although we take a just pride in our democracy, we need not always find ultimate wisdom in the decisions of a transitory political majority.

Much Injustice

An approach to the problem of the ultimate check on judicial power is to return to our original question: How does the Constitution establish justice? We all know the answer to that question: it does not. As a society, we have been working at establishing justice on and off for 200 years, and we still have not accomplished it. We can take some pride in that effort—but not too much. Although America is a more just society than most today or that we know historically, our society still contains much that is an affront to justice, too much to warrant any self-satisfaction.

The U.S. Creed

The United States has a creed . . . set forth with dogmatic and theological lucidity in the Declaration of Independence; perhaps the only piece of practical politics that is also theoretical politics and also great literature. It enunciates that all men are equal in their claim to justice, that governments exist to give them that justice, and that their authority is for that reason just. . . . The point is that there is a creed, if not about divine, at least about human things.

G.K. Chesterton, *What I Saw in America,* 1922.

That is another way of saying that justice, like any other animating human ideal, can never be achieved. Indeed, it can never even be comprehensively defined.

What the framers established was a process for seeking after justice. It is a process in which law and judges, rightly I think, play the central role. Alexander Bickel reminded us of Alexander Hamilton's statement that the judiciary is "the least dangerous branch"—and I would add the most powerful: least dangerous, because the judgment of a court, like poetry, "makes nothing happen."

But why the most powerful? Richard Neustadt said, "The power of the President is the power to persuade." And if that is true of the power of the president, how much so of the power of the courts? Nothing the Supreme Court does or says really makes anything happen unless it ultimately persuades us that it is right. That was Bickel's basic point.

Basic Values

Unlike the president, the Court does not seek to persuade bureaucrats or legislators or even voters about immediate responses to this or that program or crisis. It speaks to all of us, and it speaks about the basic values that define us as a nation and a society. It seeks to persuade us at the deepest and most fundamental level. That is why, in the long run, it is the most powerful branch.

Let me conclude with a story. Learned Hand was visiting Washington and went out to lunch with Justice Oliver Wendell Holmes. They walked back to the Capitol, where the Court still sat. As they parted, Hand called after Holmes, "Do justice."

The old man turned on him fiercely, eyebrows bristling: "What's that? What's that? That's none of my business. *Law* is my business." What else would we expect of the Holmes who promulgated the "bad man theory of the law" many years earlier in *The Path of the Law*? The point is the same: law and justice inhabit different worlds.

But we know that is not true: we know that law is inevitably concerned with justice. There is no way to talk about law without coming in the end to talk about justice.

The Discourse of Justice

It is not that we agree on what justice is—although it is interesting how often our ideas and instincts converge. The idea of justice, however, provides a point of view outside the system from which we can criticize it, an Archimedean platform for exerting leverage to change it.

Of course, the joke of the story is on Holmes. We revere him and celebrate him not because he was a superb technical lawyer and judge—although he certainly was. He is a folk hero —America is the only country in the world that has judges for folk heroes, and they all share this characteristic. Holmes is a folk hero because he was a fighter for justice or we see him so. What resonates for us are the great cadences of the *Lochner* and *Abrams* dissents and others in which he used his craft in the law to explore the meaning of justice. His utterances—and those of the other hero-judges—help keep the discourse of justice alive for us.

That is how the Constitution establishes justice.

"*The truth is there is no justice in America for the people.*"

America's Courts Do Not Provide Social Justice

Gerry Spence

Once a corporate lawyer himself, Gerry Spence is now famous for defending common people in cases against large corporations. Corporations use their money and power to win courtroom decisions, Spence maintains in the following viewpoint. Corporate power and influence in the courtroom have made justice elusive, he contends, and have turned the phrase "justice for all" from an American reality into an American myth. Spence, a practicing attorney for more than thirty-five years, is the author of *Gunning for Justice*, *Trial by Fire*, and *Of Murder and Madness*. This viewpoint is an excerpt from his book *With Justice for None: Destroying an American Myth*.

As you read, consider the following questions:

1. Why does Spence think Americans cling to the belief that there is justice for all?
2. How has the power of corporations changed the judicial system, according to the author?
3. Why does the author feel it would be wrong to accept the myth that justice is available to all?

Every day, I meet people who have been bullied or cheated or injured. They say they're going to hire a lawyer. They say they're going to sue and get justice. But they'll likely be disappointed, and that hurts me, especially when I see how people innocently cling to the belief that justice is theirs for the asking. Sometimes when I talk about justice, I get angry, and people tend to turn off when you're angry. They think you're mad at *them*. Or you seem unreasonable or—because you think differently than they—radical. Nobody wants to hear some firebrand raging about what's wrong in America when there are so many things right. You see these wild-eyed screamers all the time in the cities, standing on boxes while the people walk on by without even turning their heads. But the fellow on the box is there for himself. He'd say what he has to say even if he were only hollering into the wind. I love the guy. It takes a certain courage to be a fool, and there is still a need in this country for the pariahs and the common scolds. That they irritate us often tells us more about *us* than about them. And that they tell only part of the story is better than their not having told us anything at all.

No Illusions

I would prefer to assure you that there's nothing wrong with justice in America. After laboring in the system for over thirty-five years, I love it the way the farmer loves his pile of rocks and his old mule. But he doesn't have any illusions about them. He knows that the mule is likely to kick hell out of him whenever he feels like it, and that the forty acres only grows a reasonable crop of oats every fifth year or so. Sometimes the truth is hard to listen to. It can be cold and plain and sad, and we do the best we can to hide from it. We buy face-lifts and youthful clothes, and when the truth finally catches up with us, they haul us out under a sheet and pay someone to make us look alive and then bury us fast. We stay the hell out of the ghettos so we don't have to see the filth and poverty and pain, and we never visit the asylums where the people are screaming, and we buy a lot of worthless things in pursuit of our pervasive goal—happiness. So the farmer, too, had just as well go on hoping for a miracle—that one day he'll get one hell of a bumper crop off his forty acres behind his old mule. That's the way it is with justice in America. The system doesn't often deliver justice to the people, and it never has, but we cling to our hopes and to old myths that are much more comforting than the truth. . . .

The truth is there is no justice in America for the people. And there never has been—not from the beginning. There is no justice for the wealthy surgeon at Mercy Hospital, or the scrubwoman who cleans up after him. There is no justice for the dregs of our society who plague us with their crimes, or for the workers, or for women. There is no justice even for Jerry Falwell, who loves God and votes Republican, or for the poor in the ghettos. They've never heard of it. There is no justice for the farmer who works his guts out for the banks. And don't forget the children—there has never been justice for them.

Fear and Justice

We search for justice in fearful places—in cities encrusted with crime, in the workplace where people are mere units on the production line, in a world where justice, if it exists, has become only another commodity for sale. We huddle behind barred doors, wired to expensive burglar alarms, and when the wind blows and rattles the door in the night, we awaken, our hearts in our throats, because nothing can make us feel safe anymore. Yet fiercely we cling to old myths that give comfort —justice is out there. Somewhere.

A Promise Unfulfilled

The promise of equal justice engraved in the Constitution and defined by the Supreme Court remains unfulfilled, leaving a poor person at the mercy of a system which works a tragic injustice upon the innocent and threatens the constitutionally protected freedoms of us all.

American Bar Association Standing Committee on Legal Aid and Indigent Defendants, *Project to Monitor the Alternative Delivery Study of Legal Services Corporation,* 1978.

What has happened to justice in America? There stands the courthouse, solid, stately. Inside, we still find great judges, men and women dedicated to the law, presiding over our cases. In the courtrooms, we hear our hometown lawyers pleading to a jury of our neighbors. But there will be no justice, for a new king dominates justice in America, a sovereign whose soul is pledged to business and whose heart is geared to profit. The new king, an amorphous agglomeration of corporations, of banks and insurance companies and mammoth multinational financial institutions, maintains a prurient passion for money and demands a justice of its own, one that is stable and predictable, one that fits into columns and accounts and mortality tables, one that is interpretable in dollars, so that a little justice is a few dollars and a lot of justice many. The new king cannot deal with the soul, the fire, and the unpredictability of human justice. Profit is the lifeblood of business, and if there is no profit in justice, people are not likely to receive it.

Like the citizens of any kingdom, we tend to take on the style of the sovereign. In this corporate world, people have become corporatelike themselves. Our hearts have become synchronized with the corporate heart that beats in dollars, and with the corporate spirit that worships dollars. In the Age of the Yuppie, we have become so insanely obsessed with things that we have willingly pawned the heritage of generations, battered the earth, and poisoned the oceans in order to possess whatever dollars will buy. We seek to become salable commodities ourselves; students pursue an advanced degree, not because they yearn to learn, but because they wish to make themselves more marketable. Businessmen buy respect with the dollars they accumulate and with which they score the game of profit. Ideas seem valueless unless they are salable. Workers have become expendable parts for sale in the ordinary course of commerce. The detection, punishment, and prevention of crime are fungible goods. Rapists and robbers and thieves and their victims have become wares that stock the system's shelves. Lawyers are too often expediters, and judges are dedicated to keeping the cases flowing in deference to the commerce of law. Our leaders are often elected because of their purchasable images on television. Even eternal salvation has become something sold in the marketplace. And justice—whatever it is, and it is different for each of us—has finally become a mercantile matter, where profit is the paramount concern of all.

Judging the System

Yet a steady gnawing in the night awakens us. It is an awareness that the love of *only* money, and devotion to *only* things, leaves us as empty and dead as dollars, that the worship of *only* property transforms the living into the dead—dead forests, dead rivers, dead towns and deserted communities. When we petition for a *human* justice, one that does not sell us like so many pork bellies, we often make demands on the system to which it cannot respond. But every system must finally be judged by the character of justice it delivers, and a justice attuned to the needs of only the nonliving, to the demands of the new king, provides justice for none.

What is justice? Clarence Darrow insisted, "There is no such thing as justice. In fact, the word cannot be defined." Darrow was right. Justice, like life, cannot be adequately defined. Justice is the divine mist, and is something inexorably connected to the state of being. But Darrow understood clearly the meaning of *injustice*, and all his life fought against it. The black child in the ghetto begging for his supper knows the meaning of that word, and so does the innocent man rotting in prison. Even the coyote chained to a stake near the gas pumps to entertain the tourists understands the meaning of injustice.

Yet justice usually fails without law, for it is the office of the law to restrain the powerful. The black child, given power, may, in turn, starve the children of his oppressors, and the innocent, once freed, may, given power, kill those who have wrongfully imprisoned him. Justice is not a willow in the wind; justice is the great tree that stands immutable against unjust forces, and the law, the massive trunk of the great tree, must resist the tempests that storm upon it. . . .

Profit over People

Justice requires atonement, and justice demands reform. It teaches its lessons and insists that we change. I remember when our small Wyoming town was stunned by the death of one of its most exceptional progeny—a beautiful young woman I'll call Donna. She was a gifted and popular student, and a loving daughter. She died in the wreck of a new car her father had given her for her birthday. The manufacturer's own tests had shown that the car went out of control under certain braking conditions, and we were prepared to prove these conditions existed in her case, that the company knew of the defect but had refused to correct the design before the car was marketed to millions of unsuspecting drivers. The evidence I saw supported our allegations (and those made by hundreds of others in similar court cases) that the manufacturer's haste to market the car, despite its knowledge of the dangerous design, was motivated by its desire to beat the Japanese to the marketplace. It was the same old story—profit over people. We filed suit on behalf of the girl's stricken family. All they wanted, they said, was justice.

The Reality of Justice in America

While the American system of justice was founded upon the noble ideal of equity, fairness and justice, the reality of its workings has traditionally had little in common with that ideal. The quality and manner of justice received in this country has generally been determined by the offender and/or victim's color, social and financial status, sex and religion.

Ron Wikberg and Gilbert Guzman, *The Angolite,* March/April 1987.

A few days before the trial, we settled. These are, indeed, hard cases to win. The car manufacturer has teams of experts selected not so much for what they know but for their ability to convince jurors of whatever defenses the company may raise. It has skilled trial lawyers and huge support staffs. For my part, I dreaded dragging the parents through the agony of their daughter's death again, this time amid the glare and clamor of the media. Even if they won, there would be the expensive and lengthy appeals, and, in the end, the only justice they would receive would be, of course, money. At the last minute, faced with the strain of the upcoming trial and offered a sum of money by the company that permitted them to argue that they had at least won something, the parents opted to end the war. People usually do.

No Punishment

But the manufacturer's offer required that the amount of the settlement remain confidential. Hundreds of similar cases waited in the wings. Millions were at stake, and the company wanted protection. We could argue to the parents, and did, that we had beaten the company. The company claimed this was the largest settlement it had ever paid in this kind of case. Yet we did not win. There would be no punishment of the corporation, or of its officers, who had known from the beginning that the car was dangerous. There would be no admission of guilt. To the contrary, the settlement papers specifically recited that the corporation admitted no wrongdoing of any kind. Only the gross payment of money to the living for the dead marked the transaction. When the company paid up, it did not even flinch. To thus punish the manufacturer for exposing thousands to injury and death was as satisfying as getting even with the United States government at income-tax time by slamming the door at the post office.

I think of those nights I dumped myself heavily into bed and lay listening to my heart while I fought through the case. I think of the months my staff hunted down the facts and the law. I think of the family's grief, and that all of this human pain and striving should come down to a mere accounting entry made on the company's computer in some obscure room by a bored operator waiting for "Miller time."

Now that the case was settled and the money in my clients' hands, they didn't know what to do with it. How could they take money in place of their child? They did not get justice. They were delivered, instead, a bagful of guilt. A few days after the settlement, one of the dead girl's sisters wrote me:

"It's all over. It's gone, and [Donna] is too. What's left? An empty feeling with nothing to do about it . . . the money is nothing—pocket change to a corporation that makes billions of dollars. What bothers me is that we settled and that one of the conditions of the settlement was confidentiality. It is an admission of guilt on their part, but a *secret* admission. It's as if they are saying, 'Let's settle this now—we were wrong—here's some money—now let us get back to *business as usual.*'

"'Business as usual'—the business of making automobiles profitably, not safely, and hoping no one finds out that one of the decisions made in a big corporation is to make cars they know will kill. It's just not enough. Part of our lives is gone; revenge is impossible; the perpetrator is too strong . . . our silence was bought, and we all lose—all of us."

Of course we have a government of the RICH. You don't expect us to waste government on the poor, do you?

© Simpson/Rothco. Reprinted with permission.

The other sister addressed another side of the issue. "I think the settlement was definitely in my parents' best interests. I dread to think what a long ugly trial would have done to them and to me.

"All of us had ideas and dreams of how we would get justice —or revenge on the company. As you know, in different ways, we were somewhat disappointed that we couldn't really make the company pay by adverse publicity, and such. However, it dawned on me . . . that although we were unable to get justice as we know it or want it, there is, after all, *divine justice*. God sees all, and these people *will* pay, whether it be in this world, or the next. There *is* justice. This I know to be true, and it gives me a sense of hope, and resolution, and comfort." A pity, I thought, that in America we must wait until the "next world" to receive justice. . . .

45

Victims may look to the law for justice, but in criminal cases many report that getting satisfaction in the nation's justice system is equivalent to leaving the Church in charge of sex. We are taught, correctly, that forgiveness is sublime, but often forgiveness leaves us unjustly suspended in emotional conflict. When the state mumbles its bland rationalizations about reforming and rehabilitating those who have harmed us, and when vicious criminals are coddled and turned loose on the streets to again pursue their commitments to evil and to injury, we, the victims, feel abandoned, and, worse, we feel injured again. While we could not live in a society where the citizen is free to torture and kill at will to gratify a vengeful heart, try to explain that to a husband whose wife has been brutally raped and murdered. The state's bargain for clemency is yet another crime against him. The husband craves revenge. He must have it or his sorrow will spoil like milk left in the sun.

I can no more precisely define that phenomenon we call *justice* than could Darrow, or the Byzantine emperor and codifier of law, Justinian, who himself was able to come up with no better definition than "delivering to every man his just dues." Yet I have learned certain things: I know that the human need for revenge and the mysterious powers of forgiveness that oppose it have waged their battles, one against the other, throughout the history of man, and in my career they have proven to be inseparably entwined. . . .

Justice for None

I feel like a man groping through a dark and dangerous room. Even though my eyes are adjusted to the dark, I can still see very little. I stumble, although I've passed through this room long ago, often in the same places as before. I rely mostly on my feelings. I am afraid. Sometimes I recognize a danger and call out a warning. Occasionally a brief beam shines through the window denying the dark. "Justice for none" is as much a slogan as "justice for all." Still, in a society in which we are free to explore for better ways, to embrace the fiction of "justice for all" terminates the search.

Distinguishing Bias from Reason

When dealing with controversial issues, many people allow their feelings to dominate their powers of reason. Thus, one of the most important critical thinking skills is the ability to distinguish between statements based upon emotion or bias and conclusions based upon a rational consideration of the facts.

The following statements are taken from the viewpoints in this chapter. Consider each statement carefully. *Mark R for any statement you believe is based on reason or a rational consideration of the facts. Mark B for any statement you believe is based on bias, prejudice, or emotion. Mark I for any statement you think is impossible to judge.*

If you are doing this activity as a member of a class or group, compare your answers with those of other class or group members. Be able to defend your answers. You may discover that others come to different conclusions than you do. Listening to the rationale others present for their answers may give you valuable insights in distinguishing between bias and reason.

> R = *a statement based upon reason*
> B = *a statement based on bias*
> I = *a statement impossible to judge*

1. The United States should spend little time celebrating the Constitution. It treated blacks as less than human, ignored women, and permitted religious intolerance.

2. The U.S. Constitution includes everyone, women, minorities, and Jews. The Constitution is all-inclusive because it singles out no group to exclude.

3. The text of the Constitution excludes women because it contains only the pronoun "he" to describe the president, members of congress, and supreme court justices, among others.

4. Everyone in the U.S. gets due process of law, even the hardened criminals who don't really deserve it.

5. People say they are going to hire a lawyer to sue someone and get justice. They will be disappointed because there is no real justice in the United States.

6. Most court judges are from the upper classes of American society. This partially explains why poor people are less likely to have their view heard and respected in court than, say, corporate officials.

7. The framers of the Constitution were silent about so many topics because they believed the Constitution applied only to them, the white, male elite. Women were considered so inferior that the founding fathers never thought anyone would apply the Constitution to them.

8. The original Constitution permitted some injustice to continue. It tolerated slavery, didn't guarantee women the right to vote, and didn't protect religious freedom.

9. The Constitution guarantees that all people in the U.S. have equal rights. This in turn guarantees that the only legitimate political power in the U.S. comes from the people.

10. The U.S. judicial system is just. The Constitution and the laws of state and local governments ensure most people fair treatment.

11. Minority men cannot obtain a fair hearing in the courts. They are automatically judged to be guilty because of their skin color.

12. Obtaining justice for women is difficult because there are so few women judges.

13. No one reads the Constitution anymore. It is meaningless. It only serves to justify the existence of politicians.

14. Minorities are flagrant welfare abusers.

Periodical Bibliography

The following articles have been selected to supplement the diverse views presented in this chapter.

Business Week	"The New America," Special section, September 25, 1989.
Henry Cisneros	"The Demography of a Dream," *New Perspectives Quarterly*, Summer 1988.
Bruce Fein	"A Court That Obeys the Law," *National Review*, September 29, 1989.
Robert Heilbroner	"The Triumph of Capitalism," *New Perspectives Quarterly*, Fall 1989.
Wade Hudson	"To Abolish Demoralizing Poverty," *Christian Social Action*, January 1989.
Paul Johnson	"The Capitalist Commandments," *Crisis*, November 1989.
Ryzsard Kapuscinski	"America as a Collage," *New Perspectives Quarterly*, Summer 1988.
Michael A. Lebowitz	"Social Justice Against Capitalism," *Monthly Review*, May 1988.
Walter Russell Mead	"Capitalism Bound," *New Perspectives Quarterly*, Summer 1988.
William Lee Miller	"The Spirit of '89," *The New Republic*, June 26, 1989.
Michael Novak	"Boredom, Virtue, and Democratic Capitalism," *Commentary*, January 1990.
Claes G. Ryn	"The Democracy Boosters," *National Review*, March 24, 1989.
Robert J. Samuelson	"The Irony of Capitalism," *Newsweek*, January 9, 1989.
Alain Sanders	"Enter, Stage Right," *Time*, October 9, 1989.
Scholastic Update	"The Supreme Court: 200 Years of Wrestling with the Big Question," January 26, 1990.
Herman Schwartz	"Consolidating the New Majority," *The Nation*, October 9, 1989.
Daniel Singer	"The Specter of Capitalism," *The Nation*, August 21-28, 1989.
Utne Reader	"A Constitutional Convention: History Repeats Itself," September/October 1989.
Karl Zinsmeister	"Is Poverty the Problem?" *Crisis*, July/August 1989.

Does America's Economy Promote Social Justice?

Social Justice

Chapter Preface

The U.S. has one of the highest standards of living in the world, with a 1986 median family income of $29,460. This high standard of living attracts hundreds of thousands of immigrants to America every year. Some immigrants come with excessive expectations—like those immigrants who came in the 1800s after hearing a rumor that America's streets were paved with gold. Although they soon found that this was untrue, they and later immigrants nonetheless discovered economic opportunities in the U.S. that existed in few other countries.

Many people believe that America is still the land of opportunity. They maintain that America's economic system is the best at distributing wealth and goods fairly—those who work hardest in the system are most likely to succeed. Because the U.S. government does not maintain strict control over the economy, they contend, Americans have the freedom to participate and succeed as they choose.

Others, however, say that America's high standard of living does not reflect a land of opportunity. They maintain that although some Americans who work hard may be rewarded, those who are disadvantaged in any way are punished. The disabled, the ill, and those born into poverty all suffer under America's economy. As evidence these critics point out that in America, 1 percent of the people own 50 percent of the wealth; 20 percent of the children live in poverty; and half a million citizens are homeless. America's economy provides opportunities only for the fortunate, many believe. They argue that few opportunities exist for the less fortunate.

America has long been known as the land of economic opportunity. Many people question whether this is still true. The authors in the following chapter discuss this issue and debate whether America's economy promotes social justice.

"Our moral heritage includes a common respect and concern for our fellowmen, and an unselfish consideration for the rights and welfare of others."

America's Economy Promotes Justice

David Beers

David Beers is a fellow at the Center for the Study of Market Processes in Caldwell, Idaho, and a doctoral student in economics at George Mason University in Fairfax, Virginia. In the following viewpoint, Beers argues that America's traditional market-oriented economic system provides equal opportunity and justice for all citizens. He cautions against government interference intended to establish programs to aid the needy. Beers believes such welfare-state policies do not promote justice, and that justice is best served when Americans have the freedom to make their own economic decisions.

As you read, consider the following questions:

1. What arguments against capitalism have some critics made, according to Beers?
2. What does the author view as the true tragedy of the War on Poverty?
3. What are the benefits of a free society, according to Beers?

David Beers, "Social Consciousness and Individual Freedom," *The Freeman*, September 1989. Reprinted with permission.

One way to look at the progress of a society or even of civilization itself is to see that progress in terms of the development of moral values. Alexis de Tocqueville, the great French social philosopher and observer of American society in the 1830s, noted that the power behind America's great progress as a society and the wellspring of its creative energy was the body of values to which Americans held. To Tocqueville, the individualistic, self-reliant character of the Americans and their passion for individual freedom had more to do with the success of the fledgling nation than even its vast natural resources. Holding to the same values which had inspired its Declaration of Independence from the British Crown, American society had quickly grown to equal, and in many ways surpass, its European forebears.

New Rights

The moral underpinnings of our society have undergone gradual change over its history, but never so great as in the last three decades. The 1960s brought new values to the fore in the minds of many Americans. There were growing perceptions of the inequalities that exist among Americans—particularly inequalities of income—and a greater awareness of the welfare of the disadvantaged. From this new "social consciousness" sprang a desire that new rights be recognized in addition to the fundamental rights to life, liberty, and property. People had a right to a certain minimum standard of living, it was argued, and more was done to try to guarantee this right through government action than had ever been done before. In the face of the wide disparities in income among Americans, the government, in the words of Lyndon Johnson, was to guarantee "not just equality as a right and theory but equality as a fact and equality as a result" (Howard University commencement address, 1965).

Behind the great changes in public attitude and public policy during this time was a rising tide of anti-capitalism, the currents of which are still with us today. Implicit (and often explicit) in the demands that social inequalities be addressed by government welfare programs is the argument that the capitalist system is "socially unjust." It is a system in which factors such as luck, birth, inheritance, physical or mental impairment, or impersonal economic factors may determine an individual's welfare. It allows one man to bask in luxury and comfort while another strives in vain just to find food and shelter. In this way, it is alleged, the capitalist society, while successful in producing prosperity for many, fails in its moral duty to many others.

Here is a different sense of the word "moral" from what Tocqueville had in mind. What Tocqueville referred to as the great strength of American society was the common commitment of individuals to the value of freedom. What is meant in the phrase "society's moral duty," on the other hand, is something altogether different, for "moral" in this case is a collective imperative. The "moral failure" of our society does not consist primarily in the failings of its individual members; rather, "the system is to blame." Consequently, the moral responsibility to the disadvantaged belongs to society as a whole, or more accurately to the recognized agent for carrying out social purposes: the government.

The Benefits of Competition

In a competitive economy, citizens are able to acquire more goods and services for their dollars. After buying such basics as food, clothing, and shelter, they have more money for consumption of additional goods and services. . . .

A competitive economy offers more job opportunities and an increasing share of jobs at increasing real wage levels. It is because U.S. firms generally employ labor more efficiently than businesses in other countries that they can pay high wages, allowing workers to share the prosperity. In a competitive economy, new job creation is high. Additional population thus is an asset, not a burden. And, the quality of jobs improves.

James V. Lacy, *Mandate for Leadership III: Policy Strategies for the 1990s,* 1989.

Although the heady days of the Great Society are past and the utopian visions of the 1960s have cooled to something that one would like to think is sober realism, the idea that the United States as a society owes a moral debt to the victims of a system based on "profits rather than people" is still almost universally held. Discussions about social programs such as Aid to Families of Dependent Children, Social Security, and unemployment benefits focus on "how much," never "whether or not." In fact, even under the Reagan Administration's budget "cuts," debates over these programs were not usually so much about "how much" as about "how much more."

Such unanimous acceptance of this ethic of social consciousness is surprising considering that a scant 40 years ago it would have been almost inconceivable to most Americans. Its acceptance is nothing short of shocking, given the performance of the burgeoning system of transfers to the poor, which by the most accepted standards of measurement has been dismal. Flying in the face of all expectations, the consistent reductions in poverty that had been occurring throughout the 1950s and early 1960s actually ground to a halt in 1968 as anti-poverty legislation came into effect. Moreover, as Charles Murray notes in *Losing Ground*, the proportion of people who depended on government transfers to keep themselves above the official poverty level began to grow steadily from that year on.

The Power to Persuade

All statistics aside, though, the most remarkable point about the great rise of social consciousness in American culture is its apparently overwhelming persuasiveness—despite the fact that such an ethic is logically and pragmatically antagonistic to some of the most basic values of our society. Granted that there are many people who by some misfortune are unable to support themselves or their families, the act of using the coercive machinery of the federal government to enforce public "giving" is a flagrantly immoral invasion of the individual's right to hold property. Very few Americans would consider themselves Marxists today, yet on this issue nearly all cling to the essential spirit of Marxism embodied in the motto "from each according to his ability, to each according to his need."

Capitalism is often depicted as a system which eats away at the moral fiber of a culture. It is a system allegedly driven by self-interested behavior and one that rewards selfishness at the expense of compassion. Blind to anything but the "bottom line," it supposedly encourages the notion that success is the accumulation of material wealth, rather than the nurturing of spiritual values. Such allegations of moral decay in the free society, even if they were true, would carry little weight in view of the moral bankruptcy of welfarism.

Motivated to Be Poor

The tragedy of 20 years of the War on Poverty is not that its measures have been too small to reduce the poverty rate today to anything less than it was in 1968. The tragedy is the multitude of able people who became welfare recipients every year when they would have found their way out of the poverty trap in the absence of these programs. Social programs may supply some important benefits to the genuinely helpless. But the inevitable irony of government transfers to the poor is that they induce other people to qualify for them—people who could work for a decent living, but choose idleness and a welfare check instead. More tragic still are the children of welfare families whose role models are parents who can't or won't hold a job or who have given up trying. Not only do these children fail to learn the importance of work and self-reliance, but the value of education—already hard for a child to appreciate—becomes incomprehensible to them. Not surprisingly, this situation results in poorer attendance, more frequent classroom disruptions, higher dropout rates, lower literacy and overall competence levels, and higher juvenile crime rates. Many children of school age in our inner cities now are third-generation welfare recipients.

The prevalence of the confused notion of "society's moral duty" is revealing. It demonstrates the awareness of a grave social problem, but at the same time betrays an unwillingness to admit to the individual moral imperative presented by the problem. Invoking the moral obligations of society is a subtle way of getting others to make the sacrifices to help those in need. Taking a stand for social justice by advocating government transfers to the disadvantaged is less costly than "putting one's money where his mouth is" and donating time or money to a private charity, since the government makes sure that the burden of "contributing" to new social programs is shared by all tax-paying members of society.

Chuck Asay, by permission of the *Colorado Springs Gazette Telegraph*.

This is not meant to imply that there are not sincere, committed advocates of the underprivileged who make genuine sacrifices for the cause of helping the poor, homeless, and disabled. Certainly there are. But as government plays an ever larger role as the official agent of charity, it is sure that such altruists will become fewer in number. In a way analogous to the erosion of the work ethic among welfare recipients, the values of compassion and concern for one's fellowmen are diminished among potential benefactors. Just as the availability of welfare benefits removes the burden of responsibility on the recipient for his own well-being, the provision of welfare benefits by the government relieves the would-be giver's sense of responsibility for helping his fellowmen. The idea that the relief of poverty is "society's responsibility" and is thus in the domain of government action rather than individual action, then, tends to stunt the development of individual altruism and compassion.

Opportunity and Incentive

The free society lays no claim to any particular distribution of income, nor does it rule out misfortune or failure. But it does allow every opportunity and incentive for recovering from misfortune and failure, and furthermore, it forces people to face up to their own moral commitments toward helping others, rather than abdicate responsibility behind a facade of ineffective government programs. It promotes healthy self-examination since the results of one's actions or lack of actions to help others are more readily seen in the free society than under the bureaucratic morass of the welfare state.

By relegating the act of giving to the category of paying one's income tax, the welfare state serves only to insulate individuals from the moral decisions of whether to give and how to give. One never knows what part of his taxes is going to social programs, much less how the money is spent, or on whom. Yet the taxpayer is given some satisfaction in knowing that, like everyone else, he has done his part—even if in reality "his part" went to a perfectly able recipient who couldn't resist the temptation to take a free ride at the expense of the system. . . .

A Moral Heritage

The strength of American society lies in the values upheld by its individual members—not just values embodied in its laws, or even in documents like the Bill of Rights and the Declaration of Independence. Many of the poorest and most oppressive societies of the world have constitutions which are nearly identical to ours. The difference is one of moral heritage. Contrary to the grim caricature of the capitalist society as ridden with selfishness, callousness, and graft, our moral heritage includes a common respect and concern for our fellowmen, and an unselfish consideration for the rights and welfare of others. These elements of the American character are not undermined by a principled adherence to the rights of property and voluntary exchange. On the contrary, the freedom guaranteed by adherence to these rights is a necessary condition for the growth of that character. Unselfishness and compassion entail a moral independence and an honest self-examination that can only exist in the context of individual freedom.

"It is only when we restrict the forces of the market that we begin to have any meaningful and valuable degree of freedom."

America's Economy Is Unjust

Paul L. Wachtel

In the following viewpoint, Paul L. Wachtel argues that America's economic system does not provide justice because only the wealthy have the freedom to choose what to buy and where to live and work. He contends that the freedoms espoused by defenders of the market-oriented system are myths. Wachtel advocates government control of the market to ensure equal distribution of wealth and to establish justice. He is the chairperson of the graduate division of clinical psychology at the City University of New York. Wachtel founded the Society of Socioeconomics, a New York organization that studies how the U.S. economy influences society.

As you read, consider the following questions:

1. What does Wachtel mean when he refers to the "invisible hand"?
2. How does a market economy differ from a democratic election, according to the author?
3. How are third parties affected by the economic exchange between two other parties, according to Wachtel?

Excerpted from *The Poverty of Affluence: A Psychological Portrait of the American Way of Life* by Paul L. Wachtel, with permission from New Society Publishers, 4527 Springfield Ave., Philadelphia, PA 19143.

The market has served us as a model not only for our economic system but for our thinking about democracy as well. Phrases such as "the market place of ideas" reflect the way in which our identities as citizens and thinkers lean upon our identity as consumers. . . .

Over the years we have introduced many features into our economic set-up designed to provide a little guidance to the "invisible hand." It would be nice to think that the reasons for those interventions have lain in considerations of social justice and of human relations, that it was recognized that it was demeaning and ultimately destructive of the social fabric to organize our daily activities so centrally around the idea of trying to get the best of others. But in fact it was largely the economic misfunctioning of the market system that has led to its modification through the years. . . .

The "invisible hand" moved much like the hand on a ouija board. It depended for its credibility on the illusion that it moved quite apart from the will of men. But those who understood what went on under the table could make it spell out what they wished. If the distribution that resulted was due to an "invisible hand," it was invisible only because most people never got into the boardrooms where they might actually see the hands that fed them (though, of course, only to the degree the market would bear).

Controlled by the Market

The illusion of the "invisible hand" enabled all to feel that they had no responsibility for the way goods were distributed. We must, after all, bow before the objective laws of economics. It is sad that some have so little while others have so much, but little can be done about that. To "interfere" with the distribution that results from market forces is to tamper with nature. That, we are assured by our high priests, is an exceedingly dangerous thing to do. The wrath of the "invisible hand" is great. Bite the hand that feeds you—worse, call into question its existence, or accuse it of being a puppet hand controlled by people who know just how they want it to move—and it will take revenge. Pestilence and boils are nothing compared to the "leveling down" it will wreak. Try to help the poor gain some of what the rich have and we will *all* be poor, we are told. Men don't create unequal distribution of wealth; the "invisible hand" does. And men dare not run an economy, because only the "invisible hand" knows how. If the results seem harsh, we can at least be sure they are just, for they are meted out by the "invisible hand" in its infinite wisdom and ultimate, if inscrutable, love of mankind. . . .

Proponents of the market system tell us that in such a system decisions about what is produced and how it is distributed are the product of uncoerced choices by autonomous individuals. Each person is free to buy or not to buy what he pleases. On the basis of these individual choices, a certain aggregate demand is manifested, and on the basis of that demand other individuals conclude that it will be profitable to try to meet that demand. The glue that binds together and coordinates all these millions of individual choices is the price system, and it functions to signal to millions of individuals what is the most profitable activity in which to engage. The sovereign consumer, by buying or not buying as he sees fit, sets into motion an economic machine that is custom-tailored to his desires. No dictator or bureaucrat tells the manufacturer what to make. Autonomous individuals do that, and woe betide the businessman who does not listen to the voice of the people.

The New Inequality

Poverty, Michael Harrington wrote in *The Other America*, is "invisible." It is a tribute to the impact that Harrington's book had on public discussion and policy alike that poverty has since become, at least episodically, visible. The new inequality, however, is intrinsically invisible. People may sense that they are losing power; many know that they are losing money. But the extent of their loss becomes apparent only in statistical comparisons. The three fifths of the population experiencing little or no gain in after-tax income is not angry at the top twentieth. Those on the losing end aren't demanding remedies, because they aren't aware that there is a collective problem. Thus, silently, with no public protest, inequality gets younger every day.

The cold language of statistics is about numbers, not people. But keep the people in mind. Their troubles are not the stuff of TV documentaries. Inequality won't make today's headlines or lead to tomorrow's riots. Its manifestations are subtle: marginally frustrated hopes, a mocking disparity between the good life available to the few and the life that the many settle for—resignation, guilt, social hopelessness.

Thomas Byrne Edsall, *The Atlantic Monthly*, June 1988.

There is certainly a measure of truth in such a picture. At times consumers do say no to what is offered, and manufacturers who have improperly gauged the public mood bear the burden of their error. The Edsel is probably the classic example of this, with the more general difficulty in peddling gas-guzzlers a more widespread recent instance. This classic portrait of the market economy also has some phenomenological validity. People often do *feel* they are freely choosing, even where their desires are manipulated and their options foreclosed.

Nonetheless, there is a great deal in this vision of the sovereign consumer and of the thoroughly voluntary nature of market exchanges that is misleading, and this must be made clear in order to compare the risks and benefits of our present system with those of a potential alternative.

Differences in Wealth

For one thing, some consumers are more sovereign than others. Vast differences in wealth and income create vast differences both in the degree of influence any individual or group of individuals exerts on what is produced and in the leverage that any participant can bring to bear in an exchange. Parallels are frequently drawn between the votes individuals cast in an election and the votes they cast in the market place by what they buy or don't buy. The implication seems to be that just as political democracy protects us against tyranny in the political sphere, so too does the market, as a kind of permanent, floating voting booth, assure us of freedom in the economic realm. Indeed, some worshipers of the market go so far as to argue that it is a far better guarantor of personal freedom than are democratic elections.

We are told by William F. Buckley, Jr., for example:

> Let the individual keep his dollar—however few he is able to save—and he can indulge his taste (and never mind who had a role in shaping it) in houses, in doctors, in education, in groceries, in entertainment, in culture, in religion; give him the right of free speech or the right to go to the polling booth, and at best he contributes to a collective determination, contributes as a rule an exiguous voice. Give me the right to spend my dollars as I see fit—to devote them, as I see fit, to travel, to food, to learning, to taking pleasure, to polemicizing, and, if I must make the choice, I will surrender you my political franchise in trade, confident that by the transaction, assuming the terms of the contract are that no political decision affecting my sovereignty over my dollar can be made, I shall have augmented my dominance over my own affairs.

Now of course Mr. Buckley, the son of a millionaire, may be just a mite self-serving in this argument. His poignant defense of the right of the ghetto dweller to choose to spend his dollars "indulging his taste" in houses, travel, education, culture, and so forth, just as freely as Mr. Buckley can with his seems but a prelude to a defense of the equal right of the rich and poor to sleep under bridges. Buckley's rather cavalier attitude toward the political franchise sets him off here from many other believers in the virtues of the market as society's principal means of regulation. . . .

There is, however, another crucial difference between the operation of the market and that of a democratic election—a difference less convenient for market advocates to cite. Elections operate essentially on the principle of one person-one vote. The market doesn't even begin to approximate this principle. In the market place, a Rockefeller has thousands of times as many votes as the average citizen. Both in the money he spends for personal consumption and the money whose investment he controls, such an individual has incalculably more to say about how the society's resources will be deployed. The market works on the principle of one dollar-one vote, and those on the top have garnered far more extra votes for themselves than Mayor Daley or Boss Tweed could ever have dreamed of.

Wasserman © 1989, Los Angeles Times Syndicate. Reprinted with permission.

This means that in a market economy the products and services produced and offered are not those needed or desired by the largest number of people but those desired by those who control the most dollars. This is relevant not only to the questions of fairness and control over one's life that we are considering here. It bears as well on ecological concerns. While urban housing and mass transit, relevant to large numbers of people with relatively few dollars to vote with, go wanting, environmentally damaging luxury items are voted for in the market place by those with dollars to spare.

The realities of the market economy differ substantially from the picture offered by its apologists. As they present it, it is a wondrous thing indeed. Milton Friedman, for example, following a line of argument traceable at least back to Adam Smith, tells us that two parties will not engage in an exchange unless each sees some gain in it. Thus, no one loses; everyone comes out with more than he would otherwise have had. According to Friedman, "Most economic fallacies derive from the neglect of this simple insight, from the tendency to assume that there is a fixed pie, that one party can gain only at the expense of the other."

The real fallacy comes in elevating this pious tautology into a defense of the unmodified market. Yes, given any particular distribution of wealth and power, and any particular set of rules, two parties will not voluntarily agree to an exchange unless each expects to benefit from doing so. But that does not mean that the results of such an exchange will benefit him more than those of a different exchange which might be possible under a different set of rules and with a different distribution of power and wealth. The poor man who takes a job at minimum wage (or below the present legal minimum under Friedman's "freer" arrangements) is, we may assume, better off than he would be not taking the job if the alternative—under the "discipline of the market"—is to starve. But the market system, which has provided him with this job and thereby staved off for the day the growls of an empty stomach, has also been responsible for the distribution of wealth and the system of reward that makes such a low-paying job his only alternative to starvation. Under a different system—one that placed limits on the sovereignty of the market—he might be guaranteed a larger share of the social pie in return for his work (and, most likely, his boss would end up with a smaller share than he would have in the first case; I am not minting my own hypothetical coin).

Money Buys Freedom

Under present arrangements it is true that all are free to take or leave what the market offers. But not all are offered the same deal. Indeed, it is not even solely a matter of more or less. With regard to employment, for example, some can refuse *any* deal, while others are desperate and must accept essentially whatever comes their way. There is indeed a sense of freedom associated with a millionaire's choice of whether to accept a particular offer for his services as chairman of the board. Upon reflection, he might decide he would rather not work at all. Such is hardly the case for the unskilled day laborer, especially if the "restrictions" on the market which Friedman so decries are removed. Indeed, even Adam Smith notes this clearly:

> It is not difficult to foresee which of the two parties [masters or workmen] must, upon all ordinary occasions, have the advantage in the dispute, and force the other into a compliance with their terms. . . . A landlord, a farmer, a manufacturer, or merchant, though they did not employ a single workman, could generally live a year or two upon the stocks which they have already acquired. Many workmen could not subsist a week.

The Panglossian picture of the market's benefits offered by Friedman and others is based on assuming that no alternative means of determining wages other than a relatively unregulated market economy are available to the person. The choice the working man makes *within* the market system is his "best" choice only if one rules out certain other possibilities, such as *changing* the market system. By expanding our view of the person's options, it may appear that he has *less* by virtue of engaging in unmodified market exchanges than he would if he instead wished to change the rules and mechanisms that determine who gets what. Under a system in which considerations of equity in the outcome of distribution tempered market mechanisms to a greater degree, he might have quite a different set of choices. Even with a model of market exchanges, if redistributive mechanisms resulted in his having more in the bank than he now has, and in his boss's having less, the wage he could hold out for would be different.

A Fundamental Error

I am not concerned here, however, only with possibilities of distributing wealth more equitably or with the impact of unregulated market exchanges on the poor alone. There is a largely unacknowledged impact on the rest of us that also is obscured by what might be called the fundamental error of individualistic calculation—focusing on each transaction separately without examining the larger context of alternatives. Again, it is (tautologically) true that an individual will not voluntarily participate in an exchange unless he or she sees some gain in doing so. But again, by narrowing their vision, analysts like Friedman exclude what they wish not to see. It is not just the poorer party to an exchange who might benefit more from a substantial modification of market supremacy. In many instances, *both* parties to the exchange might be better off if they had available certain choices that the market system just doesn't provide.

This is so because unless there are specific external restrictions, a deal between two parties does not take into account the effect of their exchange upon a third party. But we are all third parties to enormously more exchanges than we are first or second parties to. My purchase of an automobile may seem to both me and the dealer a gain. I prefer the car to the money, and he prefers the money to the car. We are both better off than before the exchange. Moreover, I may be even more pleased—in a system where the government has gotten even further "off our backs"—to pay less for a car without emission controls; knowing that my own addition to the total pollution I must breathe is negligible, my individualistic calculation is that I am better off not having to pay for what—viewed in isolation—won't benefit me very much.

The Best of a Bad Situation

But whereas I am the purchaser in this one transaction, I am a bystander in the millions of other auto sales that are made in the year. If all of these purchasers also decide to save money because the contribution of their own exhaust pollutants (viewed individually) is minimal, then the total impact on my lungs of all these transactions is very powerful indeed and is likely to greatly outweigh what I gain by saving money in my one purchase. The same is true for each of the others.

Each of us, however, who are third parties to millions of other people's transactions, are, in an unfettered market, powerless to affect their transactions. So the best we can do is make the best of a bad situation by not paying for our own emission controls, which will not after all affect what millions of others put into the air.

That is what the unrestricted market so often promotes: making the best of a bad situation, and a bad situation that is, ironically but inevitably, precisely the result of scrambling by all of us to make the best of it. Far from maximizing our freedom, the market tends to trivialize it, to leave us free to choose within a set of constraints created by the inevitable workings of the market system itself. In many instances, it is only when we restrict the forces of the market that we begin to have any meaningful and valuable degree of freedom. The freedom to face a different set of choices altogether is, for many of our social and environmental problems, the only freedom really worth having. For this opportunity—often obtainable only through laws that restrict market exchanges in certain ways—the price of such restriction is well worth paying.

"The real source [of poverty] is an economic pincer between housing and jobs."

Poverty and Unemployment Prove the U.S. Economy Is Unjust

Chris Tilly and Abel Valenzuela

Chris Tilly is a professor of economics at the University of Lowell in Massachusetts. Abel Valenzuela is a graduate student in urban planning at the Massachusetts Institute of Technology in Cambridge. They write for *Dollars & Sense,* a socialist magazine. In the following article, Tilly and Valenzuela argue that America's economic system has shifted from an emphasis on manufacturing to an emphasis on the service sector. The authors contend that many factory workers have become poor because they have lost their jobs, they cannot find new jobs that pay adequately, and they receive little help from the government.

As you read, consider the following questions:

1. What factors have affected the availability of housing, in the authors' opinion?
2. How were minorities affected by the loss of jobs in manufacturing, according to Tilly and Valenzuela?
3. What government policies do the authors believe hurt the poor?

Chris Tilly and Abel Valenzuela, "Down and Out in the City," *Dollars & Sense,* April 1990. Reprinted with permission of *Dollars & Sense* magazine, One Summer St., Somerville, MA 02143.

Something is terribly wrong in our cities. In 1968, 13% of the residents in U.S. central cities lived below the poverty line. Twenty years later, the percentage had climbed to 18%—an additional six million people.

"I've seen an increase in despair," says Candace Cason, Executive Director of Women, Inc., a Boston-based agency that helps women overcome dependency on drugs and reliance on public assistance. "Particularly since 1980, people have a sense of being in a hole they can't get out of."

No one questions that poverty in U.S. cities looks and feels different than in previous decades. Legions of homeless crowd sidewalks and shelters—something not seen since the Hoovervilles of the 1930s. The crack plague and its associated violence make the heroin epidemic of the 1960s and 1970s seem tame. Experts speak of an "underclass" permanently stuck in poverty.

Why has poverty in U.S. cities worsened so dramatically? Rhetoric about the "underclass" suggests the problem lies in ingrained pathological behavior passed down from inner-city generation to generation. That analysis evades a host of causes, however. Nor are crack and violent crime the causes of the crisis. They are symptoms—albeit symptoms that intensify the problem.

The real source is an economic pincer between housing and jobs. As affordable housing has become more and more scarce, the manufacturing jobs that provided paychecks for less-educated workers have left town. These economic causes are reversible. But the key player in any coordinated effort to eliminate poverty—the federal government—has pulled back its commitment to cities. Under the Reagan and Bush administrations, the feds have eagerly declared a "war on drugs" but have refused to challenge the loss of jobs and affordable housing hammering at poor communities.

Urban Poverty in Perspective

Inner-city poverty accounts for a minority of America's poor. But that minority is growing rapidly—from 30% of all poor people in 1968 to 43% in 1988—and is likely to become a majority soon. The population in concentrated poverty neighborhoods —areas where 40% or more of residents are poor—is growing four times as fast as the overall poverty population. Economic inequality has climbed along with poverty, both nationally and in cities. In 1986, the richest 20% of New York City residents earned 19.5 times as much as the poorest 20%—a 25% increase since 1977. Nationwide, the ratio is nearly ten-to-one. . . .

During the 1970s and the 1980s, two opposing investment strategies destroyed affordable housing in U.S. cities. On the one hand, massive disinvestment by banks and land-owners cut into the existing housing stock in low- and moderate-income communities, rendering whole areas like the South Bronx of New York barely habitable. On the other hand, booming service industries such as finance and high technology lured professionals back to the city, fueling gentrification and turning neighborhoods upscale and unaffordable for most residents.

Shifting National Priorities

Since most poor people, like most Americans, want to support themselves at a decent living standard, our society can't be serious about ending poverty until we shift our national priorities toward creating millions of entry-level jobs with a future.

Frances Moore Lappé, *Rediscovering America's Values*, 1989.

The sweep of the change was startling. In Los Angeles, between 1974 and 1985, the number of apartments renting for under $300 (in 1985 dollars) was cut in half. At the same time, apartments priced at $750 or more quadrupled.

Climbing housing costs pinched everyone, but squeezed the poor hardest. In 1978, 44% of poor renters paid 60% or more of their incomes for housing costs; by 1985, 55% did. The burden on poor homeowners grew at a similar pace.

"Even for the average working class family in the communities we serve, being able to save enough to buy a house is inconceivable—out of reach," comments Women, Inc.'s Cason.

For many, the ultimate consequence was homelessness. By 1985 there were 3.7 million fewer units of affordable housing nationwide than households earning under $10,000 needed. Families caught in the gap doubled up with family or friends, found a spot in welfare hotels, or spilled into the streets and shelters. Estimates of the number of homeless range from the federal government's conservative estimate of 250,000 to the National Union of the Homeless' figure of 2.2 million. Whatever the correct number, observers agree that the homeless population grew dramatically in the 1980s, despite the economic recovery.

Homelessness is not just deprivation; it is degradation. "You're never prepared for this," a homeless man told author Jonathan Kozol. "It's like there isn't any bottom. It's not like cracks in a safety net. It's like a black hole sucking you inside."

Blue-Collar Blues

While housing costs went through the roof, manufacturing jobs fell through the floor. Between 1968 and 1988, total U.S. employment grew 56%, but the number of manufacturing jobs stayed even. With certain industries like steel and autos particularly weakened, some cities were especially hard-hit. Pittsburgh lost an estimated 140,000 manufacturing jobs, for a wage loss of $2.3 billion per year.

"We have seen the collapse of these communities," reports Tom Croft, Director of the Pittsburgh-based Steel Valley Authority, a jobs organization created by dislocated steelworkers. "The people of these communities and the communities themselves have moved toward a much more marginal existence. Some people migrate to other parts of the country; others are bouncing around from one low-wage job to another. Some just give up."

People of color suffered disproportionately. "When you have a mass of people lose their jobs in the blue-collar field, those who benefited from affirmative action are the first to lose," Croft notes. "They just get pushed down the totem pole one more rung."

Compounding the damage from manufacturing decline, government employment—long a source of relatively decent, secure employment for people of color—slumped from a high of 19% of all jobs in 1975 to only 16% in 1988.

Service-sector growth did bring some good jobs to the city. To a large extent, though, these were white collar and professional jobs accessible to few of the less-educated workers who had swelled the ranks of manufacturing. Black and Latino males, especially, continue to hold jobs in declining industries. . . .

Government Response

Some local and state governments, as well as a wide range of community and advocacy organizations, have tried to confront these forces head-on. But more help is needed. The National Urban League called for an "Urban Marshall Plan" to physically and economically rebuild U.S. inner cities. Unfortunately, the federal government, which has the economic and political clout needed to lead this assault, has largely turned its back. . . .

Given the shortfall in federal commitment, what can be done to deal with urban poverty? Asked to comment on how to solve the problem of manufacturing decline, Croft offers a frank answer that could apply equally to all aspects of urban poverty. "What does it take to move the rock? I keep being struck by the intransigence of the system—the way the system seems to not want to deal with these problems." But, he quickly adds, public policies in Europe, Sweden, and even as close as Canada are dealing with these problems far more effectively. For the time being, adds Cason, "effective programs are going to have to be hard-fought for, and probably self-initiated."

"Most poverty in America results from behavior: regarding work, education and marriage."

Poverty Does Not Prove the U.S. Economy Is Unjust

Michael Novak

Michael Novak is the director of social and political studies at the American Enterprise Institute, a think tank in Washington, D.C. He has written many articles and books, including *The New Consensus on Family and Welfare: A Community of Self-Reliance.* In the following viewpoint, Novak argues that poverty exists in the U.S. not because the system is unfair, but because the poor do not work, do not attend school, and have children outside of marriage. He contends that the only way to help the poor is to make them change their behavior.

As you read, consider the following questions:

1. What does Novak believe is the best way to reduce poverty?
2. What happens when society thinks of the poor as victims, according to Novak?
3. Why shouldn't the government simply give each poor family money to bring the family's income above the poverty line, according to the author?

Most of the 12 million immigrants who have come to the U.S. in the 1970s and 1980s, usually nonwhite and very poor, do not long remain poor. The Census Bureau classifies as poor a family of four with an annual income under $12,092.

The Census Bureau tells us three important things about the poor. First, even in these days of severe labor shortages, 83% of poor householders did not work full time year-round in 1988. Of course, there are many reasons some householders do not work full time year-round: (mostly) retirement; disability; family responsibilities; going to school; an inability to find work, etc.

The census report also indicates that most of the officially poor have not taken full advantage of free public schooling by graduating from high school. More than 93% of those over 18 who did graduate from high school are not poor.

Finally, and most important, the officially poor tend to live outside a married-couple family. Among married-couple families, 94.4% were not poor. Looked at the other way, the simple fact of getting married and staying married, even if not on the first try, reduces one's chances of being poor to 5.6%. Marriage is one of the nation's greatest bulwarks against poverty.

Female-Headed Households

Of the nearly 66 million families in the U.S., only about 7 million were poor. More than half of the latter, however, were households headed by women, with no husband present. Only 3 million were married-couple families.

Nonetheless, in 1988 just under 32 million U.S. citizens were poor—or 28 million, depending on the calculation. Almost two-thirds of these were white. Half were either children under 18 years (almost 40%) or elderly (11%). Most of the elderly were retired, and many benefits for the elderly were not included, such as Medicare. Virtually all the youngsters were financially dependent upon their parents.

Further, some very good news is hidden in this census report. For example, half of all black married couples had a family income of $30,385 or higher. This was not as much as the top half of white married-couple families ($36,840), but it was a substantial family income just the same.

Almost half (44%) of all black families, however, are headed by a female, no husband present. Most such female householders are not working, and many have never finished high school. Such households account for a staggering 76% of all black families in poverty.

Thus, there has come to be a consensus that the single most powerful remedy for poverty in the U.S. would be to reduce steadily the number of female-headed households, no spouse present, especially those who have out-of-wedlock births. For one-third of female householders were poor in 1988, and they cared for half of the poor children in the country.

To this remedy must be added efforts to help such householders to complete high school, to help them find work and to break down the social isolation in which many of them and their children live.

In short, the new consensus has shifted attention away from mere financial assistance to a more full-bodied, humanistic emphasis upon a whole pattern of life, involving marriage, education and work. Most of the nation's poor live in families. A strategy of concentrating on family life would bring help to several persons at once, including, above all, the children.

Chuck Asay, by permission of the *Colorado Springs Gazette Telegraph*.

Moreover, it is now clear that those who think of the poor only as "victims" dehumanize them. The poor are as capable of responsibility as anybody else. Most of them, in fact, seize normal American opportunities to move out of poverty—as the recent immigrants have done. The rest of us need to believe in their capacities and design our assistance accordingly.

If poverty were merely a financial matter, we could raise every poor family in America above the poverty line quite easily: merely mail each such family a check to bring its income above the poverty line. Total cost: under $35 billion. Nobody suggests this because we actually spend more money than that each year—at least three times that sum—in various programs of financial assistance to the poor. And such assistance has not done the job.

By contrast, the Census Bureau figures show clearly that most poverty in America results from behavior: regarding work, education and marriage. Since 1962 we have virtually eliminated poverty among the elderly, who once were poorest of all, while "the new poverty" appears mostly among single women with children. That is where the nation ought now to apply fresh resources of imagination, to help the poor choose more productive behaviors and to help them contribute to the public good, instead of merely being dependent upon it. In these days of worldwide economic competition, the nation badly needs their contributions.

"The notion of an excessive income inequality is in fact a myth."

Statistics Show the U.S. Economy Promotes Equality

Robert Rector and Kate Walsh O'Beirne

In the following viewpoint, Robert Rector and Kate Walsh O'Beirne argue that the U.S. has a high level of economic equality and is not becoming a two-class society. The authors contend that government statistics on income are inaccurate because they do not count government assistance to the poor as income. Robert Rector is a policy analyst and Kate Walsh O'Beirne is a visiting fellow at the Heritage Foundation's Thomas A. Roe Institute for Economic Policy Studies in Washington, D.C. The Heritage Foundation is a conservative think tank.

As you read, consider the following questions:

1. The U.S. is becoming divided between what two groups, according to Rector and O'Beirne?
2. If the Congress and taxpayers believe that large income inequalities exist in the U.S., what do the authors feel will be the result?
3. What do the authors contend is the main reason for the small amount of income inequality that exists in the U.S.?

Robert Rector and Kate Walsh O'Beirne, "Dispelling the Myths of Income Inequality," The Heritage Foundation *Backgrounder,* June 6, 1989. Reprinted with permission.

Capitol Hill has been debating what is alleged to be an enormous income gap between rich and poor in America. Some lawmakers claim that this income inequality is excessive and reflects a flaw in federal tax and spending policies. Thomas J. Downey, the New York Democrat who chairs the House Subcommittee on Human Resources, even charges that the current income disparity in the United States threatens "the health of a democracy."

Yet the notion of an excessive income inequality is in fact a myth. Criticisms like Downey's are unfounded because they are based on faulty government data. Government income distribution statistics, for example, do not count as income a substantial portion of government assistance to low-income households. The December 1988 U.S. Census Bureau report on income distribution fails to include a staggering $98 billion of government spending on low-income and elderly persons (equal to 50 percent of all such spending). These omissions make an accurate comparison of the incomes of poor families with the rest of society virtually impossible and invite false charges about income inequality.

Remarkable Equality

If the full value of government spending were included in estimating the incomes of poor families, the figures would show not an alarming degree of inequity but a remarkable level of economic equality. When the full value of government assistance is counted, the average per capita income among households in the poorest one-fifth of U.S. society turns out to be about 60 percent of the per capita income in median American households, much higher than generally assumed.

Another factor contributing to the myth of great inequality is that government statistics fail to reflect the degree to which income disparities are offset by differences in family size or are a result of differences in the number of workers in a family. "Low-income" families generally are small. And among these families, work is quite rare, while total reliance on government is common. There are over six full-time workers among households in the fifth of the population with the highest income for each full-time worker in the lowest fifth. America is increasingly divided not between the rich and the poor but between families with two or more taxpaying workers and families dependent on government funds, in which no one works.

Future reports of income inequality by the federal government should be corrected to include all government assistance to low-income and elderly persons. Such studies also should clarify the extent to which differences in household income are affected by reasonable variations in family size, in the number of workers per family, in education, and in productivity levels.

When the Census Bureau compiles its annual statistics on income and poverty, it traditionally counts only before-tax cash income. These statistics constitute the "official" measurement of income and poverty in the United States and form the foundation of virtually all debate and policy. Yet the Bureau ignores the effect of such noncash programs as Medicaid, housing subsidies, and food stamps, which now make up about 73 percent of all government assistance to the poor. Because of these flawed procedures, the Bureau systematically exaggerates the extent of income inequity and poverty.

Age and Wealth

Much income inequality is due to age. People in their 40s tend to earn twice as much as people in their 20s. Disparities in wealth are even greater, since older people have been saving much longer and making mortgage payments much longer. More than half the total wealth of the country is in the hands of people over 50.

It is hardly a great social injustice when people who have been working longer have more to show for it. Those who are younger will, of course, become older with the passage of time and have the same economic benefits, in addition to inheriting what today's older generation leaves behind.

The political left, however, ignores these age differences and automatically treats statistical disparities in income and wealth as differences between social classes, rather than as differences between age brackets. When you are in a hot political crusade and full of moral indignation, you often don't have time to check the facts.

Thomas Sowell, *The Washington Times,* December 6, 1988.

In a special study entitled *Measuring the Effect of Benefits and Taxes on Income and Poverty: 1986,* released in December 1988, the Bureau partially corrects this glaring omission in its widely used annual report. This study analyzes the distribution of income among households, using both the official Census Bureau definition and alternative income definitions that take account of other types of cash and noncash income and subtract taxes. These alternative definitions partially count some government transfers, including some nonmeans-tested cash and noncash programs, such as Social Security and Medicare, and some means-tested cash and noncash programs, such as public assistance, Medicaid, food stamps, and housing subsidies. When these noncash benefits are included as income to the poor, the Bureau calculates that the official poverty rate of 13.6 percent for 1986 actually falls to 11.6 percent. This would reduce the number of Americans categorized as poor by 4.8 million. More dramatic, using this alternative definition, the poverty rate for the elderly would drop from 12.4 percent in 1988 to just 5.7 percent.

Although these new Census Bureau calculations constitute a more accurate estimate of the financial well-being of American families, the Bureau's latest report is still deficient. For instance, the Bureau attributes only $49 billion in means-tested benefits and services to the poor in 1986. By contrast, other government sources estimate that government at all levels spent a total of $126 billion on such assistance. Thus the Bureau dismisses $77 billion in government aid as having no income value to its low-income recipients. Similarly, $71 billion was spent on Medicare in 1986, yet the Bureau identifies only $50 billion of this as having increased the share of national income received by the elderly. Overall, the government fails to count $98 billion in government aid to low-income and elderly persons—50 percent of the total. This uncounted aid is given in four ways: cash assistance, noncash assistance, services, and Medicare benefits. . . .

The table on the next page indicates the cumulative effect of these disparities in the income calculations of the Census Bureau and those of the CRS [Congressional Research Service]. By counting virtually every possible benefit as having income value to higher-income families, while failing to count billions of dollars in government transfers to the poor, the Census Bureau's report gives a false impression of the condition of low-income Americans, and thus of the financial differences between income classes. It is this indefensible treatment of family resources by the Bureau that has ignited charges in the media and in Congress that America is an unacceptably unequal society and that government transfers have been insufficient to reduce income inequalities. This conclusion bolsters calls for further taxation and income redistribution.

Telling Policy Makers Little

In fact, using the Bureau's faulty methodology, the government could double its spending on many low-income programs and have absolutely no effect on income distribution measured by the Census Bureau. The Bureau thus should not even profess to be measuring the distribution of "aggregate household income" if it includes certain benefits as part of the income of the upper and middle class but excludes the same benefits when counting the incomes of poorer families. It cannot arbitrarily assume that billions of dollars in government spending on the poor have no "income value" and can therefore be ignored. The Census Bureau's faulty model thus tells policy makers very little about the relative well-being of U.S. families. An accurate measure of income distribution in the U.S. must represent the share of *total* economic resources made available to individuals at different economic levels.

	CRS and Other Government Sources	Census	Shortfall
Medicare	71	50	21
Means Cash	37	23	14
Means Noncash	70	26	44
Services	19	0	19
Total	197	99	98

SOURCE: U.S. Census Bureau

Charges of excessive inequality arise not only from these flaws in the measurement of income—considerable as they are—but also because the Census Bureau's comparison of families fails to take into account key differences in the characteristics of rich and poor households. This failure adds further erroneous ammunition to support the inequality myth.

A glaring problem with the Census Bureau study of inequality is that it fails to recognize the effect of differences in family size and in the number of workers per family on income inequality. Example: Suppose "the Smiths" have an income of $40,000, while "the Jones" have an income of $20,000. The conventional Census Bureau analysis would conclude that the Smith household must be "high income," while the Jones household was "low income." Some policy makers might even conclude that such inequality represents a *prima facie* case for income redistribution to correct "inequality." But if the Smith household consists of a husband, wife, and three children, while the Jones household is a recent college graduate living alone, very few Americans would feel that the Smith household should be regarded as the more affluent. Indeed, the per capita income of the Smith family would be $8,000, compared to $20,000 for the Jones.

The Census Bureau income inequality data are riddled with paradoxes of this kind. Because they do not take into account differences in family size, conventional Census Bureau measures of income inequality exaggerate its level in the U.S.

Similarly, most Americans would agree that it is quite reasonable and fair for a household with two workers to have a higher income than a household with one worker. But the Census Bureau analysis ignores the fact that much of the apparent income inequality in America is caused by households having different numbers of workers. . . .

Census Bureau Reforms

The impressions of family income and income equality provided by the Census Bureau differ markedly from reality. If the Census Bureau reports were obscure documents, used only by scholars who understood their shortcomings, that might not matter. But the Census Bureau data form the basis for media reports and for policy making in Congress. Thus the deficiencies in the Census data often lead to deficiencies in public policy. Good policy making requires that the Census Bureau measurement of income distribution be reformed in the following manner:

• The recent inclusion by the Census Bureau, on an experimental basis, of capital gains and employee health benefits, and the subtraction of federal and state income taxes and Social Security taxes, are welcome improvements. These calculations should be made a permanent feature of the annual income statistics.

• The full value of Medicare, means-tested cash aid, and means-tested noncash transfers and services should be incorporated in the Census Bureau's income data. The Congressional Research Service and other government sources have estimated that these benefits were worth $197 billion in 1986.

• Census Bureau procedures currently count a government benefit as having a certain income value to affluent families, while the same benefit is counted as having less or even no income value to lower income families. These procedures should be reformed.

• When comparing the income of American families, the Census Bureau should emphasize comparisons of per capita household income and per capita household income per worker. The Bureau should downplay the more misleading figures of total household income. . . .

More accurate income distribution data would show that the U.S. is a society with a high level of economic equality. While efforts to improve data over the past few years have been largely commendable, the current income distribution figures are still inadequate and misleading. They present an erroneous, unflattering image of U.S. society to policy makers and social commentators. Improvements in the Census Bureau income distribution data are long overdue and should be undertaken immediately.

"Not just the chasm between the rich . . . and the poor . . . but the gap between the rich and the great American middle class has grown wider."

Statistics Show the U.S. Economy Promotes Inequality

Thomas Byrne Edsall

In the following viewpoint, Thomas Byrne Edsall contends that the U.S. is becoming a society of two distinct classes: the rich and the poor. He argues that the rich are increasing not only their economic power, but also their political power. Edsall believes the power of America's once-dominant middle class is being taken over by wealthy Republicans. Edsall is a reporter for *The Washington Post,* and the author of *The New Politics of Poverty.*

As you read, consider the following questions:

1. Americans believe that inequality is constantly being remedied, according to the author. What evidence does he give to refute this notion?
2. Why does Edsall believe there have been increases in family income recently?
3. How can the poor and powerless advance their economic interests, according to the author?

Thomas Byrne Edsall, "The Return of Inequality," *The Atlantic Monthly,* June 1988. Excerpted with permission.

Social imagination often lags behind social fact. Long after farming had ceased to be the premier American occupation, for example, we thought of ourselves as a nation of farmers, and the small town still serves as a touchstone of Americanness. This essay will explore a similar lag between a picture in our minds and a quantifiable social reality—a phenomenon that challenges an image of America which is about as true to our condition as those Norman Rockwell *Saturday Evening Post* covers that move us to nostalgia. The phenomenon is not poverty. Our mental picture already has a place for that. Poverty has a claim on our moral sense; it stirs our beneficence and concern. Liberals and conservatives may disagree about its scope, but they acknowledge its existence and they join in deploring it. They don't enjoy any such unanimity on the subject of this essay, however, for the social phenomenon I mean to discuss is inequality, an old word for the dominant social fact of our times.

Textbook Pictures of Inequality

Inequality: the very word invites polemic. Tocqueville found, if anything, too much equality of condition in the early Republic. In the post-Civil War era, to be sure, inequality had its innings: our school textbooks concede as much. But within fifty to a hundred pages a *deus ex machina* known as the New Deal comes along, just in time to humanize the sweatshop capitalism of the high industrial era. Depending on their level of sophistication, the textbooks leave us with a picture of America achieving greater and greater equality in incomes and life chances since the Second World War. First, workingmen, through those still controversial institutions, labor unions, achieved a large measure of the promise of American life. They were soon joined by blacks and women. Yes, black poverty remains a grim problem. Yes, women still don't earn as much as men for performing the same jobs. But on balance, in that mental picture of ours we are closer today to Tocqueville's America than to Andrew Carnegie's. Asked if his age was a handicap, twenty-six-year-old William Pitt, the great British Prime Minister, said that if it was, it was one he was remedying every day. That, I think, expresses our notion of inequality: it's a fault we have been remedying every day.

That notion is wrong. Not just the chasm between the rich (the top five percent, defined by the Congressional Budget Office in 1986 as those families making more than $124,651 a year before taxes) and the poor (in 1986 the Census Bureau considered poor any four-person family making $11,203 or less) but the gap between the rich and the great American middle class has grown wider. From 1977 to 1988 the majority of the population has experienced a stagnating income or a net loss in after-tax income, according to an October, 1987 report by the Congressional Budget Office. Meanwhile, the top twentieth of the population has seen average family income grow by $33,895 and the top hundredth (those now earning more than $303,900) by $129,402. The important debate over whether the middle class is expanding or contracting obscures the meaning of those sobering statistics: economic and political power are flowing from the middle class to the affluent. . . .

The Electioneering Elite

Two closely linked political developments of the past twenty years lie behind the new inequality. The first is the collapse of broad-based political parties, particularly of the Democratic Party, which has left those in the bottom half of the income distribution, where families make less than $30,000 a year, with a diminished voice in the political process. This loss of political voice, in turn, has caused their economic interests to be less and less forcefully represented.

The Economy and Poverty

By every measure, poverty increased dramatically during the Reagan era. Part of the blame rests on cuts in benefits that began in the mid-1970s and accelerated during the Reagan years. Part rests on a legacy of policies that fail to attack the roots of poverty in employment, income distribution, and discrimination. Underlying both policies and cutbacks was the economy. After 1973, real wages declined; income inequality widened; productivity dropped; inflation soared; and unemployment increased. Extraordinary numbers of black men remain out of work.

Economic recovery did not wholly reverse the impact of these trends. Although the number of jobs grew, they consisted disproportionately of badly paid jobs in the service sector. As a consequence, poverty rose dramatically even among those who work. Without the minimal safety net that exists, hunger, homelessness, infant mortality, and disease would be catastrophes unimaginable to most Americans.

Michael B. Katz, *The Undeserving Poor*, 1989.

The second development is the growing dominance over politics of a new fund-raising, polling, consulting, and electioneering elite. Ward- and precinct-based organizations, whose most important function was to get out the vote in working- and lower-middle-class communities, have been replaced by technology-based campaigns dependent on television and on vast sums of money; this development has coincided with, if not encouraged, a steady decline in voter turnout, most acute among those earning less than the median wage.

The new electioneering elite is made up of approximately thirty Republican and Democratic consultants and pollsters, almost all based in Washington, who are the principal strategists in almost every presidential campaign and competitive Senate race in America; they also play significant roles in gubernatorial, House, and local referendum contests. House and Senate candidates, in addition, have become dependent on political-action committees (PACs), vehicles for the transfer of money from organized interest groups to elected officeholders. . . .

The Decline of the Democratic Party

The rise to authority of new elites that are empowered to make decisions without being accountable to the economic interests of voters is part of a much larger shift in the balance of political power involving changes in voting patterns, the decline of organized labor, a restructuring of the job marketplace, and the transformation of the system of political competition. This power shift, in turn, has produced a policy realignment most apparent in the alteration of the after-tax distribution of income.

What this points to is a reversal of the progressive redistribution of income that has underlain America's tax and spending policies since the Administrations of Franklin D. Roosevelt and Harry Truman. A study released by the Congressional Budget Office shows that from 1970 to 1986 there was an overall increase in median family income. From 1977 on, however, most of the gain was concentrated in the top quintile, and inequality grew sharply. Moreover, almost all the recent gains in family income have resulted from the entry of wives as second earners into the work force, not from substantial raises for established workers.

In the competition between the defense and social-welfare sectors a roughly parallel shift in the balance of power can be seen over the years 1980-1987. According to the historical tables of the 1987 budget of the United States, the share of the federal budget going to national defense has grown from 22.7 percent in 1980 to 28.4 percent in 1987. At the same time, the share of federal dollars going to education, training, employment, social services, health, income security, and housing has dropped from 25.5 percent in 1980 to 18.3 percent in 1987.

These priorities reflect the rising strength of the Republican Party. The Republican Party has gained the allegiance of many voters, achieving near parity by 1988; what was a twenty-three-point Democratic advantage in terms of self-identification has shrunk to a four-point edge. . . .

Relatively comfortable in their own lives, the Democratic reformers failed to recognize the growing pressure that marginal tax rates were putting on the incomes of working- and lower-middle-class voters. The progressive rate system of the federal income tax had remained effectively unchanged from the early 1950s through the 1970s, so that the series of sharply rising marginal tax rates that had originally been designed to affect only the upper middle class and the rich began to pinch regular Democratic voters whose wages had been forced up by inflation, and Democratic households whose incomes had risen only as the wives had gone out to work. By neglecting to adjust the marginal rate system for inflation while repeatedly raising the highly regressive Social Security payroll tax, Democrats effectively encouraged the tax revolt of the 1970s, which provided a major source of support to the conservative movement and to the Republican Party.

Wasserman © 1989, Los Angeles Times Syndicate. Reprinted with permission.

The effects of the ever larger tax bite on traditionally Democratic voting blocs were aggravated by the sudden halt in 1973 of what had been a steady rise in median family income since the end of the Second World War. According to data from the 1987 Economic Report of the President and from the Bureau of the Census, family income in 1981 dollars rose from $12,341 in 1947 to $17,259 in 1960 to $23,111 in 1970, and topped out at

$24,663 in 1973—a level that was not exceeded at least through 1986. Of all the blows to the Democratic coalition in the 1960s and 1970s, the stagnation of family income had the potential to inflict the most severe long-range damage. It undermined the party's basic claim that the system of government established in the years following the New Deal promised continued growth and a better life for each new generation. It lent credibility in the public mind to claims that the untrammeled accumulation of private wealth is a necessary precondition of economic growth; that regulations to protect consumers and workers—indeed, most forms of government regulation of the economy and the environment—endanger the power of the free-enterprise engines of progress; and that if efficiency is not fostered, even at the price of inequity, the last will be dragged down with the first. . . .

The New Political Underclass

Over the thirty-year period 1949 to 1979, according to Bureau of Labor Statistics figures, the number of manufacturing jobs grew by an average of three million a decade. From 1979 to 1986, however, the number of manufacturing jobs dropped from 26.5 million to 24.9 million—a loss of 1.6 million jobs. Though they were counted as employed in the government statistics, *28.9 percent* of the 59.6 million workers getting hourly wages in 1987 (as opposed to weekly salaries) received less than $5.00 an hour. For a full-time worker getting paid all fifty-two weeks of the year in 1986, it took an hourly wage of at least $5.39 to exceed the $11,203 poverty level for a family of four. . . .

While most of those who have lost manufacturing jobs have found full-time employment, such workers have in the main seen wages fall and fringe benefits decline or disappear. Given the declining voter turnout associated with dropping income, these workers have fallen into what amounts to a new political underclass. . . .

If the trends we have been discussing continue over the next twenty years, the social consequences could be severe. Egalitarianism has been the democratic answer to Marxism. Greater equality of incomes and life chances, in other words, is not just something that is in the interest of the few. It is in the national interest.

"Poverty in the United States will be eliminated only when the poor secure the right not to be poor."

Economic Equality Should Be a Legal Right

David R. Riemer

David R. Riemer is the director of administration for the city of Milwaukee, Wisconsin. He has been counsel to the U.S. Senate Subcommittee on Health and Scientific Research, and has advised many government agencies on policies for the poor. He is the author of *The Prisoners of Welfare: Liberating America's Poor from Unemployment and Low Wages*. In the following viewpoint, excerpted from that book, Riemer argues that the U.S. should provide each family with enough income to place it above the poverty line, thus establishing a legal right to an adequate standard of living. He believes such a policy would be morally sound and would benefit all Americans.

As you read, consider the following questions:

1. In what specific ways would the poor benefit from a right not to be poor, according to Riemer?
2. How does the author believe the existence of poverty in the U.S. affects America's world image?
3. What dominant moral question does Riemer ask concerning poverty?

Excerpted from *The Prisoners of Welfare: Liberating America's Poor from Unemployment and Low Wages*, by David R. Riemer (Praeger Publishers, 1988), pp. 97-107 passim, © 1988 by David R. Riemer. Reprinted with permission.

Poverty in the United States will be eliminated only when the poor secure the right not to be poor. However much we might wish poverty to be eliminated without creating such a right, the supply of jobs and the structure of wages in the U.S. economy present such an enormous barrier to the elimination of poverty that the only practical way to end poverty in this country is to create a right not to be poor, to implement that right through acts of government, and to finance the implementation by expending public funds. . . .

Neither the purpose of the Constitution, nor the language of the Constitution itself, nor 200 years of judicial interpretation, nor either of the competing schools of thought about how to go about applying the Constitution, lends support to the view that the Constitution can be fairly construed to vest America's poor with a legal right to reverse the inaction of government that permits poverty to continue or to alter the operations of the private economy (i.e., the creation of an insufficient number of jobs and the payment of low wages), which are proverty's primary cause. There is no constitutional right not to be poor, and there will probably never be one. . . .

If the poor in the United States are ever to secure the right not to be poor, therefore, the right must come through the enactment of statutes. The U.S. Constitution has been consistently interpreted over the last 50 years to permit Congress to enact, implement, and finance such a statutory right. (State constitutions would also permit state legislatures to do likewise.) We must turn, therefore, from the realm of constitutional interpretation to the realm of public policy. Should laws be enacted to grant the poor the right not to be poor? If the poor were granted specifically enforceable rights to obtain concretely defined benefits (more cash, a job, a wage supplement), which, if taken advantage of, would result in their income rising above the poverty line—and if those rights were translated into reality through the enactment of national programs and full-scale financing—would the public benefits outweigh the public costs? The question should be considered from at least three perspectives: that of the poor, that of the rest of us (the nonpoor), and that of American society as a whole.

Benefits Outweigh Costs

From the perspective of the poor, it seems obvious that the benefits would outweigh the costs. The benefits to poor people of no longer being poor would be enormous. Their intake of protein and other nutrition would increase. Their choice of housing and the quality of the housing they select would improve. Crimes related to poverty (that the poor generally commit against each other)—murder, rape, robbery, burglary, child abuse, spouse abuse, and drug-related crimes—would probably decrease. Apart from these specific improvements, the poor would benefit by an increase in the control over their own lives. Increased purchasing power represents a part of this. More money to spend not only permits the purchase of additional goods and services but greatly widens the choice of goods and services that potentially could be purchased. The poor, if no longer poor, would also gain greater control of various nonfiscal aspects of their lives. As their economic stake in society increases, their political stake is likely to increase as well. They will vote more, and thus exercise a greater influence in municipal, local, state, and federal elections. As a result, elected officials will respond to them more effectively. Agencies of government—police, fire, sanitation, streets, parks, and so forth—will also respond more promptly and effectively. Public school systems in particular will be more responsive. The former poor who dislike the education their children are getting in public schools will have an increased ability to "vote with the dollars" by enrolling their children in previously unaffordable private schools or moving to living quarters in previously unaffordable communities. Responding to the former poor will become a matter of survival for the teachers and administrators who depend for their livelihood on the public schools.

Equality of Opportunity

I'm not for imposing particular outcomes, but to achieve equality of opportunity takes a lot more than an absence of legal restraints. Equality of opportunity would require that the minimal conditions necessary to develop one's unique talents and to participate in community life be available to all. This is impossible without a floor and a ceiling in the distribution of income. Let me explain why.

The opening or closing of opportunity begins in infancy and childhood. So without a secure economic floor under families, millions of children are denied opportunity from birth. To have a fair chance in life, each child minimally would have to have good nutrition, education, and medical care. That one-fourth of young American children live in poverty, and 12 million children go hungry, proves how frightfully far we are from achieving equality of opportunity.

Frances Moore Lappé, *Rediscovering America's Values*, 1989.

While the benefits to the poor of enjoying a right not to be poor may for the most part be obvious, some potential disadvantages—to them—should also be considered. First, will not the creation of a right not to be poor reduce the motivation of the poor to exert themselves to get out of poverty? It is arguable that to the extent that self-help is rendered unnecessary to achieving a minimum living standard, many of the poor will refrain from enrolling in the schools, undertaking the enterprises, and in general taking the risks that today elevate many of them not only above the poverty line but into the middle class and beyond. The establishment of a right not to be poor could result, arguably, in the poor as a whole—or at least a substantial percentage of them —ending up economically worse off in the long run. Second, to the extent that a guarantee of nonpoverty reduces the poor's incentive to exert themselves, will there not be a parallel reduction in their innovative contributions to the economic well-being of our entire society—including the well-being of the former poor along with the well-being of the rest of us? In other words, a guarantee of nonpoverty may arguably induce the poor child—whose deprivation would otherwise have spurred the child to graduate from high school, finish college, get a Ph.D. in physics, and win the Nobel Prize for devising a way to produce cheaper energy—to refrain, because of the security offered by the guarantee, from embarking on a course that would greatly benefit all former poor people as well as society as a whole.

Balancing Benefits

In individual cases, it may indeed be true that a guarantee of nonpoverty will reduce the incentive to achieve. In other individual cases, however, the opposite may hold true. The establishment of a right not to be poor may eliminate the listlessness and aimlessness that often accompany deprivation. Formerly poor people, no longer paralyzed by want, may be more highly motivated to attend school, achieve great things, and improve not only their own lot but society's overall condition. . . .

Even if the incentive question yielded a conclusive negative answer, it would still have to be balanced against the enormous, positive, and tangible benefits accruing to the poor as a result of creating a right not to be poor. Those benefits include, at a minimum, improved nutrition, better housing, increased purchasing power, and greater influence over elected officials and public services. In the final analysis, there can hardly be doubt that on balance the poor would be much better off if they could exercise a right not to be poor.

Would the poor's possession of a right not to be poor help or hurt the rest of us, that is, the nonpoor?

There are many reasons why the elimination of poverty is in the self-interest of the rest of us. Poor people commit more crimes than other people. Sometimes we are the immediate victims. More often we suffer indirectly: spending money on burglar alarms and other security systems; choosing not to live in "bad neighborhoods" whose architecture, liveliness, and proximity to work we may actually prefer; haunted subtly but powerfully by the fear of violence or violation. Ending poverty would presumably reduce the level of crime we endure, reduce our expenditures for home security systems, expand our choices of where to live, and remove some of the fear we endure whenever we walk in the dark or return home alone or hear strange noises in the night.

Inequality Causes Poverty

Poverty ought to be viewed as an aspect of inequality, a facet of the maldistribution of wealth and income. It is the inevitable social byproduct of the concentration of wealth in the hands of a few. From this perspective, one does not pay primary attention to individuals, or propose programs aimed at correcting the deficiencies of individuals. For if inequality is the cause of poverty, the proper question is not "What is it about individuals that makes them poor?" but "What is it about the nature of the economy that creates poverty?"

Ronald D. Pasquariello, *The Christian Century*, February 18, 1987.

Poor people often do not have health insurance. When they get sick and receive care, the hospitals and doctors who treat them shift the costs to the insurance companies or self-insured employers that insure most of the rest of us. Our wages, salaries, and dividends are reduced accordingly. Ending poverty would presumably result in a more even distribution of health insurance. Low-income people already buy health insurance with their own out-of-pocket funds to a surprising extent. Lifted out of poverty, the former poor would probably increase their purchase of health insurance to the extent that current national health insurance policies remain static, and their ability to contribute to the cost of premiums would increase to the extent that current arrangements are replaced by policies that either offer individuals and firms incentives to provide health-care coverage or mandate such coverage. Under any scenario, lifting the poor above the poverty line would thus reduce the necessity for cost shifting, which in turn would make it possible for insurance companies to reduce the premiums (or at least the premium increases) they charge the rest of us, and for self-insured employers to curb the growth of their per-employee health expenses. This in turn would permit employers to pay the never-poor majority higher wages, salaries, or dividends.

Poor people, indeed, impose a host of other costs on the rest of us. Committing more crimes, they make police protection more expensive. Setting more fires, they make fire protection more expensive. Raising more handicapped, violent, and other "problem" children, they make public education more expensive. Committing more child abuse and spouse abuse, they make publicly funded social services more expensive. Unable to care as well for themselves, their children, or their parents when mental illness or other disabilities strike, they make not only public programs but private charities more costly than would otherwise be true. Ending poverty would greatly reduce—though hardly eliminate—all these fiscal burdens on the rest of us.

Widespread poverty also results in the imposition of a disproportionate burden of taxation on the nonpoor. Because poor people maintain their homes less well than other people, the valuation of the property owned by the rest of us accounts for a disproportionately higher share of property taxes. If poverty were ended, the formerly poor would take better care of their homes, their property would increase in value, and the burden of property taxation would be redistributed. Similarly, because poor people earn less, they pay lower income taxes, thus shifting the burden of income taxation to the rest of us. If poverty were ended, the formerly poor would pay higher taxes, and the rates the rest of us pay (all other things being equal) could decline. . . .

Benefits to American Culture

The establishment of a right not to be poor would benefit American society as a whole. We are more than a nation of self-interested persons, each seeking to maximize our personal advantage. We are also a culture. Admittedly, we constitute a mixture of many separate subcultures with divergent and even conflicting histories and aims. Yet all (or at least the great majority of us) also belong to and consciously adhere to a common set of values, a common vision of our past, a common purpose for our future.

At the heart of our culture are the twin concepts of freedom and equality. Every observer of U.S. society, from Alexis de Tocqueville on down, has noted this. Freedom and equality pervade our rhetoric, define our social and political debates, permeate our institutions. Reconciling the drive for liberty and equality with each other, with the other values of the U.S. system (powerful local government, the rule of the majority), and with the imperatives of government itself (the need for law, the need for stability) has been the ongoing challenge of U.S. history. Though liberty and equality have suffered as many defeats as victories, in the end they have consistently triumphed in

American history (though the cost, as in the Civil War, has included the slaying of hundreds of thousands of men and the laying waste of half the nation).

Hunger in America

Clyde Peterson. Reprinted with permission.

The advancement of liberty and equality—the liberation of the colonies from British rule, the emancipation of the slaves, the movements for equal rights for racial minorities and women, the elevation of the status of the worker during the New Deal—defines not only the U.S. view of itself but its image of its role in the world. Since our creation as a self-made nation, we have offered ourselves as a model for the world. Today most of us still view the United States as a model. While we recognize that our appeal to other countries has diminished during the last several decades, we sense that some nations (or, at least, large numbers of people in other nations) still share our view of ourselves. The model we offer is a model of liberty and equality. . . .

None of these inquiries, unfortunately, disposes of the question, Should the poor have a right not to be poor? None of these inquiries can settle the question. In the final analysis, it is neither a legal nor a utilitarian issue. It is a moral issue. Legal and utilitarian considerations inform the answer, but they alone cannot provide an answer. Moral judgments must be made to come to a final resolution.

The dominant moral question is, Is poverty just or unjust? More particularly, do we as a society believe that poverty is just or unjust?

More than a third of the poor are children. Do we as a society believe it just that children, poor through no fault of their own, should remain poor? Or do we believe that impoverished children should be lifted out of poverty as a matter of justice?

A tenth of the poor are over 65. Do we as a society believe it just that old people, regardless of the cause of their poverty, should remain poor? Or do we believe that impoverished elders should be raised out of poverty as a matter of justice?

Most of the poor adults under 65 either want to work or are working, many full-time and year-round. Do we as a society believe it just that people who want to work, or who are doing work, should remain poor? Or do we believe that the working poor should—if they work full-time and year-round—not be poor, as a matter of justice?

A Matter of Decency

If we conclude that whether the poor remain impoverished or get out of poverty is not a matter of justice—the attitude toward the poor that prevailed in the United States and most societies until the twentieth century—the matter comes to an end. The poor can be left to their fate. If they remain poor, justice has not been offended. If they climb out of poverty, that is wonderful, but justice has in no way been enhanced.

If we believe, however, that because poverty (or at least most poverty: the poverty of children, the handicapped, the elderly, those who seek but cannot find work, and those who are already working) is unjust, we can proceed to the next step. Should the injustice be ended? And, if so, how?

Poverty is unjust and affording every poor American a means by which that person can easily escape from poverty is required as a matter of decency, fairness, and equity in a wealthy society such as ours. Some reasonable people will no doubt disagree. Most will agree. There is no way to prove the proposition in an objective manner. It is a matter of values and belief.

"Policies that attempt to use the state to redistribute goods or increase equality will tend to fail."

Economic Equality Cannot Be a Legal Right

Charles Murray

Charles Murray is a Bradley Fellow at the Manhattan Institute for Policy Research in New York. He is the author of several books, including the controversial *Losing Ground: American Social Policy 1950-1980,* and *In Pursuit: Of Happiness and Good Government.* In the following viewpoint, Murray contends that the government cannot eliminate economic inequalities. Because people are born with different abilities, he argues, different levels of income will always exist. Not only is it impossible for the government to even out these inequalities, it would also be devastating to a free nation's economy, Murray concludes.

As you read, consider the following questions:

1. What does the author see as the difference between the 18th-century definition of inequality and the 20th-century definition of inequality?
2. Why are factions necessary evils in any democratic society, in Murray's view?
3. What problems result when a society attempts to solve social problems through a centralized government, according to the author?

In 1987, the celebration of the bicentennial of the American Constitution prompted lavish invocations of what the Founding Fathers would and wouldn't think of contemporary American problems. . . .

The founding of the nation was an affirmation of the potential of individual human beings and in that sense was profoundly optimistic. Two features of man especially captured the imagination of Americans of the Revolutionary era: his capacity to act as an autonomous being, and his equality as an actor.

Man as an Individual

The Founders' ringing defense of man's *right* to act independently is different from their analysis of man's *capacity* to act independently. The Declaration hailed the inalienable right, in the words that were once part of the secular catechism of every school child. The theory that undergirded it drew from John Locke's theory of natural rights as expressed in his *Second Treatise of Government.* But along with the right of man to be free and independent (no matter whether he used that freedom wisely), there was a strong sense that man was at his best operating as an individual. . . .

The other revolutionary aspect of the Founders' optimism regarding the nature of man had to do with that word which has in the twentieth century been used to mean so many things, "equality."

The Founders were not egalitarians nor even very good democrats. Men *are* unequal, they observed, and these inequalities should affect the way a government is structured. This is a far different thing from saying that the inequalities are unjust and should be reduced (the twentieth-century issue), for the inequalities that concerned them were inequalities of virtue, accomplishment, and judgment, not inequalities of material condition. When it came to government and what was meant by "the consent of the governed," the Founding Fathers were generally persuaded that one could easily go too far. Thus Thomas Jefferson could write easily of a "natural aristocracy" of virtue and talents that "I consider as the most precious gift of nature, for the instruction, the trusts, and government of society." James Madison took as the limit of his "great republican principle" that the common people would have the good sense to recognize the rarer men of virtue and wisdom who were fit to serve as their representatives. Such features of the Constitution as the electoral college and provision for the selection of senators by the state legislatures were a few of the concrete expressions of the Founders' doubts about the masses.

In the twentieth century, the Founders' unflattering vision of the common man has come under sustained attack. One history widely used as a university text, *The American Political Tradition* by Richard Hofstadter, is a good example, pointing out that an essential purpose of the Constitution was "cribbing and confining the popular spirit." The Founders "did not believe in man," the author wrote, and had "a distrust of man [which] was first and foremost a distrust of the common man and democratic rule."

Blaming Society

Years ago, there was far more pride and self-respect in America. Someone who had two or three illegitimate children was seen as their own worst enemy. Today we blame society. People who refused to work were considered bums; today they're helpless "victims" of society, and you and I must be taxed for their indiscretions and sustain them in their mistaken lifestyle.

It's about time we recognize that the government cannot provide the basic ingredients for upward mobility. Child-rearing practices in which parents make children do their homework, behave in school, and go to bed on time are beyond government policy.

Personal pride, ambition, perserverance, and self-respect can't be given by the government, but they can be weakened by handout programs. Government is no match for the family, church and civic organizations for instilling success-oriented values. That's something we have to teach the "experts."

Walter E. Williams, *Human Events*, June 10, 1989.

Hofstadter was right. The Founders *were* distrustful of democratic rule. But the Founders believed that men *were* equal in another and crucial sense, and the affirmation of that equality was perhaps the most revolutionary and optimistic aspect of the Founders' conception of man.

Their view was revolutionary first in that it broke with the assumption that inequalities were governed by class. The few who were fit to govern were not necessarily to be drawn from an economic or social aristocracy. Alexander Hamilton, in many ways the most elitist of the Founders, wrote matter-of-factly that "experience has by no means justified us in the supposition that there is more virtue in one class of men than in another." On the contrary, he continued, the only difference among the social classes is the type of vice that predominates, not its quantity. But beyond this pragmatic recognition that virtue and intelligence can reside in anyone was a broader affirmation of equality. The nobility of the American experiment lay in its allegiance to the proposition that everyone may equally aspire to happiness.

This seems hardly a radical position to modern eyes, but radical it was. From the most ancient times until the Founding Fathers broke ranks, governments had been based on the opposite premise, that only a few men have the potential for (in modern terms) self-actualization. All men may exhibit rudimentary good qualities or experience primitive feelings of pleasure, it was believed, but attributes such as virtue and meaningful happiness might be achieved by only an exceptional few. A primary function of government was to nurture these few. "The classical idea of human nature is, as it were, aristocratic," as Martin Diamond put it. "All men are human but some are more so, and that is the crucial political fact." The Founding Fathers began a new tradition that is now as unquestioned as the old one: "The modern idea of human nature is democratic: No difference among us can reach so far as to alter our naturally equal humanness, and that is the crucial fact," [according to Martin Diamond]. That also is the underlying assumption of equality and democracy that makes it reasonable to seek the best of all possible worlds in one that makes the enabling conditions for pursuing happiness available to everyone.

A Level Playing Field

In terms of practical politics, the Founders' prescription was simple. Equality meant that all men shared as their birthright the same natural rights of liberty. All were equally immune by right from the arbitrary coercion of the state. This did not have anything to do with equality of outcome. Edmund Burke expressed the prevailing view when he wrote that "All men have equal rights, but not to equal things." The essence of this constrained vision of equality, as Thomas Sowell has pointed out, is process—providing a level playing-field, to employ a modern analogy. Even this formulation permits semantic games, but the underlying meaning is reasonably clear. If your competitor comes to the playing field after months of practice, with professional coaching and superior ability, it is no doubt true that you will not derive much advantage from a level playing field. But there is a qualitative difference between your disadvantage under those circumstances and the disadvantage if *the rules* specify that the referee give you three strikes and your competitor four, or (worse) that no matter what, your competitor *must* win. For if you have superior abilities or even just superior determination, what you need most of all is a level playing field. What is deadening to the soul is not to lose, but to be forbidden to win. Until relatively recently in American history, such logic was taken for granted. . . .

The nation was founded as an affirmation of the private man but was to survive because of profound pessimism about the public man. The construction of the American polity was grounded in the understanding that men acting as political animals are dangerous, and that what men might do innocuously as individuals is far different from what men might do innocuously as groups. Man's potentialities are grand; his human nature constantly threatens to prevent him from realizing those potentialities.

Government Takeover

If we had in our Constitution, as some nations do, a guaranteed right to an adequate diet, to adequate shelter at a reasonable rent, to a job, and to other things, how would the government honor these guarantees? I am talking about taking the guarantees *seriously*, as something the government is pledged and *obliged* to do. When unemployment rises, it will not suffice just to increase appropriations for unemployment insurance. It will be necessary for the government to generate jobs, either on the public payroll or by controlling industry. . . .

Where the state guarantees the right to a job and takes it seriously, it is hard to see how it can stop short of controlling the entire economy—the training and placement of workers, the allocation of resources for investment, the opening and closing of workplaces.

Robert A. Goldwin, *Why Blacks, Women, and Jews Are Not Mentioned in the Constitution and Other Unorthodox Views*, 1990.

This understanding was expressed in the Constitutional Convention, in the minutes of the state ratifying conventions, in the public and private correspondence of the leading figures, and (in a losing but influential cause) by the Anti-Federalists. But to a remarkable degree the theory has been handed down to us in a single text, *The Federalist*, the collection of eighty-five letters written to newspapers in New York State in an effort to persuade the voters of New York to ratify the Constitution. The byline on the letters was "Publius," the nom de plume of Alexander Hamilton, who instigated the project, John Jay, who soon had to drop out because of bad health (he was injured in a street riot), and James Madison, a Virginian who chanced to be in New York that winter of 1787-88 for the sitting of the Continental Congress. It was a haphazardly conceived and hastily conducted effort that gave birth to the most enduringly influential document in American political history save only the Constitution itself. . . .

Republics don't last. Democracies don't last. This was the stark empirical truth that faced the Founders. It is a fine thing to say that government derives its just powers from the consent of the governed, but it is exceedingly difficult to translate this aspiration into policy.

The reason why it is so difficult, Publius concludes, is that men, given a chance, will destroy their freedoms under a representative government. The bludgeon with which they do so is called faction, defined by Madison in No. 10 as "a number of citizens, whether amounting to a majority or minority of the whole, who are united and actuated by some common impulse of passion, or of interest, adverse to the rights of other citizens, or to the permanent and aggregate interests of the community." Faction is something with which the political system must live, because eliminating the phenomenon is out of the question. To endure, the system would either have to suppress faction—which requires a totalitarian state—or else convince everyone to share the same opinions and interests, which is impossible even in a totalitarian state. . . .

If the Founders Were Wrong

There are many able proponents of the proposition that the Founding Fathers were wrong. Indeed, in the twentieth century it has been intellectually fashionable to believe that they were, joining in Hofstadter's opinion that "No man who is as well abreast of modern science as the Fathers were of eighteenth-century science believes any longer in unchanging human nature. . . . Modern humanistic thinkers who seek for a means by which society may transcend eternal conflict and rigid adherence to property rights as its integrating principles can expect no answer in the philosophy of balanced government as it was set down by the Constitution-makers of 1787."

And that is the kernel of the debate over policy choices. Most of what we know as contemporary social policy is based on the tacit assumption that the Founders were wrong. It is believed, apparently by a large majority of people, that humans *can* act collectively with far more latitude than the Founders believed they could.

If the Founders were wrong, we may conduct social policy on the assumption that if humans seek a more even distribution of resources, for example, they may achieve it. If humans want an end to racial inequality or sexual inequality, it is within their grasp to have it; all they have to do is pass the right laws. The world can be made constantly fairer if human beings use the instruments of government to reduce unfairness. If the Founders were wrong, we may continue to be optimistic in the face of failures, and assume that when one attempt at a solution doesn't produce the desired results, the proper response is to try again with another and better political solution. Most importantly: If the Founders were wrong, then we may assume that this expansive use of a centralized government *can continue over the long run*, because men have it in them after all to act collaboratively in their public capacity.

Suppose, however, that the Founders were right. If one accepts their optimistic view of private man, then centralized governmental solutions are not attractive. What allows man to fulfill his own nature in the Founders' vision is the process of individual response to challenge, risk, and reward. Each of those words—"individual," "challenge," "risk," "reward"—grates against the rationale for centralized solutions. Centralized solutions from the left urge that the collective society has a moral claim on the individual; they seek to dampen risks and increase predictability, and use as primary measures of success the achievement of security and equality. Centralized solutions from the right urge that the state has the right to impose beliefs on individuals; they seek to restrain by law individual variations in social behavior, and use as primary measures of success the degree of conformity to the righteous way. If man has the autonomy and equality that the Founders saw in him, these goals are not "bad" but wrongheaded. They do not liberate humans to fulfill their potential. They do not nourish the human soul.

If the Founders were right about *public* man, then the practical options for seeking solutions to social problems through a centralized government are highly constrained for two reasons.

Solutions, Not Rights

Declaring the right to an adequate diet does not augment the supply of food or improve its distribution. If we think of the plight of desperate peoples, with hundreds of thousands dying of malnutrition, can it help to insist that these people have a right to an adequate diet? The question is not whether they have the right, but how to get food to them, how to correct the problems that led to the lack of food, and how to put their agricultural production on a sounder footing. Surely no one seriously asserts that a significant part of the problem of hunger in the world stems from a denial that people have the right to an adequate diet.

Robert A Goldwin, *Why Blacks, Women, and Jews Are Not Mentioned in the Constitution and other Unorthodox Views,* 1990.

First, such solutions will be impossible to sustain over time without also sacrificing democracy. If Publius was right, republics collapse when a faction is able to use the state to impose its vision of the good on the rest of society. And a relentless use of the state in just that fashion—to let a majority faction decide what is right for everyone and impose that vision on everyone—is the very essence of legislation that requires either school prayer on behalf of religious values or school busing on behalf of social justice.

Accepting Publius's analysis, one should view the Western democracies as in a process of transition. Sooner or later the genie will get out of the bottle. If one permits the government to do one thing for everybody in the country because it is the "right thing" to do, every once in a while the government will do another thing for everybody in the country that is the wrong thing. And as time goes on, and as the limits on what it is permissible for government to do are loosened, there will be no defense against any number of bad things being done in the name of good.

Unintended Outcomes

Second (and less apocalyptically), policies that attempt to use the state to redistribute goods or increase equality will tend to fail. The ubiquitous "unintended outcomes" that have been found by the evaluators of social programs would not have mystified Publius. Constituencies of persons, Publius already knew, would seek to use the reforms for their own ends. They would form factions, bringing pressures to bear on the politicians who design the policies and the bureaucrats who implement them. The politicians and bureaucrats themselves would have ambitions that affect the way that the programs are run, not to mention other human frailties of vanity, ineptitude, and foolishness that would obstruct the implementation of the great schemes. And if all that were not enough, Publius knew, the very definition of what constituted "serving the common good" would be impossible for anyone not omniscient and of Olympian detachment to discern. A central message for modern times to be drawn from *The Federalist* is that one cannot use central governments to do such things—not just "ought not" use them but *cannot*, successfully. To work, to be just, to be stable, centralized social reforms demand every quality of public man that the Founders did not believe in.

Recognizing Statements That Are Provable

From various sources of information we are constantly confronted with statements and generalizations about social and moral problems. In order to think clearly about these problems, it is useful if one can make a basic distinction between statements for which evidence can be found and other statements which cannot be verified or proved because evidence is not available, or the issue is so controversial that it cannot be definitely proved.

Readers should be aware that magazines, newspapers, and other sources often contain statements of a controversial nature. The following activity is designed to allow experimentation with statements that are provable and those that are not.

The following statements are taken from the viewpoints in this chapter. Consider each statement carefully. *Mark P for any statement you believe is provable. Mark U for any statement you feel is unprovable because of the lack of evidence. Mark C for any statement you think is too controversial to be proved to everyone's satisfaction.*

If you are doing this activity as a member of a class or group, compare your answers with those of other class or group members. Be able to defend your answers. You may discover that others come to different conclusions than you do. Listening to the reasons others present for their answers may give you valuable insights into recognizing statements that are provable.

> *P = provable*
> *U = unprovable*
> *C = too controversial*

1. Poverty in the United States will be eliminated only when the poor secure the right not to be poor.
2. Poor people often do not have health insurance.
3. A tenth of the poor are over age sixty-five.
4. Affording every poor American a means to escape from poverty is required as a matter of decency, fairness, and equity.
5. The only difference between social classes is the type of vice that predominates.
6. Policies that attempt to use the state to redistribute goods or increase equality will fail.
7. The U.S. Census Bureau report on income does not include a staggering ninety-eight billion dollars of government spending on low-income and elderly persons.
8. Most Americans would agree that it is quite reasonable and fair for a household with two workers to have a higher income than a household with one worker.
9. America is a remarkably just nation.
10. Young children brought up in poverty are more likely to remain in poverty.
11. In the not-too-distant past, being born poor usually meant dying poor almost everywhere in the world but in the U.S.
12. Most of the officially poor have not taken full advantage of free public schooling by graduating from high school.
13. It is now clear that those who think of the poor only as "victims" dehumanize them.
14. The nation ought to help the poor become more productive members of society.
15. In 1968, 13 percent of the residents of America's inner cities lived below the poverty line.
16. The federal government has pulled back its commitment to cities.
17. The U.S. government provides less financial aid to cities today than it did in 1975.
18. Many of the poorest, more oppressive societies of the world have constitutions which are nearly identical to ours.
19. In a market economy, the products and services produced and offered are not those needed or desired by the largest number of people but those desired by the people who control the most dollars.

Periodical Bibliography

The following articles have been selected to supplement the diverse views presented in this chapter.

Walter Block	"Analyzing the Welfare System," *Vital Speeches of the Day*, March 15, 1989.
Mario Cuomo	"Will the Poor Always Be with Us?" *New Perspectives Quarterly*, Fall 1989.
E.J. Dionne Jr.	"The Idea of Equality Is Proving Unequal to the Demands of Today," *The Washington Post National Weekly Edition*, May 7-13, 1990.
Marian Wright Edelman	"Invest in Our Young—Or Else," *Human Rights*, Summer 1989.
Thomas Byrne Edsall	"The Return of Inequality," *The Atlantic Monthly*, June 1988.
Robert Greenstein	"Making Work Pay," *Christianity & Crisis*, March 6, 1989.
John Huey	"War on Poverty," *Fortune*, April 10, 1989.
Mickey Kaus	"For a New Equality," *The New Republic*, May 7, 1990.
Jack Kemp	"Liberate America's Other Economy," *The Wall Street Journal*, June 12, 1990.
Robert W. Lee	"Charity Begins at Home," *The New American*, September 26, 1988.
Amata Miller	"Envisioning a Just Economy," *Christian Social Action*, December 1989.
Claudia Mills	"Charity: How Much Is Enough?" *Utne Reader*, March/April 1990.
Daniel Patrick Moynihan	"Toward a Post-Industrial Social Policy," *The Public Interest*, Summer 1989.
Charles Murray	"Here's the Bad News on the Underclass," *The Wall Street Journal*, March 8, 1990.
Robert B. Reich	"As the World Turns," *The New Republic*, May 8, 1989.
Warren J. Samuels	"The Pursuit of Economic Quality," *Society*, September/October 1989.
David Whitman	"The Surprising News About the Underclass," *U.S. News & World Report*, December 25, 1989-January 1, 1990.
Walter E. Williams	"Fairness and Justice: Process vs. Results," *The Freeman*, October 1988.

Does the U.S. Provide Equal Opportunities for Minorities?

Social Justice

Chapter Preface

Since slavery was first debated during the Constitutional Convention of 1787, America has struggled with the question of how to treat its minority members. Over the years, amendments have been added to the Constitution, aiming to ensure that all members of society, whether minority or majority, have the same legal rights.

Many Americans, however, contend that these legal guarantees have not eliminated the racism and discrimination that prevent many blacks from succeeding. They maintain that racism is the cause of black poverty, the rate of which is three times that of whites, and of the high black unemployment rate, which is double that of whites. University of Colorado professor Manning Marable states, "The American economic and political system promises equality, but has never delivered for the African-American."

Other Americans disagree with Marable's contention that American society is to blame for the failure of many blacks to succeed. They believe that success and failure are determined by the efforts of the individual and not by race. They quote Booker T. Washington's statement that "it is a mistake to assume that one man can . . . give freedom to another. Freedom . . . every man must gain for himself." As evidence that any American, regardless of race, can succeed, these people cite as examples blacks such as Colin Powell, the head of the Joint Chiefs of Staff; Thurgood Marshall, a U.S. Supreme Court justice; and Douglas Wilder, the governor of Virginia.

Is American society to blame for minority failures, or does success depend solely upon an individual's initiative? The following chapter addresses this question and debates the broader issue of whether America is a society in which minorities receive justice.

"African Americans start out further behind and all too often slip backward because racial differentiation and discrimination still exist."

Racism Denies Minorities Equal Opportunities

John E. Jacob

John E. Jacob is the president and chief executive officer of the National Urban League, an organization whose goal is to eliminate racial segregation and discrimination. In the following viewpoint, Jacob contends that racism is still prevalent in the U.S. and that it is the root cause of the economic, educational, and social problems of many black Americans. He argues that eradicating racism is the only solution to these problems.

As you read, consider the following questions:

1. What legacies did the Reagan administration leave the U.S., according to Jacob?
2. How does the author explain the success of some blacks despite the existence of racism?
3. What steps does Jacob suggest the U.S. take to rid itself of racism?

John E. Jacob, "Racism and Race Relations: To Grow Beyond Our Racial Animosities," a speech delivered to the Conference on Public Policy and African Americans, Kalamazoo, Michigan, October 21, 1989.

There is a school of thought—perhaps the dominant one in America today—that says there is no racial problem. There is a poverty problem. A housing problem. A health problem. An urban problem. Other problems. But no racial problem. That's been solved.

How wrong can you get?

Those "problems" people talk about without mentioning race are simply euphemisms for race. African Americans are only about twelve percent of the population, but we're a third of the poor. More whites may be poor, ill-housed, and uneducated. But that is only because there are so many more of them.

Race Is the Issue

African Americans suffer disadvantage in numbers grossly disproportionate to our share of the population.

And because we are concentrated in urban centers, any talk of urban problems, education or poverty amounts to a euphemism. We're really talking about race, the effects of racism and racially based disadvantage.

We have to be clear about that. So many people are trying to deal with so many problems—but they ignore the central, core issue—race. That indicates they no longer even understand what the problem is.

When today we talk of the problems of the underclass, of the urban poor, of the disadvantaged, we are talking about the same people we talked about 25 years ago when we spoke of racial disadvantage and discrimination.

The vocabulary has changed, but the people remain the same. And the change in vocabulary has masked the real, potent effects of racism and the extent to which it has permeated our society.

We've just emerged from eight years of an Administration that insisted we are a colorblind society. That Administration has left a triple legacy that may take decades to undo.

Its first legacy is the effect it had on people's attitudes. They bought the theory that we are a colorblind society and that if many African Americans remain mired in poverty and disadvantage, it is their own fault.

A second devastating legacy is the social and economic policies of the 1980s that tore away programs that enhanced African American access to job, education, and other programs. The result was to drive more African Americans deeper into poverty.

The third legacy is the Supreme Court, which was high-jacked by the Reaganites and now boasts a 5-4 majority that is actively dismantling civil rights guarantees.

In effect, the clock has been turned back two decades, and African Americans—who have been behind for four hundred years—are today even further behind.

Too often, we approach racial issues in a conceptual vacuum. We take an historical view. We forget that while most Americans' forebears came to this nation seeking freedom and opportunity, ours came in chains and were enslaved and oppressed.

From Overt to Covert Racism

We forget that the Constitution defined blacks as "three-fifths of other people" and today black family income is still three-fifths of white family income.

We forget that emancipation didn't lead to forty acres and a mule but to sharecropping and segregation.

A Heavy Burden

Who pays the cost for the legacy of racial discrimination? And indeed, racial discrimination has wrought and continues to place a heavy burden on all black people in this country. A major function of racial discrimination is to facilitate the exploitation of black labor, to deny us access to benefits and opportunities that would otherwise be available, and to blame all the manifestations of exclusion-bred despair on the asserted inferiority of the victims.

Derrick Bell, *Human Rights*, Fall 1988.

We forget too, just how recent America's emergence from the dark ages of racial backwardness has been. Twenty-five years ago African Americans could not vote, could not attend schools or hold jobs reserved for whites.

It took a massive national grass roots movement of blacks and whites to change that. But the various laws, executive orders, and court decisions that followed did not eradicate racism. They didn't change disadvantage. They didn't eliminate discrimination.

They made all those things harder. For the first time, blacks had constitutional rights that had to be respected. But the main change in white America was that overt racism became unfashionable and covert racism became the new trend.

The Klansman with his hood and burning cross was rejected. But the smooth, subtle racism of people in three-piece suits continued to keep African Americans out of schools, jobs and neighborhoods.

We have to remember that history as we deal with our subject today, because it provides the context for the present . . . the environment that shapes today's issues and solutions.

And part of that history has to be the extraordinary gains

African Americans have made. Black people today sit in mayors' offices in many of our largest cities. . . .

And beyond politics, we see African Americans in senior executive positions at corporations that once refused to hire blacks. We see an emerging black middle class holding professional positions, educated at the best universities, and living in integrated neighborhoods.

We see these people because they are so visible.

But their presence raises important issues related to our topic today.

Few Succeed

One issue is the claim that the existence of appreciable numbers of blacks who have made it indicates that racism is no longer a factor.

I strongly disagree with that assumption. The group that has made it in our society is a very small one.

It is comprised of individuals whose extraordinary gifts allowed them to take advantage of the breakthroughs of the 1960s—the access to education and jobs mandated by law, and affirmative action practiced by institutions who sincerely wanted to change and by those who had to change to conform to legal requirements.

Their success in no way suggests racism is dead. Rather, it suggests that racism is capable of being suspended temporarily in the presence of both superior ability and the law.

As for those who have made it, racism merely takes on a different aspect. They are relatively immune from the institutional racism that locks others into poverty and disadvantage. But they continue to face racism's ugliness daily.

No matter how successful an African American is, he or she cannot escape the consequences of being black in this society. Successful blacks may drive a Mercedes—but they can expect to be pulled over by highway police convinced that a black behind the wheel of such a car has to be a car thief.

They can rise to the vice presidencies of their corporations, but most understand they've reached a ceiling on their career aspirations and must resign themselves to seeing whites, including some with lesser abilities than they, move to the faster lane of career promotion.

When *USA Today* surveyed black views on racism, it found that four out of five blacks earning more than $50,000 said race was a determining factor in job mobility. And only three out of five said they expected opportunities to increase.

That's a devastating view of racism from the people most affected by it. It's based on first-hand experience and while such conclusions may shock those of us who truly believe racism is dying, it is clear that racism is alive and well—affecting even those who have overcome its worst effects.

Last month, my friend Earl Graves, the publisher of *Black Enterprise Magazine*, caused a bit of a furor because in only one paragraph of a 20-page speech, he mentioned the fact that Westchester County, New York, clubs exclude blacks from membership.

Exclusive Inner Club

Now I suppose that's a measure of how far we've come—that we can add to our long list of disadvantages the relatively new one of not being able to join country clubs.

But that's not as frivolous as it seems because as much business gets done on the golf course as in the boardroom. When you are excluded from the country club you are also excluded from the inner club that wields power in our society.

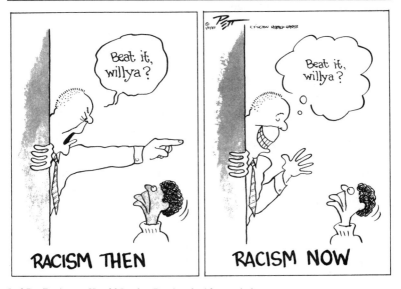

Joel Pett/Lexington Herald-Leader. Reprinted with permission.

There is a second issue raised by the emergence of African Americans in power positions today. And that is—if they made it, why can't others?

This is a concept that has taken deep root in America today. The barriers have been lifted and those left behind have only themselves to blame.

This view is especially popular among black conservatives, some of whom have made careers out of it. I saw one article by a black academic that said that if racism no longer existed at all, African Americans would remain far behind because of the disorganization in our communities.

Look at the crime, the drugs, the teenage single mothers, and the other pathologies of the ghetto, he wrote. And he went on to say that if all we had to worry about was being brutalized by whites, we would have no real problems because we do so much damage to ourselves.

That's a seductive argument, especially to those who don't want to face the issue of racism.

There is no doubt that many people in what has become known as the underclass exhibit dysfunctional behavior patterns that prevent their own advancement and even impede the progress of others.

There's no news in that. But to approach such people and situations in a vacuum, without taking into consideration the racial factors that caused their poverty and antisocial attitudes in the first place, is irresponsible.

For much of what appears to be self-destructive behavior unconnected with race is in fact behavior deeply affected by economic and social realities that are molded by racial factors.

Economic Trends

Let me give you one example of what I mean.

The "blame-the-victim" crowd is fond of saying that blacks are disproportionately poor because of the growth in female-headed households. They'll usually follow that with a condemnation of lifestyles, irresponsibility and promiscuity.

The trouble with that is that there's been a growth in single female-headed-households not because of the individual irresponsibility of young women but because of unemployment among young black men.

In 1960 almost three-fourths of black families were intact and almost three-fourths of black men had jobs. In 1988 only half of black families are intact and only about half of black men have jobs.

Among employed young black men, real income adjusted for inflation has fallen by about 50 percent since 1973. Where the typical income was once sufficient to support a family, it no longer is enough.

So black poverty and family dislocation are largely determined by negative economic trends that have destroyed opportunities that once were more readily available.

Today's economy requires skills and educational attainment beyond the reach of many youngsters who grow up in poverty and in impacted neighborhoods, isolated from the mainstream world.

112

It's a vicious circle—dysfunctional behavior is caused by economic, educational, and social factors. And those in turn are caused by the heritage of racism.

African Americans start out further behind and all too often slip backward because racial differentiation and discrimination still exist.

We start out behind because the typical white family has ten times the wealth of the typical black family. In addition, the single biggest asset of white families is usually a house, which appreciates in value. Among blacks, it's a car—which depreciates in value.

Why the disparity in wealth? Because when America abolished slavery it forgot to give the slaves a pension. By law and by custom, African Americans were relegated to the lowest paying tasks and denied access to the better paying ones.

The result is a reservoir of poverty and behavioral attitudes that impede progress. But you can't say the poor are at fault—it is racism that put them where they are and helps to keep them there.

Values for Survival

That some escape is a tribute to their ability and to the steps we've taken to become a more open society. But we're far from being the open, pluralistic, integrated society the Urban League has sought to secure.

We'd be a lot closer to that goal if we could untangle ourselves from the interrelated problems we face and acknowledge that racism is at the root of those problems.

Simply to assert that the poor are poor because they don't have middle class attitudes and characteristics is to say nothing of value. The question is why so many of the poor *do* have those values and fail to make it in our society.

Very often what we label a dysfunctional characteristic is actually a survival mechanism that doesn't work in the larger society. Drugs as an escape from unbearable reality is one such. Crime is often another.

I spend a lot of my time telling young people to get skills that make them employable and then have to listen to them tell me they can't buy big cars and gold watches on what legitimate jobs pay.

Is that distorted value system a part of their racial heritage —or is it a macabre version of the value system of a society that exalts material wealth and greed?

In some ways the underclass is a mirror image of the upper class—a caricature of an upper strata of society, many of whom are also into drugs, suffer unstable family life and often act in antisocial ways. The big difference is that the underclass is black and poor and the overclass is white and wealthy.

So while there is some validity in the views of those who say if racism were to disappear overnight, nothing would change for many black people—there is also great falsehood.

If racism were to vanish, a lot would change for virtually all African Americans. Despite the apologists for racism, it is the prime factor in the lives of African Americans today.

Racism pervades our society to such an extent that many people who believe they are free of it actually practice it. They can't escape thinking in stereotypes—thinking that every black male is a potential mugger, that black workers aren't as good as whites, that a black family moving next door signals the end of the neighborhood.

Behavior Is the Key

Some will deny it. Jackie Mason, you'll remember, even boasted that he sent a check to the NAACP [National Association for the Advancement of Colored People].

But those attitudes get translated into behavior that reduces black opportunities to schooling, jobs and education. Behavior that imposes upon black children the premature knowledge of limits and barriers in a society from which they are all too often isolated by color, wealth and status.

Let me be clear however, that our argument is not with attitudes. It is with behavior.

I don't care what someone may think of me—so long as his attitude is not translated into denying me a job or a cab ride or a club membership.

The Urban League confronts racism through that behavioral side. We have taken as our theme, racial parity by the year 2000.

To measure how far we are from that goal and what we must do to achieve it, we conducted a research study that measured the distance between whites and blacks in key areas of life—employment, health, housing and other indicators.

We found that it would take many years, even hundreds of years, to catch up in some areas. And in others, we found that at the current rate of change, there will never be parity.

We also developed a Racial Parity Index that pulls all those numbers together. A Racial Parity Index of 100 would indicate absolute parity between the races.

In 1967, the Racial Parity Index was 51.2—in 1985, it stood at only 47.

We're moving backward because racism is moving forward. Whatever the excuses and the smokescreens of those who would deny its impact, racism is a cause of our present predicament and a major factor in perpetuating it.

"The basic nature of this problem of the underclass is not discrimination, but inadequate performance."

Racism Does Not Deny Minorities Equal Opportunities

Richard D. Lamm

Richard D. Lamm is the director of the Center for Public Policy and Contemporary Issues at the University of Denver in Colorado, and a former governor of Colorado. In the following viewpoint, taken from a speech before the Denver Rotary Club, Lamm argues that the economic, social, and educational failures of minorities in the U.S. can no longer be blamed on racism. He contends that the successes of some minority individuals prove that racism can be overcome, and that cultural factors are more to blame for the failures of minorities.

As you read, consider the following questions:

1. How did the first minority underclass form, according to Lamm?
2. What immigration reforms does the author suggest?
3. Why does Lamm believe that new or additional civil rights laws are not the solution to minority problems?

Richard D. Lamm, "Confronting Minority Failure: A New Priority to Solving the Problem," a speech delivered to the Rotary Club, Denver, Colorado, January 26, 1989.

It is our purpose today to expand the dialogue about race relations in the United States. We feel that this is a problem that is festering: not getting better but getting worse. We feel that America will not remain a great country unless we help all of our people succeed; and that the underclass is today a social cancer which will have grave long-term negative effects on the body politic.

We believe that the existing dialogue is not adequate given the scope of the problem. It is our desire to expand the scope of the inquiry—for the challenge of assimilating the underclass has staggering implications to America's future. We feel that racism is no longer the primary roadblock and that schools are not the primary solution. We shall not "solve" this problem here today but we would like to suggest a few areas in which progress can be made.

Minority failure is a problem larger than white racism. We do not think that America is a racist society: there are racists, but the overwhelming percentage of Americans are fair, tolerant, committed to pluralism, and recognize the great stake they have in improving the conditions of minorities. Martin Luther King did not understate when he said "we shall either learn to live together as brothers, or die as strangers."

Minority Failure

There must be some non-racist way to raise the issue of minority failure, and start to explore how society can better help. A problem well defined is a problem half solved and, conversely, a problem misdefined is a problem made worse. If we attribute minority failure solely to racism we misdefine the problem and look in the wrong direction for the solutions. Like the man who looks for his keys under the lamp post, even though he lost them in the dark, we shall search for the wrong solutions.

As Glenn C. Loury, a black author, put it:

> It is now beyond dispute that many of the problems of contemporary black American life lie outside the reach of effective government action, and require for their successful resolution actions that can only be undertaken by the black community itself. These problems involve at their core the values, attitudes, and behaviors of individual blacks.

After citing staggering statistics on black illegitimacy, crime and incarceration rates, Loury states:

> Too much of the political energy, talent, and imagination abounding in the emerging black middle class is being channeled into a struggle against an 'enemy without' while the 'enemy within' goes relatively unchecked.

We suggest that Loury's assessment is correct. Advancement

116

of minorities by civil rights laws has reached diminishing returns. We have to sensitively and compassionately look to a range of new solutions, at the same time we continue to enforce our civil rights laws. Where then can we look for our new solutions?

I believe that first we must be aware that the demographic forces which helped create the first underclass is now forming to create a second underclass. The United States has just granted amnesty to over two million illegal immigrants as a part of our new immigration law. I suggest there is a substantial chance that soon America will have *two* unassimilated, undereducated, underemployed minority groups within its society.

An Improper Diagnosis of Discrimination

Civil rights organizations and feminist organizations are quick to assert that discrimination explains income, and other, differences. But can race discrimination alone explain the fact that black median income is only 59 percent that of whites? Can sex discrimination alone explain why female median income is only 61 percent that of males?

An improper diagnosis can lead to an inappropriate policy prescription. If we diagnose the high rate of black teenage unemployment (45 percent) as the result of employer racism, when, in fact, poor education is a more significant factor, then any anti-discrimination policy will produce disappointing results.

If high crime rates, high illegitimacy, the breakdown of the black family, and the destruction of black neighborhoods are interpreted as a result of racism, we will suffer the same disappointment. Whether racial discrimination exists or not is not the critical issue; more important is how *much* of what we see is caused by racial discrimination and how much is caused by other factors.

Walter E. Williams, *All It Takes Is Guts: A Minority View*, 1987.

The black sociologist William Julius Wilson found that the origins of the black underclass were caused by the rapid migration from the South during and after WWII. Then as a proud result of our civil rights laws, the black middle class moved, like their white counterparts, to the suburbs and, in the words of one author, "took their coattails with them." That left large numbers of poorly educated, unskilled poor people with few social support systems and no positive role models. The results have been disaster.

Patrick Burns of FAIR [Federation for American Immigration Reform] suggests that the pattern is being repeated. He writes:

This pattern is being repeated in crowded barrios across the nation. Middle class Hispanics are leaving old ethnic neighborhoods for less crowded suburbs. Left behind are large numbers of poorly educated immigrants many of whom are without the social, language or job skills needed to succeed in an increasingly sophisticated domestic economy.

He suggests that we shall soon have both a black underclass and a Hispanic underclass.

We have so focused on the individual success stories of some immigrants, that we have ignored the fact that most immigrants, particularly from South of our border, have low educational levels. Of recent illegal aliens, 25 percent have less than five years of education. Of Mariel boatlift Cubans, 33 percent have less than six years of education. (By contrast, the first generation of Cubans are some of our most successful businessmen and women.) The rates of unemployment of Southeast Asian refugees is the highest in California. Demographers have found that while poverty among Americans in general is in decline, poverty in immigrants is on the rise.

A Microchip Society

Now it is true that throughout history immigrants often came to America without an education, but that was mostly when America was an empty continent, and where we needed many strong backs. Today we live in a computer and microchip society where one has to have a skill to get a good job. Again, Patrick Burns:

> When it comes time for the children of today's legal and illegal immigrants to find their place in an increasingly sophisticated labor market, what will we have to offer them? What does the future hold for a person raised in poverty, trapped between languages, and who is a member of a racial minority?

The original immigrants are often very grateful to be in America, and they suffer in silence, but their children are American born and have American expectations. They do not suffer in silence. They are brought up in crippling poverty and have the highest dropout rates in American history, an increasing involvement in gangs, but they do not suffer in silence. Increasingly, they channel their frustrations into anti-social, self-defeating behavior. Gang involvement, drug and alcohol abuse, teenage pregnancy and street crime become the outlets for their frustrations.

So our first emphasis would be to start selecting immigrants more for their skills and less on the basis of "family reunification" and to limit immigration to absorbable and assimilable numbers.

It is axiomatic that the most valuable resource of a country is its human resources. The country that is second best educationally, second best in skills, will soon be a second rate economic power. Demography is destiny. We are as a nation ultimately dependent on an educated, motivated and creative workforce to compete in this new world of international competition. We have absorbed nearly eight million immigrants during the 1980s. Schools that are already strained and falling behind are being inundated by legal and illegal immigrants. And they are mostly immigrants with marginal skills. Seventy-two percent of all adult Mexican immigrants entering southern California during the 1970s had an 8th grade education or *less*. Only 2 percent had a college degree or better. In contrast more than one half the Asian immigrants had attended college.

America has already undertaken a staggering social agenda and we must educate and assimilate the people we have already accepted before taking millions more.

Blacks Must Help Themselves

In an era of abundant prosperity for many American blacks, where every measure of white racism shows it to be in sharp decline, where the crying imperative is no longer equal political rights but economic empowerment among a marginal black underclass, there is only so much white America can do. In its next phase black ambition must focus urgently upon economic activism, and black Americans must ask themselves what they can do for themselves and for their brothers. Repairing the tattered fabric of black family life, in particular, will require self-healing. The obstacle is no longer a simple "Them."

Karl Zinsmeister, *Public Opinion*, January/February 1988.

It is also essential that we help all immigrants assimilate into America and learn English. One clear reason for minority failure is failure to learn English. You can't come into a job market without a high school degree, not speaking English or speaking inadequate English, and without marketable job skills, and then claim discrimination. Equal opportunity requires some level of self help and that includes proficiency in English.

One study put it this way: "When earnings of Hispanics are considered, the question of how they compare with earnings of Anglos naturally arises. If attention is restricted to those in our most English-proficient group, we find no evidence of statistically significant differentials" (with Anglos).

So we must use our immigration laws to ensure that we do not grow a second underclass while we are working hard to solve the problems of the current underclass.

Second, we must recognize that the problem of minority failure will not be remedied merely by new or more civil rights laws. We need strong enforcement of existing civil rights laws, but the basic nature of this problem of the underclass is not discrimination, but inadequate performance. Too many nonmajority people succeed brilliantly in America to continue to classify this as a problem of discrimination. The most economically successful groups in America are Japanese Americans and Jews —people who have overcome discrimination and succeeded brilliantly. Too many blacks and Hispanics have themselves succeeded brilliantly not to recognize that others could if they had the right skills. Discrimination, where it still exists (and it does), is a hurdle, not a barrier.

We have a large and growing underclass of about five million black Americans (out of a total of 30 million) who are enmeshed in a cycle of welfare, drugs, alcohol, crime, illiteracy and disease. It is not Jim Crow who is keeping them in the ghetto— that is too often the excuse and seldom the real reason. Millions of immigrants from Korea, Pakistan, India, Africa, Cuba, Haiti, Indochina, Afghanistan and elsewhere come from economically poor circumstances but prosper in America. They leapfrog over the black underclass.

Slavery Is Not the Cause

It is true that slavery is a very heavy burden for the black underclass. But that will only go so far. Too many black families are in worse shape today than they were during the height of Jim Crow. There is far more drug use, far more crime, far more illegitimacy, far more family breakdown. Black sociologist William Julius Wilson points out that in 1940 only 17.9 percent of black American families were headed by women and today that figure is closer to 45 percent. Slavery cannot carry the responsibility for the situation getting dramatically worse.

Next we would look at the family. . . . Washington, D.C. already spends 50 percent more than Iowa and Minnesota, yet they graduate only 57 percent of their students from high school while Iowa and Minnesota graduate about 90 percent of their students. Schools need more money, but neither more money nor better schools is a panacea. Schools, even at their best, cannot salvage wholesale the product of broken homes, teenage mothers, neglected children. There is an old saying that "one mother is worth a hundred teachers." Broken homes too often produce broken children. We use the schools too often as the answer to problems which weren't caused by the schools nor are truly correctable there. The deterioration of the family is, at the same time, a cause and an effect of the growing underclass. It is essential to recognize that no society, no matter how well intentioned, can ever replicate the nurturing role of a stable family.

Third, and this will offend some of you, but I believe that all women, including all welfare women, should have access to family planning and abortion. They should have the same control over their reproductive functions as other women do. The one time our average welfare family size went down dramatically was when we made birth control and abortion available to women on welfare. There is no public policy reason to force unwilling welfare women to have unwanted children.

Focus on the Children

I believe also we have to spend more on the next generation and less on the last generation. The elderly are 12 percent of America, and yet they get 57 percent of federal entitlements, and they have more disposable income than the average non-elderly. Poverty in America is much more of a problem of children than of the elderly. We have to stop giving our tax monies to those who lobby us the hardest and start giving it to those who need it the most.

Lastly, I suggest that we look to culture as a dominant factor in the success of people. All people were created equal and I believe entitled to equal opportunity. However, some people, some cultures, succeed in large numbers and others fail in large numbers. I believe that this is partly due to the cultural signals that are sent to people. Those cultures that stress education, delayed gratification and hard work create wealth. Those cultures which send opposite signals are often left in an economic backwater. I would love the opportunity to expand on this subject sometime.

In summary, we feel that America has a great stake in solving the problem of inadequate performance of *all* its citizens. Our children as a group are falling behind in many areas. However, we have a special challenge with our minority children. They are failing in record numbers and if we fail to come to grips with this failure, we shall have unprecedented social strife. We feel that the problems will *not* be solved by areas today given major emphasis: i.e. new civil rights laws and leaving the solution to the schools. Those are important but inadequate. We must put a new emphasis on immigration to ensure that the problem does not grow; we must put a new emphasis on assimilation and the need for the melting pot to truly melt; we must find ways to dramatically cut down on illegitimacy and single-parent families and stop the breakdown of the black family, and we have to put a new priority to solving this problem.

"A great deal of what is evil in America . . . originated in a deep enmeshment with the culture of slavery and its positive evaluation of racism."

The Legacy of Slavery Denies Minorities Equal Opportunities

Orlando Patterson

Orlando Patterson is the author of numerous books and novels, including *Slavery and Social Death: A Comparative Study* and *The Children of Sisyphus*. In the following viewpoint, Patterson discusses slavery and its continuing tragic effects on black society. He states that all Americans are responsible for slavery and racism, and that consequently all Americans must work to fight racism and help the black working class and underclass.

As you read, consider the following questions:

1. According to Patterson, how was American slave society unique?
2. How did slavery affect the black family, according to the author?
3. Why does Patterson believe that all Americans are responsible for the heritage of slavery?

Orlando Patterson, "Toward a Study of Black America." Reprinted with permission from the Fall 1989 issue of *Dissent*, a quarterly publication of the Foundation for the Study of Independent Social Ideas, Inc., 521 Fifth Ave., New York, NY 10017.

No understanding of black American society is possible without a clear grasp of its origins in slavery. Yet sadly, the thrust of most historical scholarship on American slavery since the seventies has been to undermine the critical importance of these two and a half centuries of the black, and American, experience. How this happened constitutes an essential preliminary chapter on the sociology of American historical knowledge. We do not have the space here to explain this paradoxical development, except to point out that black scholars and Marxists have been the most prominent in this subversion of the explanatory potency of slavery. Black bourgeois historians, anxious to prove that the group has had a past like all other Americans—one that can be shown to go back in an unbroken line to African culture, or out of the mistaken belief that the only dignified history is one that demonstrates near complete control of one's life—have hopelessly obfuscated the fundamental cultural tragedy, the nightmarish social catastrophe, and the sustained economic exploitation that was American slavery. . . .

Unique Culture of Slavery

The study of slavery must begin where almost no American student of the subject has chosen to begin: with an understanding of what is unique about the slave relationship itself. Slavery is distinctive in being a relation of personal domination based on direct and indirect violence, in which the dominated is utterly excluded from all independent involvement in the wider community, and is parasitically dishonored, by which I mean that the master gains ego enhancement from his personal debasement of the slave, and all nonslaves gain collective honor from the degradation of the slave group.

While not alone in its racist ideology, American slave society was unique in the complexity and sophistication of the culture of slavery that it developed and in the extraordinary role slavery and the slave culture played in that development. The culture of the South became not simply a culture with a racist ideology, one conveniently justifying the enslavement of people, as was the case all over Latin America, the Caribbean, and the Islamic world, but rather a chronically racist culture. There is a critical difference between the two. England and France today both have racist ideologies in that many people there, perhaps the majority, believe in the inherent superiority of whites over non-white peoples. Yet they are not racist cultures, because this ideology is a minor component in their systems of belief; it serves no indispensable cultural or socioeconomic functions and is not a critical element in the way people define themselves physically and socially. Not so in America.

A great deal of what is evil in America, and—a point that cannot be overemphasized—a great deal of what later emerged as highly desirable, even for blacks, springs from, or originated in, a deep enmeshment with the culture of slavery and its positive valuation of racism. Gunnar Myrdal opened his famous study of black America with the much-cited observation that there is a conflict in the American democratic commitment to equality. Ironically, this is the most questionable statement in that great work, and to the extent that this view informed the work to that degree it obscured understanding of its subject. For the truth, the depressing, paradoxical truth about American history is that without slavery, and without the chronic, structurally reinforced racism generated by the system of slavery, there would either have been no democracy in America, or, at the very least, its whole character would have been fundamentally different from what we experience today. . . .

Slaves of Society

Though slavery was abolished, the wrongs of my people were not yet ended. . . . And yet the government . . . felt it had done enough for [the freedman]. It had made him free, and henceforth he must make his own way in the world. Yet he had none of the conditions for self-preservation or self-protection. He was free from the individual master, but the slave of society. He had neither money, property nor friends. He was free from the old plantation, but he had nothing but the dusty road under his feet. . . . He was . . . turned loose, naked, hungry and destitute, to the open sky.

Frederick Douglass, *My Bondage and My Freedom,* 1855.

Consider the seeming paradox of what I have called our confounding fathers. Almost every one of these noble founders of the nation and of our democracy was a major slaveholder. And yet they were not hypocrites. All were men of the utmost integrity. How? Why? What was going on in the making of America? Yale historian Edmund Morgan . . . has laid bare the paradoxical truth: Slavery both enabled and defined the very character of Virginian democracy. Studies such as Eric Foner's *Free Soil, Free Labor, Free Men,* have further shown how by means of the antebellum propaganda war in which both sides used antiblack racism in defense of freedom, and the war itself that followed, the oppression of blacks became the decisive element in generating and reinforcing the nation's commitment to democracy and the more general ideal of freedom. . . .

Racist culture not only constrained blacks directly in the thoroughgoing way it poisoned the minds of all nonblack Americans, natives *and immigrants*, to black folks, by imprinting upon the national consciousness the view that blacks did not, and could not and would never belong; but also offered a free collective cultural resource to all whites, one that was not only psychologically and economically useful, but politically generative. As W. J. Cash insightfully observed in *The Mind of the South*: "Negro entered into white man as profoundly as white man entered into Negro, subtly influencing every gesture, every word, every emotion and idea, every attitude.". . .

Four Black Communities

There was not a single mode of response, no such thing as "the American slave"; any "composite biography" of the slave must be seriously called in question. There were at least four modes of adjustment to the slave system leading to the emergence of four distinct types of black American subcommunities from at least the early nineteenth century. First, there was a distinct underclass of slaves. These were the people who were not only broken by the system, but who lived either fecklessly or dangerously. They were the "incorrigible" blacks of whom the slaveholder class was forever complaining. Descriptions of them abound. They ran away. They were idle. They were compulsive liars. They seemed immune to punishment. There is independent evidence from the slave autobiographies and interviews that clearly indicates that a distinct group of shiftless, economically and socially deviant slaves existed. What is more, they persisted after slavery. We can trace the underclass, as a persisting social phenomenon, back to this group. . . . The black underclass has always been with us. And the white one too.

However, this class was then, as now, a small minority of slaves, at the very most five percent or so, if one may hazard a guess. Larger in size was the group that I call the dependent or accommodating class of slaves. These were the perfect slaves, the kind of blacks that made absent planters pine for home—the Uncle Toms and Aunt Jemimas. They constituted a distinct subgroup and they too have left their mark on black American culture. They worked out a symbiosis with the white group, usually within the context of the household. They accepted fully the superiority of the whites. And yet, they did so without necessarily abandoning all dignity. Uncle Tom was real, and he deserves our sympathy, if not quite our respect.

Unsung Heroes

Third, there was the majority of the slave population. These are the true, and still largely unsung, heroes of American history. For not only did they survive the horrors of slavery, but whenever and wherever the system offered the slightest openings one finds clear evidence of social and cultural creativity. . . .

Although it is good to applaud the quiet achievements of this group, we should be careful not to make supermen of them by failing to take account of those areas where the system was simply too overwhelming, resulting in compromises and problems that lingered long after slavery. Let me take the most important case in point: family life. This is in need of serious rethinking and restudy. Conventional scholarly wisdom is now dominated by what can only be called the simplicities of demographic reification. It used to be thought that the female-headed family was the norm for this group. Revisionist studies during the seventies and eighties have shown persuasively that something very similar to the nuclear family was the norm among them. From this essentially demographic finding all sorts of claims have been made, in effect, that the black family in the dominant group of blacks was alive and well during the period of slavery, and that this then formed the basis of stable extended rural families in the post-emancipation South.

Joel Pett/*Lexington Herald-Leader.* Reprinted with permission.

This is highly questionable. A house, as the saying goes, is not a home. A demographic unit is no more than a unit of reproduction. . . .

The worst horror of slavery, its single greatest crime against the slave population, was its systematic ethnocidal assault on the inner workings of the complex rules, roles, meanings, and relations of the black family. It did not attack the basic form of the institution.

Indeed, like a highly evolved parasite that instinctively recognizes that the death of its host would entail its own demise, slavery reinforced the reproductive potential of the slave union even as it ate away at its inner institutional core. It systematically undermined the marital and parental bonds, especially focusing on the male role. It did so not only by the formal legal denial of all marital rights and custodial claims in children and parents, but in the countless open as well as more subtle humiliations of spouses, parents, and children in their relations with each other, and in the delegitimation of all familial authority. . . .

The institutional fragility of the black family, even within its most stable class, has always been and remains the group's most serious liability, the most pernicious heritage of its slave past. Until the black family is fully rehabilitated, American society has a serious debt to repay the black American. That black leaders and their liberal allies are today among the most serious critics of this view must surely be the most tragic irony of present commentary on the black condition.

There was a fourth distinct group of blacks during the period of slavery: the freed blacks on and off the plantations and the favored mixed group of slaves. A fair amount has been written on this group. Even when freed they were truly "slaves without masters," as Ira Berlin has ably shown. What interests me is their distinctive mode of accommodation to the system of slavery and post-emancipation society: the complex of values, meanings and expressions they developed and passed down to their inheritors, the black bourgeoisie. Their chronic hostility and ambivalence to working-class blacks, and their notorious color prejudices, are well known and have been thoroughly analyzed, perhaps too much so.

Emancipation and Today's Blacks

The abolition of slavery marked only the end of a long beginning for black Americans. The schema above indicates the key points and structural developments of the group. Several important aspects of this development must now be noted.

The first is that when slavery was abolished only the personal, legally enforceable relation of slavery was removed. The racist culture of slavery not only continued but was compensatorily emphasized as never before. Indeed, one may seriously argue that the culture of slavery, by which I mean the whole set of values, meanings, and expressions directed at the black American as a slave and ex-slave, continued right down to the 1960s. Only with the civil rights movement was the culture of slavery finally demolished. The civil rights movement, in succeeding where it did, marked the close of the abolition movement in America. It did not, however, mark the end of America's culturally entrenched racism.

Second, it is clear now that from right after slavery blacks always faced two sets of constraints: those of the overarching racist culture and those of the underlying social structure. This underlying structure was not necessarily overtly racist but it invariably had the effect of undermining the position and opportunities of the black population. Rural peonage, as we will argue shortly, was covertly racist, even though set up as a means of controlling both black and white labor. Its deleterious impact on the blacks reinforced pre-existing disadvantages, and the incapacity of blacks to move from under its weight reinforced the racist view of the group. What this all means is that what is today called institutional racism was always with the black population. It is a cardinal error to argue that it has only recently emerged as the critical constraint on the black group as overt racism declined. Throughout the history of the black experience in America, institutional (indirect) racism and direct overarching culturally based racism have reinforced each other. . . .

Leftover Americans

The inner-city poor are poor because they have been scarred more deeply by the legacy of slavery than the rest of us. Racism has always hurt some blacks more than others. . . .

Some blacks came North before Emancipation and others were slammed back into semislavery during and especially after Reconstruction. Some of their descendants remained illiterate peasants in the South in the sixth and even seventh decades of this century. They were driven off the land by the mechanization of agriculture.

When they got to the major cities, millions of the unskilled jobs that the underclasses from Europe and earlier black émigrés from the South had used as ladders to the middle class were disappearing. Some survived this transition while others became disoriented and redundant in the cities' hard and dirty backwaters.

It is the children and grandchildren of these leftover Americans that Dr. Samuel D. Proctor, the retired pastor of the Abyssinian Baptist Church, mentioned when I asked what the biggest lesson of his years in Harlem had been.

Roger Wilkins, *The New York Times*, August 22, 1989.

This situation leads to the following conclusions:

(1) A return to history and some serious rethinking of recent revisionist historiography on the black past are essential prerequisites for any understanding of the present crisis.

(2) Cultural analysis must inform our attempts to understand the external racist environment that constrains all black Amer-

icans as well as the internal problems that beset, in different ways, the various classes among them.

(3) All white Americans share the burdens and responsibilities of slavery and its racist heritage. Post-emancipation immigrants and their descendants fully exploited racism, and even were they model liberals the fact remains that becoming a citizen of another country is like buying into a company: one enjoys the profits of its material and moral economy, but equally, one shares all its liabilities and moral burdens. If the present descendants of post-emancipation immigrants wish to be relieved of the moral burden of slavery, they had better stop cheering on the Fourth of July.

(4) We must eschew gross aggregation in our discussion of the black population. It makes little sense to discuss this complex population of over thirty million people, spread over a vast continent, in dualistic terms.

(5) The underclass is not a new phenomenon, having persisted from the days of slavery. Exaggerating its importance can serve and has served racist purposes. In our consideration of this group there ought to be greater concern with the segment of the black population most exposed to its violence and destruction.

(6) Which leads me to close with an appeal on behalf of the black working class, the silent, near-forgotten plurality of the black population. . . .

As concerned Americans, it is time that we started taking the lives, the fears, and the aspirations of black working people seriously. And as scholars it is time we began to recognize their existence.

"The existence of racial disparity . . . is not, ipso facto, evidence that we have failed to achieve equality before the law for the descendants of slaves."

The Legacy of Slavery Does Not Deny Minorities Equal Opportunities

Glenn C. Loury

Glenn C. Loury is a professor of political economy at Harvard University's Kennedy School of Government in Cambridge, Massachusetts. He is the author of many publications on race problems, including *The Moral Quandary of the Black Community* and *The Need for Moral Leadership in the Black Community*. In the following viewpoint, Loury states that blacks should no longer blame slavery for social problems, but should instead recognize that each individual is responsible for his or her own success and failure.

As you read, consider the following questions:

1. Why does Loury believe that the Constitution's obligation to blacks has been fulfilled?
2. According to the author, what prevents full equality of opportunity from being achieved?
3. What does Loury believe blacks give up when they blame the "system" for their failures?

Glenn C. Loury, "'Matters of Color'—Blacks and the Constitutional Order," in *Slavery and Its Consequences: The Constitution, Equality, and Race*. Washington, DC: AEI Press, 1988. Reprinted by permission of the American Enterprise Institute for Public Policy Research.

In his treatise on the early development of American legal doctrine affecting slaves, U.S. Circuit Court Judge Leon Higginbotham observes: "This new nation, 'conceived in liberty and dedicated to the proposition that all men are created equal,' began its experiment in self-government with a legacy of more than one-half million enslaved blacks—persons denied citizenship and enslaved, not for criminal infractions, but solely as a matter of color." The United States, in other words, was born with the burden of a sinful, "peculiar" institution that belied the very ideals the founders sought to affirm. That a group of colonialists, proclaiming themselves fathers of a new nation built on Jefferson's "self-evident truths," were prepared to legitimate in law the brutalities requisite to a commerce in human beings is an irony that forms the heart of a powerful indictment of the American legal tradition by Judge Higginbotham. He goes on to cite a conversation with Earl Warren shortly before the chief justice's death, in which the two jurists agreed that "there is a powerful nexus between the brutal centuries of colonial slavery and the racial polarization and anxieties of today. The poisonous legacy of legalized oppression based upon the matter of color can never be adequately purged from our society if we act as if slave laws had never existed." But no matter what our actions, can this "poisonous legacy" ever be purged from our civic life? Is the Constitution an aid or an obstacle to the removal of this legacy? Are the precepts and structures of American government capable of eradicating the consequences of the "original sin" that was African slavery? This is an old question, raised 150 years ago by Tocqueville, who wrote: "The most formidable of all the ills that threaten the future of the Union arises from the presence of a black population upon its territory." This astute observer of early American life further noted that the difficulty was more than a legal one, that "the prejudice which repels the Negroes seems to increase in proportion to their emancipation . . . and inequality is sanctioned by the manners while it is effaced from the laws of the country.". . .

Blacks and the Founders' Vision

It is worth noting that, until quite recently, the black champions of the struggle for equal citizenship have placed great faith in the capacity of the Constitution to deliver on its promise. . . . Martin Luther King, Jr., while leading a mass movement to eradicate Jim Crow in the South, spoke eloquently and often of "that magnificent promissory note," which was the as yet unfulfilled obligation to blacks implicit in the American civic creed.

But has not *that* obligation now been fulfilled? Do not the Civil Rights Acts of the 1960s, the Supreme Court decisions running from *Brown* through *Bakke*, the most recent cases upholding affirmative action, the political failure of those in the Reagan administration to change the direction of the country on civil rights issues, the near-universal affirmation of the inadmissibility of racial prejudice in public political discourse, the broad acceptance throughout the private sector of the legitimacy and necessity of exerting special efforts to include "previously excluded groups" when making employment or educational admissions decisions, even the historic campaign for the presidency of Jesse Jackson himself—do not all of these things, and many more that could be mentioned, confirm that Martin Luther King, Jr., did not "dream" in vain?

Regaining Moral Codes

Any hope of fundamentally ameliorating the predicament of poor blacks will derive from their ability to perceive the enhanced opportunities and alternatives that are possible for those who opt for discipline and self-control. These are the qualities that were central to the success of earlier generations of blacks. The moral codes, which have never died in black communities, will regain their former influence when the most visible and vocal leadership ceases to make racial oppression a greater demon than it is and commits itself instead to making unequivocal distinctions between creditable and disreputable behavior.

Elizabeth Wright, *Critical Issues: A Conservative Agenda for Black Americans,* January 1990.

Is it not therefore ironic indeed, at the bicentennial of the U.S. Constitution, with the faithful visions of Frederick Douglass, Charles Houston, King, and countless others vindicated by the successes of the civil rights movement, that there should be so many questions raised about the ability of the American constitutional order to accommodate an equal citizenship for blacks? For although there can be little question that, on the whole, black Americans have not as yet attained full equality—in economic, social, or political standing—within our society, it is hard to see how the principles of government codified in the Constitution, as now being interpreted and administered throughout the land, can be faulted for this incomplete success. But, if this is so, how can we ever expect to be finally free of the enormous burden arising out of the "original sin" that was black slavery?

Emancipation Is Not Enough

We will never escape the specter of the "original sin" of slavery until we understand that the liberalization of the legal framework—the fulfillment of the promise of equal rights implied in the founders' vision of American government—is a necessary, but not sufficient condition for the attainment of equal citizenship for the descendants of the slaves. As Tocqueville and Gunnar Myrdal both saw clearly, and as the problem of "white flight"—which has plagued public schools and, to a lesser extent, residential desegregation efforts—further attests, the inequality of condition that black Americans endure is rooted in *social* as much as in *legal* practice. And the ability of the law to undo what the racially discriminatory associational behaviors of white and black Americans have wrought is extremely limited.

We are, of course, intimately familiar with these socially discriminatory behaviors because we all engage in them daily. We choose our friends and neighbors, decide upon our business partners and professional associates, select the schools our children will attend, influence (to the extent we can) the prospective mates of our children, and, of course, choose our own mates. Moreover, for the great majority of us—black and white—race, ethnicity, and religion are factors in these discriminating judgments. The statistics on interracial marriages show this to be so, as does the extent of social segregation in the ostensibly integrated environments of today's colleges and universities. The preservation of our distinct ethnic communities, once thought to be a parochial, even reactionary, objective has, in the wake of the "black power movement," the "rise of the unmeltable ethnics," and the advent of bilingualism, become the respectable (and occasionally government-mandated) pursuit of "pluralism.". . .

It is crucial to realize that what is involved here is in the main not a legal or even an attitudinal problem, but an inescapable social fact. If people are left with the liberty to choose their social environments, then their exercise of that liberty will inevitably produce a situation in which only mutually advantageous associations can be sustained. As a result, some persons will be deprived of the benefits of an association that, while desirable from their point of view, is perceived as undesirable from the point of view of the other. When the association at issue is that between an employer and an employee, the antidiscrimination mandate of the Civil Rights Acts of 1964 requires that race play no part in the calculation of mutual advantage. But when the association is that between two prospective neighbors, mates, business associates, or friends, no such statutory restraints apply.

Private Prejudices

Our legal and philosophical traditions are such that we are unwilling to undertake the degree of intrusion into the intimate associational choices of individuals that would be required to achieve a full equality of opportunity between individuals or the members of various ethnic groups. Such choices, in our law and in our ethics, lie beyond the reach of the antidiscrimination mandate. They are private matters that, though susceptible to influence and moral suasion about the tolerance of diversity and the like, are not thought to constitute the proper subject of judicial or legislative decree. Freedom to act on the prejudices and discriminations that induce each of us to seek our identities with and to make our lives among a specific, restricted set of our fellows is among those inalienable rights to life, liberty, and the pursuit of happiness enshrined in the Declaration of Independence. . . .

Slavery as an Excuse

As I travel around the country speaking to young people, the question that I raise is this: If you don't want to be judged by the color of your skin, what is the content of your character? For some people, when they sell drugs to little children, when they ride by and shoot other people on the street, when they rape women in Central Park, they would be better off judged by the color of their skin because they have no character.

Throughout history, black preachers never used slavery as an excuse to justify negative behavior. You can't find one sermon where a black preacher in the 18th or 19th century said, "Well, I know you folks have been slaves, so drink all you want. I know that it's been tough. It was hard coming over on the slave ship, so make as many babies as you want." You will never find one black leader justifying immoral behavior, anti-social behavior, self-destructive behavior by using slavery as a rationale. And they were on the back steps of slavery. Whereas now, 200 years after slavery, we are now reverting back and using slavery as an excuse for the behavior of some people today.

Buster Soaries, *The Heritage Lectures*, February 8, 1990.

As a practical matter this means that we will have to accept that some of the inequality results from the fact that even the best Head Start program is an expensive and imperfect substitute for the advantages freely conveyed to a youngster born to middle-class, well-educated, attentive, and concerned parents. And we shall have to live with the fact that some subgroups inculcate attitudes and values that leave their youngsters better prepared, and more inclined, than others to pursue careers as university professors, entrepreneurs, or engineers. . . .

One aspect of the "poisonous legacy" of slavery and the subsequent denial of equal rights has been that blacks are disproportionately represented among those whose "social background resources" are comparatively deficient. In view of this history of racial oppression under which we as a political community labor, the ongoing fact of group disparity is bound to be attributed by those advocating the interests of the dispossessed to a failure to make good on the promise of the American civic creed. Our slavery-laden past will naturally be evoked as cause of our unequal present. And the failure of special actions on behalf of blacks, legitimated by reference to the constitutional requirement of "equal protection," to bring about an equality of status in the present may well be seen as evidence that the process of emancipation remains incomplete.

Yet the existence of racial disparity in contemporary economic circumstances is not, ipso facto, evidence that we have failed to achieve equality before the law for the descendants of slaves. Those who look to the Constitution to provide a remedy for group inequality, which originates in historical discrimination but is perpetuated through social organization, are doomed to be disappointed, and sometimes bitterly so. When opportunity for success in life is linked to parental and communal circumstances, and when individuals employ racial criteria among others in their decisions about private associations, group inequality can go on for a long time, notwithstanding the fact that the original source of the disparity, remediable through the law, has long since been addressed. Complete emancipation, in the sense of the attainment of the full legal rights and privileges associated with citizenship, does not imply an equality of standing in the social and economic order.

Unfortunately this point is not sufficiently well understood or accepted by contemporary advocates of racial equality. They continue to seek a constitutionally secured "freedom and equality" for blacks, as if these goals could be ordained by a government endowed with sufficient nobility of spirit and clarity of purpose. There is something tenuous, and ultimately pathetic, about the position of blacks in this regard. Do not recoil here at the use of the word "pathetic"; that, after all, is what this practice is all about—evoking the pity, and the guilt, of whites. But, for that very reason, the practice is inconsistent with the goal of freedom and equality of blacks. One cannot be the equal of those whose pity, or guilt, one actively seeks.

Slavery and Sociology

Booker T. Washington, that much maligned figure who rose to prominence as a black leader and spokesman some ninety years ago, understood this matter clearly. "It is a mistake," Washington wrote, "to assume that the Negro, who had been a slave for two hundred and fifty years, gained his freedom by the signing, on a certain date, of a certain paper by the President of the United States. It is a mistake to assume that one man can, in any true sense, give freedom to another. Freedom, in the larger and higher sense, every man must gain for himself."

Unnatural Relationships

Experts wring their hands debating this and studying that about what's wrong with the large and increasing black underclass in our cities. But the answer is simple. Relationships and behaviors among people in black neighborhoods, once natural, are now unnatural. Let's look at it. Isn't it unnatural for adults to be afraid of kids? Kids cursing and assaulting teachers? Healthy people refusing to work? Teenagers and preteens engaging in sex?

Isn't our response to all this unnatural? Not punishing kids who curse and assault teachers? Subsidizing healthy people who refuse to work? Establishing nurseries in schools to take care of teenagers' babies? We invent excuse after excuse for irresponsible and reprehensible antisocial behavior. Given these unnatural acts and our unnatural responses, should anybody be surprised to see exactly what we see?

Walter E. Williams, *Lincoln Review*, Spring/Summer 1989.

How long can blacks continue to evoke the "slavery was terrible and it was your fault" rhetoric and still suppose that dignity and equality can be achieved thereby? Is it not fantastic to suppose that the oppressor, whom strident racial advocates take such joy in denouncing, would, in the interest of decency and upon hearing the extent of his crimes, decide to grant the claimants their every demand? The evocation of slavery in our contemporary discourse has little to do with sociology, or with historical causation. Its main effect is moral. It uses the slave experience in order to establish culpability. Why should others—the vast majority of whom have ancestors who arrived here after the emancipation, or who fought against the institution of slavery, or who endured profound discriminations of their own—permit themselves to be morally blackmailed with such rhetoric? How long can the failures of the present among black Americans be excused and explained by reference to the wrongs of the past? Must not, after some point, there begin to be resentment, contempt, and disdain for a group of people that sees itself in such terms? Consider the contradictions: Blacks seek general recognition of their accomplishments in the past and yet must insist upon the extent to which their ancestors were reduced to helplessness. Blacks must emphasize that they live in a nation that has never respected their humanity, yet expect that by so doing, their fellow countrymen will be moved to come to their assistance. . . .

For too many blacks, dedication to the cause of reform has been allowed to supplant the demand for individual accountability; race, and the historic crimes associated with it, has become the single lens through which to view social experience; the infinite potential of real human beings has been surrendered on the altar of protest. In this way does the prophecy of failure, evoked by those who take the fact of racism as barring forever blacks' access to the rich possibilities of American life, fulfill itself: emphasis on the determinative effects of the "poisonous legacy" in the struggle to secure redress for past oppression requires the sacrifice of a primary instrument through which genuine freedom might yet be attained.

The Price of Playing the Victim

Thus does the decision to play the historical victim extract its price. The acknowledgment by blacks of the possibility, within the American constitutional order, of individual success, and the recognition of the personal traits associated with such success, comes to be seen, quite literally, as a betrayal of the black poor, for it undermines the legitimacy of what has proved to be their most valuable, if too often abused and rapidly depreciating, political asset. There is, hidden in this desperate assertion of victim status by blacks to an increasingly skeptical white polity, an unfolding tragedy of profound proportion. Black leaders, confronting their people's need and their own impotency, believe they must continue to portray blacks as "the conscience of the nation." Yet the price extracted for playing this role, in incompletely fulfilled lives and unrealized personal potential, amounts to a "loss of our own souls." As consummate victims, blacks lay themselves at the feet of their fellows, exhibiting their own lack of achievement as evidence of their countrymen's failure, hoping to wring from the American conscience what we must assume, by the very logic of their claim, lies beyond the ability of individual blacks to attain, all the while bemoaning how limited that sense of conscience seems to be. This way lies not the "freedom" so long sought by our ancestors but, instead, a continuing serfdom.

"To deny the influence of the culture of poverty is to deny a powerful reality."

Culture Prevents Minorities from Overcoming Poverty

Don Wycliff

In the following viewpoint, Don Wycliff presents the case of Jerry Carter, whose life Wycliff believes is an example of how black culture and poverty are related. Wycliff contends that a lack of family structure and the absence of discipline and traditional values such as hard work and responsibility may be some of the causes of black poverty. Wycliff is a member of the editorial board of *The New York Times.*

As you read, consider the following questions:

1. What does the author mean that the Committee on the Status of Black Americans had demolished a "straw man"?
2. The author mentions thrift as a mainstream attitude. What other attitudes do you think the author would describe as mainstream?
3. Why does Wycliff believe that it is important to acknowledge that the culture of poverty is a powerful reality?

Don Wycliff, "A Culture of Poverty," *First Things*, March 1990. Reprinted by permission of the Institute on Religion and Public Life.

I hadn't thought of Jerry Carter for at least five years.

I probably wouldn't have thought of him for at least another five if it hadn't been for the report of the National Research Council's Committee on the Status of Black Americans.

I met Jerry in 1982. I was a reporter for the *Chicago Sun-Times*. He was a kid in trouble with the law. Specifically, he was one of a gang of twenty teenagers and thirteen young adults from Chicago's vast, grim Robert Taylor Homes public housing project arrested for pickpocketing at Churchill Downs in Louisville on Kentucky Derby Day. I was sent by my newspaper to cover their hearings and learn what I could of their lives and the adult "Fagin" who supposedly masterminded their crimes.

The National Research Council report ("A Common Destiny: Blacks and American Society") reminded me of Jerry because his life seemed to refute one of the book's principle claims: that the "culture of poverty" has little or nothing to do with persistently high rates of black poverty.

I suspected when I first heard this claim that the Committee on the Status of Black Americans, loaded as it was with social scientists, had demolished a straw man, a bloodless construct so rigidly defined as to be meaningless in terms of the actual lives of the humans who inhabit the nation's ghettos and who, for the most part, make up what has come to be called the underclass. After reading the pertinent parts of the 608-page volume, my suspicion was confirmed.

Modern Artful Dodger

The committee describes the concept fairly enough at first: the culture of poverty is "a distinctive set of beliefs, values, and behavior patterns that tend to perpetuate (the) condition" of those who are poor and segregated. But the discussion quickly degenerates into an exercise in semantic hairsplitting, finally concluding that "taken as a whole, the data and analyses we have examined throw serious doubt on the validity of the strong thesis that the culture of poverty is a major cause of self-perpetuating poverty."

Against the committee's data and analyses, I would set the life of Jerry Carter. When I wrote about him for the *Sun-Times*, I didn't use his name. After all, he was a minor—at least chronologically. Instead, I borrowed the title Dickens used for his young pickpocket in *Oliver Twist*, the Artful Dodger.

Jerry told the police and the juvenile court judge in Louisville that he was twelve, and he looked as if he could have been. He later told me, however, that he was fourteen.

He tearfully told the judge that his mother was a maid in a Chicago hotel who worked from 6 a.m. to 6 p.m. every day except Sunday and couldn't afford to come and escort him home, the condition that the judge demanded for each youngster's release. Yet when I as a surrogate delivered Jerry to his apartment at midday on an ordinary Friday, his mother was there, washing greens at the kitchen sink. So were three grown men, at least two of whom were introduced to me as Jerry's brothers.

Holding Blacks Responsible

To hold blacks responsible for their lives, we have been told, is "blaming the victim." Before such arguments, liberals fell silent; and the crisis of the underclass deepened.

The long silence seems to be coming to an end, however. Both the NAACP and the Urban League have begun to speak about the need to break the trap of welfare dependency. Michael Lomax, chairman of the Fulton County Commission in Atlanta, said: "There are problems within our community that were not imposed upon us by white society. Intravenous-drug abuse, teen-age pregnancy and sexual promiscuity are behaviors that are pathological in our own community, and we must come to grips with that, to take responsibility."

That last word is the key.

Pete Hamill, *Esquire*, March 1988.

"We sure do appreciate you bringing him," one of them said to me, as if I had found him lost at an amusement park or some other equally innocuous place. There was no parental reprimand, just smiles and kisses and some jocular banter with the men about having gotten caught.

That was the crazy part: Jerry's criminal activity seemed taken for granted, in his household and his neighborhood. As we approached his building, he was surrounded by children and other teenagers who knew where he had been and what he had been doing and found it not the least bit unusual.

Worldly Wisdom

At fourteen, Jerry had been in the pickpocket business for a year and a half, mostly working the streets of downtown Chicago but making an occasional out-of-town foray to an event like the Derby where the pickings would be good. He was a skilled and effortless liar. And he possessed a certain worldly wisdom: He didn't begin telling me the truth about himself until our flight had landed at O'Hare airport and he was safely back "in my own town."

If he shared any mainstream attitude, it was thrift. "If I get more than $100, I save it," he said, describing his work. "If I get less than $100, I spend it, mostly on clothes."

It's possible that Jerry, who would be twenty-one now if he has survived, may have been successful enough at crime to lift himself and his family out of poverty. He wouldn't be the first American to have done so; some have even made it to respectability. I suspect, however, that Jerry and most of his neighborhood friends are no better off now than they were in 1982. And I suspect that their "distinctive set of beliefs, values, and behavior patterns" has much to do with that.

Jerry Carter has a female counterpart in the culture of poverty. She is the young, pregnant teenage girl, who dreams of being of the age when she can "get my own (welfare) grant and get my own apartment." I wish I could count the number of times I heard that line as a reporter.

Denying Reality

Of course, the culture of poverty doesn't exhaust the explanations for persistent black poverty and the underclass. No single explanation does. Indeed, as James Tobin, the Nobel laureate economist who was a member of the Committee on the Status of Black Americans, said at the press conference where the report was released: "Everything is a cause and everything is an effect."

Yet to deny the influence of the culture of poverty is to deny a powerful reality. To deny reality is to assure that one will be defeated by it.

"The only difference between white pathology and black pathology is that white pathology is underreported."

Culture Does Not Prevent Minorities from Overcoming Poverty

Ishmael Reed

In the following viewpoint, Ishmael Reed contends that black culture is not the reason many blacks are socially disadvantaged. He argues that the media focus on the problems of blacks, ignore the crimes of whites, and use blacks as scapegoats for the widespread problems in American society. Reed heads the Oakland, California media committee of PEN, an international organization of poets, playwrights, editors, essayists, and novelists that promotes freedom of expression. Reed is a poet whose works include *Cab Calloway Stands In for the Moon* and *The Terrible Threes*.

As you read, consider the following questions:

1. Why do network news shows exhibit black pathology, according to Reed?
2. What statistics does the author cite to support his contention that black youth are being used as scapegoats?
3. What comparison does Reed make between the political campaigns of today and those of the 1880s?

Ishmael Reed, "The Black Pathology Biz," *The Nation*, November 20, 1989. Copyright © 1989 The Nation Company, Inc. Reprinted with permission.

Black pathology is big business. Two-thirds of teenage mothers are white, two-thirds of welfare recipients are white and white youth commit most of the crime in this country. According to a survey, reported by *The Oakland Tribune*, the typical crack addict is a middle-class white male in his 40s. Michele Norris of *The Washington Post* has cited a study that discovered "no significant difference in the rate of drug use during pregnancy among women in the public clinics that serve a largely indigent population and those visiting private doctors who cater to upper-income patients." Yet in the popular imagination blacks are blamed for all these activities, in the manner that the Jews took the rap for the Black Plague, even in countries with little or no Jewish population.

Now that network news shows have become "profit centers," news producers have found a lucrative market in exhibiting black pathology, while coverage of pathologies such as drug addiction, child abuse, spousal battering and crime among whites and their "model minorities" is negligible. According to the news shows, you'd think that two black gangs, the Crips and the Bloods, are both the cause and the result of the nation's drug problem, even though this country was high long before these children were born.

When it comes to singling out blacks as the cause of America's social problems, NBC and CNN are the worst offenders. (The owner of CNN, Ted Turner, once proposed that unemployed black males be hired to carry nuclear warheads on their backs; when pressed he said that he was only kidding.)

Unfair Focus on Blacks

Let's look at just one month: October of 1988. General Electric's *NBC Nightly News* ran stories on child abuse, drug trafficking and cocaine pregnancy. Blacks were the actors in all these news shows, yet the August 30, 1988, front page of *The New York Times* reported that there is as much cocaine pregnancy in the suburbs as in the inner city. That same October, it was revealed on CNN's business program, *Moneyline*, that U.S. bankers have laundered $100 billion in drug money, $90 billion of which ends up overseas, contributing to the trillion dollars in debt owed by the United States, mugging millions of Americans of jobs and endangering the economic stability of the country.

Also in October 1988, CNN did a series called "Crime in America." According to this series, whites don't commit crimes. They're either victims or on the side of the law—the line promoted by *The New York Times*, a black pathology supermarket that regularly blames crack use, crime, welfare and illegitimacy on black people and whose journalists and columnists still use the term "black underclass" even though studies, including

Blacks and American Society, by the National Research Council, and *The Persistence of Urban Poverty and its Demographic and Behavioral Correlates,* by Terry K. Adams and Greg J. Duncan, have been unable to locate this underclass. Its neoconservative house organ, *The New York Times Magazine,* printed a puff piece about the ex-editors of the anti-Semitic, anti-black *Dartmouth Review.*

Blaming the Victim

Instead of addressing the structural factors that are producing inner-city dislocations, including the tenacious and rising economic insecurity of meager pay and joblessness, policy advocates have fastened on the personal characteristics of ghetto residents. As a result, policy initiatives have mistakenly focused on devising renewed incentives or means of administrative coercion to reform the assumed habits of the apathetic, deviant, and destructive individuals that supposedly make up the "underclass." Such *disciplining,* in Michel Foucault's sense of the term, will do little to alleviate the plight of inner-city minorities.

Loïc J.D. Wacquant, *Dissent,* Fall 1989.

CNN aired a special about drug-crazed Los Angeles street gangs. It proposed that gang activities were inspired by rap music. If rap music is forcing people to sell drugs, then how does one explain the participation in this industry of a Gregorian chant-loving ex-Vatican diplomat, the Rev. Lorenzo Zorza?

Cost of Corporate Crime

How convenient it is to blame everything on a scapegoat, in this case black youth, who, according to public superstitions, are responsible for all the crime in this country. Yet Gerry Spence, citing a Bureau of National Affairs estimate, writes in his book *With Justice for None: Destroying an American Myth,* that "the cost of corporate crime in America is over ten times greater than the combined larcenies, robberies, burglaries and auto-thefts committed by individuals. One in five of America's large corporations has been convicted of at least one major crime or has paid civil penalties for serious misbehavior. One way the Crips and the Bloods can improve their image is to do what the big crooks do, buy advertising on TV news shows so that their crimes will rarely be reported." The only difference between white pathology and black pathology is that white pathology is underreported.

By putting out the lie that U.S. crime is black, the networks contributed millions of dollars in free advertising to Lee Atwater's 1988 racist political campaign.

Presenting the fact that pathologies are widespread in American society and that American society itself might be pathological would be like showing films about lung cancer to the millions addicted to cigarette smoking. To portray America as a pathological society would interrupt the country's cozy fetal sleep, which requires that the shrill half-wits it elects to office run the sort of campaign that former Confederate officers ran in the 1880s: They threatened whites with a black rapist in every bedroom, an image that's been commercialized by some millionaire feminists in novels and movies for the last decade, proving that the black pathology industry is an equal opportunity gold mine.

"The plight of African Americans cries out for emergency action. Billions of dollars can be diverted to a massive federal bailout of the inner cities and depressed rural communities."

Increased Government Spending Will Give Minorities Equal Opportunities

Ron Johnson

In the following viewpoint, Ron Johnson states that a crisis of poverty afflicts black Americans, a crisis that can be solved by dramatic increases in government spending. The author contends that the defense budget could be drastically cut to free funds for job programs, public housing, health care, and improved schools, which would help solve the crisis of poverty blacks face. Johnson is the African American affairs editor for *The People's Daily World,* a socialist newspaper that supports the views of the Communist Party USA.

As you read, consider the following questions:

1. How does capitalism affect blacks, according to Johnson?
2. What political gains have blacks made, in the author's view?
3. What steps does Johnson suggest blacks take to ensure that civil rights laws are enforced?

Ron Johnson, "The State of African Americans as the New Decade Begins," *Political Affairs,* February 1990. Reprinted with permission.

The crumbling of the Cold War presents new opportunities for a better material and spiritual existence for people around the globe, including African Americans, who have seen a large segment of their people held hostage at, and even below the poverty level by Reaganism.

Massive Fight Needed

But the opportunities cannot be realized without a massive fight in every aspect of life to bring about a restructuring of U.S. society. Whether that can happen by the year 2000 is an open question, but fundamental societal reforms cannot be precisely scheduled. They are gains of peoples' struggles in which, as Lenin once said, "twenty years may be as one day and one day as twenty years."

The crisis of everyday living for African Americans has depressed their standard of living, cut their life span, and resulted in higher percentages of homeless children and prison convicts relative to their numbers in the total population. African Americans are special victims of exploitation as corporations seek maximum profits, utility companies seek maximum profits, real estate developers seek maximum profits and bankers seek maximum profits.

African Americans are exploited on the job as workers and at home in their communities as consumers. On the small business level, unlike other national minorities, African Americans find themselves lagging behind and/or locked in place, even within their own communities.

Crises of Capitalism

While U.S. capitalism's cyclical crises have trapped generations of African Americans below the poverty line in the inner cities and Southern rural areas, there are tens of thousands of African Americans who once held industrial jobs and who have been swept by the structural crisis into the ranks of the poor. Added to these economic conditions is the prevalence of institutionalized racism—from segregated housing and school systems to hospitals and courts.

Although class differences exist among African Americans (most of whom are workers), racism cuts across class lines and binds African Americans together in a special way as a nationally oppressed people. For the working class this means that its struggle must include a fight for the affirmative, democratic demands of African Americans.

The late Henry Winston, national chairman of the Communist Party USA, said,

> An example of institutionalized racism's saturation of every aspect of life in this country can of course be found in dictio-

147

naries which ignore the distinctions existing in real life between the white "ethnic" groups and the oppressed minorities. What determines the status of Black people in this country is not "common customs" but common oppression. If one equates white "ethnics" with Black and other oppressed minorities, the special struggle to remove the racial barriers facing the oppressed can be dispensed with. The concept of "ethnicity" sets an ideological atmosphere in which affirmative action programs for jobs and education of Blacks can be twisted into "racism in reverse." When one substitutes "ethnicity" for class, one projects race against race—instead of projecting struggles of the multi-racial, multi-national working class and the oppressed minorities against the white ruling class.

In order to advance democratic rights for the vast majority of Americans, to ensure that the crumbling of the Cold War is irreversible and for the working class to gain state power, the struggle for African American equality in all aspects of life is key.

Battle Being Lost

We must advocate certain socioeconomic prerequisites for full participation in a democracy, such as the right to a job, not to starve, and to have decent housing and free medical care. Martin Luther King would insist that the battle today against racism is being lost, and that all Americans lose when blacks' median incomes are barely 55% of whites'. Poverty is directly connected with urban crime. And the answer to urban chaos, King would tell us, is not more police and capital punishment. The termination of drugs, crime and social unrest will come about only with total reconstruction of the inner cities, which requires shifting millions of dollars from the military budget.

Manning Marable, *The Witness*, February 1990.

As long as inequality exists, those forces who lust for profits will try to divide working people along racial lines. . . .

The Fightback Underway

An unprecedented fightback is underway by African Americans for winning a better life: in their organizations—civil rights, trade unions, communities, and churches; and by their allies—women, youth and others. The 1988 presidential campaign of the Reverend Jesse Jackson, which garnered seven million votes, was an impressive display of this growing fightback movement's clout. The nationwide election that followed, and which saw advances in African American, trade-union and women's representation, also showed the growing strength of the people's fightback.

The 1989 election featured the coming together of Black and

white voters to elect David Dinkins as mayor of New York City and Lawrence Douglas Wilder as governor of Virginia. They became the first African Americans to win those posts.

John Jacob, president of the National Urban League, has called for an Urban Marshall Plan, to be funded by $50 billion in savings from the Cold War thaw, that "develops our economic infrastructure, renews our cities, and moves people out of poverty."

African Americans are playing a leading role in the fight to reverse the Supreme Court's rulings, during its 1988-89 term, against civil rights and affirmative action. . . .

The NAACP [National Association for the Advancement of Colored People], which has played a leading role in the fight for the new legislation and in campaigns for equality throughout the South, has come under siege from white supremacists. Robert Robinson, a Savannah, Ga. alderman and a member of the local NAACP board of directors, was killed by a mail-bomb in December, 1989. NAACP offices and officers have received death threats. White supremacists picketed the NAACP national headquarters in Baltimore on New Year's Day, 1990. The NAACP has responded by stepping up its involvement on all levels—from sponsorship of its annual Image Awards for Black Americans to its Economic Justice for Workers campaign in Myrtle Beach, Virginia.

The 1990 celebrations for Dr. Martin Luther King Jr.'s birthday made a clearcut statement that growing numbers of African Americans and whites are working together to win equality for Black people and put an end to racism and other forms of bias.

Some 15 states now have laws calling for tougher penalties against those who commit racist, anti-Semitic and other biased crimes. . . .

These are a small sampling of what is happening among African Americans.

The Road Ahead

The plight of African Americans cries out for emergency action. Billions of dollars can be diverted to a massive federal bailout of the inner cities and depressed rural communities by cutting the war budget as the Cold War recedes. Such funds could go into job creation, repair of the infrastructure, to building low- and middle-income housing, to affordable health care from conception to the grave, to day care, to improve schools, and much more.

Corporations which discriminate should be liable for large fines which could be made available for victims of bias. Corporations which defy the law should be subject to federal takeover and run by public boards.

Laws which call for jobs and/or income, including for first-time job seekers, are needed.

Zero-interest loans and more grants to youth seeking to attend college should be legislated.

Laws that establish human rights to jobs, housing, education, day care, health care, etc. would also go a long way to solidify the legal basis on which equality can be built.

Laws are needed to outlaw racist violence and discrimination in all areas of life.

But passing laws will not suffice. They must be enforced. The Bush administration, like Reagan's before it, shows that it will undercut, not enforce civil rights. This calls for mass actions, strikes, boycotts, voter education, registration, and mobilization to win advances. More trade unionists, African Americans, Latinos, peace activists, farmers and other forces for progress should seek public office. Building independent organizations based on issues while working within existing political parties lays the basis for successful people's politics. The Rainbow Coalition serves as a sterling example in this regard. . . .

As part of the human rights process, as part of the concern for African Americans, the nation owes it to itself to get a booster shot to secure reforms now that will ease the pain among African Americans, not only because it is morally right, but also because it will improve the health of the whole nation.

"Unless blacks come to appreciate conservative principles and practices, they are likely to continue falling behind."

Promoting Self-Reliance Will Provide Equal Opportunities

Joseph Perkins

Joseph Perkins is the deputy assistant for domestic policy in the Bush administration. In the following viewpoint, Perkins contends that the problems faced by black Americans would be solved if blacks became self-sufficient and morally responsible. He maintains that black communities should adopt such conservative policies as supporting private enterprise and getting tough on crime.

As you read, consider the following questions:

1. What does Perkins believe is the main aim of a conservative agenda for blacks?
2. Why does Perkins feel that education is better without help from the federal government?
3. What problems does the author see in government set-aside programs for black businesses?

Joseph Perkins, "An Agenda for Black America," in *Critical Issues: A Conservative Agenda for Black Americans.* Washington, DC: The Heritage Foundation, 1990. Reprinted with permission.

Three decades of liberal policy have wreaked havoc on black families, black communities, and black institutions. Thirty years ago, before the unprecedented expansion of the welfare state, more than three-quarters of black families were intact, meaning that households included both husband and wife. By 1985, only half of black families could make that claim.

As recently as 20 years ago, fewer than 20 percent of black births occurred out of wedlock. Today, more than half of black births are illegitimate. The black poverty rate now is triple that of whites, and the unemployment rate, double. The black high school dropout rate in many urban areas tops 30 percent. In some inner-city areas, the rate is more than 50 percent. More than 40 percent of the inmates in federal and state prisons are black. More than 40 percent of all murder victims are black, and 95 percent of these black victims are murdered by other blacks.

By almost every measure, blacks are losing ground. Unless blacks come to appreciate conservative principles and practices, they are likely to continue falling behind. The task at hand is to make it easier for blacks to understand what conservatism offers and thus enable blacks to make the transition from reflexive liberalism to the conservative camp. This requires a conservative agenda for black progress—an agenda that seeks to help blacks strengthen their families, build their communities, unleash their creativity, and reinforce their vital mediating institutions.

Encouraging Self-Sufficiency

The agenda's aim must be to sever black dependency on government transfer programs and to encourage self-sufficiency. It should seek to reverse those academic policies that ensure that blacks receive a substandard education and doom black graduates to mediocrity. It should bring more blacks into the economic mainstream by supporting initiatives that encourage private sector involvement in the creation of jobs in economically distressed areas. It must aim to nurture black businesses in a way that teaches them how to compete in the free market without government subsidies. And it should seek to ensure that hardworking black Americans are protected from criminals who would prey upon them.

The challenge of bringing all blacks into the American mainstream is formidable, but not impossible. The following specific agenda could promote such black progress.

A Call to Arms for Black Conservatives

Challenge the demagoguery of black liberals.

If not, poor blacks—whose political capital black liberal leaders freely expend—will pay the price.

Continue to emphasize self-help prescriptions.

The liberal black leadership aims to co-opt self-help and claim it as their own. Conservatives must not allow them to do so. Conservatives need to develop even closer working relationships with black self-help organizations.

Make it clear that personal moral responsibility is expected.

Elders in the black community should use their collective strength to confront destructive behavior. Conservatives must repudiate the notion that there exists a special set of ghetto norms that supersede the accepted morality of the larger society.

Moral Challenges

As I look around the country, the people who are making a difference in the lives of young people, who get the needles out of their arms, who get the young women not to have babies—don't do so because they have better programs. They do so because they challenge young people morally and spiritually to become what they can, and what God intended them to be. . . .

You can have all the fancy treatment programs in the world, but the only way things are going to change is when you convert the hearts of people. And those who are best able to do that are the people that have a proprietary commitment to doing it, not because they are being paid by some program. Now I am not against programs. I am merely saying programs should come at the end of a process of self-liberation that comes from within one's own moral and spiritual value system.

Robert L. Woodson Sr., *The Heritage Lectures,* February 6, 1990.

Encourage frank debate within the black community.

Disenchantment with scores of failed liberal policies has sparked an outbreak of open debate and dialogue among blacks. This changing climate makes it less possible for the black liberal establishment to stifle the contrary views of black conservatives.

Dealing with Black-on-Black Crime

Support research, especially by black social scientists and criminal justice experts, that seeks to define the problem of black crime in terms of victimization, rather than as racial discrimination or lack of economic opportunity.

Blacks are as unsympathetic to criminals as are any other group of Americans. Conservatives need to address crime in black communities from the perspective of black victims.

Support black law enforcement administrators as they attempt to run their departments or agencies professionally and effectively.

Police departments should not become the objects of attack by liberal politicians who probably have no interest in tough or effective law enforcement. Conservatives need to voice strong support for police efforts to reduce crime in black neighborhoods.

Support professional organizations, such as the National Organization of Black Law Enforcement Executives (NOBLE).

Such groups need more backing to counter effectively those liberal black leaders who maintain that black crime results from white oppression.

Support community-based and neighborhood crime prevention programs.

Such programs have been extremely successful in reducing crime in inner-city neighborhoods and public housing projects.

Support tough law enforcement measures that significantly increase the risks involved in committing ordinary street crimes.

Conservatives should oppose policies that cause law enforcement agencies to ignore such minor offenses as drug use and vandalism. Near disregard for minor offenses implies that they are unofficially condoned.

Support tough law enforcement measures that remove violent and repeat offenders from the street.

Many of the criminals who victimize the black community are repeat offenders. They need to be given long sentences.

Support the fair and racially neutral application of the death penalty.

The death penalty needs to be strictly enforced to make the penalty more certain and to eliminate disparities.

Back to Basics for Black Education

Reduce the federal government's role in elementary, secondary, and higher education.

The authority of the federal government to intervene in academic affairs and to influence the composition of student bodies should be limited because education is a local matter, not an appropriate one for federal micromanagement. Black Americans would gain from this because education would be controlled by neighborhoods, where black parents often are in the majority, rather than by Congress, where they are perpetually in the minority.

Reemphasize equal opportunity, rather than equal results, in education.

Conservatives must reverse liberal policies that emphasize equal results, such as forced busing, preferential treatment, hiring goals, quotas, and timetables. Instead, conservatives must assure equal opportunity by such actions as pressing for vouchers and strict testing of teachers.

Support higher academic standards.

Liberal education policies have lowered or eliminated high

school graduation standards, devalued the importance of standardized tests, eased college entrance requirements, and replaced substantive academic courses with those of questionable academic merit. The biggest losers in this may be blacks who are condemned to mediocrity because of substandard educations.

Time for Reassessment

We spend 140 billion dollars a year, but what we spend it for and how we spend it is not always to our best interest. But for all of our spending power, we do not have a strong financial base. We need to form more investment clubs, credit unions, and co-ops, etc. We need to learn to pool our resources and seek greater economic control of our community. We must develop an economic base and learn to be producers and not just consumers. It's time for reassessment. A Korean who had just gotten off the boat a few years ago said, "We all worked 16 hours a day and saved our money to buy a business." Is it any wonder that Orientals are acquiring many businesses? A group of Indians are buying up small hotels across this nation. We cannot afford to stand still and cry about our condition; we, too, must be about that business. . . .

Racism is not preventing us from doing this—it's us. And we are going to have to answer to God for how we use His money.

Walter Bowie Jr., *Lincoln Review*, Fall 1988.

Challenge the efficacy of the Chapter 1 program.

Compensatory education programs have in many ways failed the black community. Conservatives should strongly support education vouchers that would allow parents to take the money the school district spends on their children's education and use it at the school of their choice, public or private, sectarian or nonsectarian, within or outside the school district.

Stress the strengths of traditional schools.

These strengths include knowledgeable teachers, a strong principal, an emphasis on traditional subjects, a clear mission, an orderly quiet learning environment, frequent monitoring of student progress, parental support, effort, persistence, responsibility, and strict behavioral standards. Such schools inculcate the basic values that have been undermined by today's welfare state. Conservatives need to work with black independent schools, and parents in black communities, who endorse these values.

Assist those community efforts that are the product of neighborhood initiatives and that have demonstrated the ability to mobilize local resources and sustain an organization to deal with local issues.

Those most affected by problems must be active participants

in the solutions to those problems. This requires the creation of coalitions to mobilize the poor to address these issues.

Explore welfare assistance approaches that enable recipients to invest public assistance payments in small businesses or job training programs.

Welfare could be restructured to stimulate general economic improvement in poor communities. Some welfare payments, for instance, could be converted into vouchers available to employers to encourage them to hire welfare recipients.

Stimulate alternative service delivery by neighborhood-based organizations.

Federal and state initiatives could be undertaken to encourage cities to contract with neighborhood organizations to provide such services as basic street maintenance, basic health servicing, and day care.

Explore private sector alternatives to assist families that leave AFDC [Aid to Families with Dependent Children] *and lack private health insurance.*

The loss of medical benefits is one of the most significant barriers to welfare recipients seeking to enter the labor force.

Rely more on institutions within the black community, such as churches and neighborhood organizations, to coordinate and deliver social services.

Foster care could be a starting point. Public officials could transfer to traditional institutions in the black community (such as the churches) the authority to recruit and approve potential black foster and adoptive families.

Creating a Climate for Black Business

Pare minority set-aside programs.

Not only are such programs wracked by fraud and corruption, but they have failed to accomplish their original purpose—to increase black self-employment. Conservatives should continue to attack set-asides as demeaning to black Americans and as the wrong way to spur entrepreneurship.

Reemphasize advice and training of black entrepreneurs.

The Commerce Department's Minority Business Development Agency should return to its original function as a center for development, collection, and dissemination of information helpful to minority business enterprises.

Fight regulations that prevent entrepreneurs from competing or that raise the cost of their doing business.

Conservatives should work with small businessmen to target labor laws, restrictive licensing requirements, and other rules that frustrate black entrepreneurs.

While deemphasizing set-asides, focus on reasonable alternatives, such as privatization opportunities.

Many black firms have profited from decisions of local governments to contract with private providers for such services as maintenance of office buildings, trash hauling, and data processing. Conservatives should encourage cities to explore such privatization initiatives.

Encourage self-help.

Black entrepreneurs can help themselves through joint ventures, risk sharing, and investment. By pooling resources, black businessmen can find more opportunities in the market. Conservatives should highlight such opportunities, in contrast to government assistance.

Encourage joint or partial ventures with non-black companies.

The fastest growing black enterprises happen to be those attracting not only black investment but non-black capital as well.

Attainable Goals

Even if they were to follow this agenda to the letter, conservatives could not, of course, cure all the ills of black America and, in the process, bring vast numbers of blacks into the conservative fold. On the other hand, this agenda would make a significant contribution both to removing the political barrier between conservatives and black Americans and to improving conditions within the black community. Moreover, the goals identified—providing blacks a way out of poverty and dependency and convincing blacks of the virtues of conservatism—are far from unattainable. Conservatives can demonstrate their interest in improving the lives of the mass of blacks by pressing this conservative agenda for black progress. When blacks are convinced of the sincerity of this interest, they will surely be inclined to be a part of the conservative movement.

Recognizing Stereotypes

A stereotype is an oversimplified or exaggerated description of people or things. Stereotyping can be favorable. Most stereotyping, however, tends to be highly uncomplimentary, and, at times, degrading.

Stereotyping grows out of our prejudices. When we stereotype someone, we are prejudging him or her. Consider the following example: Mr. Smith believes all ethnic minorities in the U.S. are drug abusers who would rather steal money and deal drugs than do an honest day's work. If he sees young black, Asian, or Hispanic men idle, he tells them to get a job. He disregards the possibilities that they may not be able to find work for a variety of legitimate reasons or may have jobs but work a different shift than Mr. Smith. Instead, he labels them lazy criminals. Why? He has prejudged all minorities and will keep his stereotype consistent with his prejudice.

Part I

The following statements relate to the subject matter in this chapter. Consider each statement carefully. *Mark S for any statement that is an example of stereotyping. Mark N for any statement that is not an example of stereotyping. Mark U if you are undecided about any statement.*

S = stereotype
N = not a stereotype
U = undecided

1. We forget that emancipation didn't lead to forty acres and a mule but to sharecropping and segregation.
2. We need to make changes in our basic institutions so they become inclusive and reflect a society that is made of diverse peoples of all races, backgrounds, and beliefs.
3. Asian immigrants are joining blacks as an undereducated, underemployed minority group that drains our welfare system.
4. White people have been oppressing African-Americans for centuries, even now refusing to share power or wealth with anyone with dark skin.
5. Many people of all races are working together to end racial oppression in the U.S. and to achieve social justice for everyone.
6. Black and Hispanic cultures do not encourage the work ethic in their young people, so the underclasses perpetuate their own poverty.
7. White people don't commit crimes. They're either victims or on the side of the law.
8. How convenient it is to blame everything on a scapegoat, in this case, black youth, who, according to public superstitions, are responsible for all the crime in the country.
9. The only difference between white pathology and black pathology is that white pathology is underreported.
10. Black girls are doomed to become pregnant and poor in their teen years.
11. Mexican-Americans have large families.
12. Cubans and Haitians are responsible for the high crime rate in Miami, Florida.
13. Blacks are more hardworking than whites.
14. Minorities are flagrant welfare abusers.

Part II

Based on the insights you have gained from this activity, discuss these questions in class:

1. Why do people stereotype one another?
2. What are some examples of positive stereotypes?
3. What harm can stereotypes cause?
4. What stereotypes currently affect members of your class?

Periodical Bibliography

The following articles have been selected to supplement the diverse views presented in this chapter.

Wendell Berry	"True Integration," *Mother Jones,* June 1989.
Clint Bolick	"Fight the Power," *Reason,* July 1990.
John H. Bunzel	"Exclusive Opportunities," *American Enterprise,* March/April 1990.
Michael Dyson	"The King Holiday and American Moral Life," *Z Magazine,* January 1990.
Frye Gaillard	"On and Off the Bus in Charlotte," *The Progressive,* April 1988.
Gus Hall	"The Ideology of Racism and National Oppression," *New Left Review,* February 1990.
Kathryn Harris	"Money Talks," *Forbes,* May 28, 1990.
Dorothy Height	"Self-Help—A Black Tradition," *The Nation,* July 24-31, 1989.
Susan Jacoby	"The 'Logic' of Racism," *Present Tense,* April 1990.
Morton M. Kondracke	"The Two Black Americas," *The New Republic,* February 6, 1989.
Lincoln Review	"The Disturbing Re-Segregation of America," Spring/Summer 1989.
Frederick R. Lynch and William R. Beer	"You Ain't the Right Color, Pal," *Policy Review,* Winter 1990.
John Paul Newport Jr.	"Steps to Help the Urban Black Man," *Fortune,* December 18, 1989.
Stephen Powers, David J. Rothman, and Stanley Rothman	"The Myth of Black Low Self-Esteem," *The World & I,* March 1990.
Thomas Sowell	"'Affirmative Action': A Worldwide Disaster," *Commentary,* December 1989.
Stephen Steinberg	"The Underclass: A Case of Color Blindness," *New Politics,* vol. II, no. 3, Summer 1989.
Chris Tilly	"The Politics of the 'New Inequality,'" *Socialist Review,* January/March 1990.
Thomas Toch and Joyce David	"Separate but Equal All Over Again," *U.S. News & World Report,* April 23, 1990.
Frank Trippett	"Broken Mosaic," *Time,* May 28, 1990.
Robert L. Woodson	"A Vision for Black America," *The World & I,* January 1990.
C. Vann Woodward	"The Crisis of Caste," *The New Republic,* November 6, 1989.

What Policies Would Promote Social Justice for Women?

Social Justice

Chapter Preface

U.S. Department of Labor statistics show that women who work outside the home earn seventy cents for every dollar men earn. Many people conclude from these figures that American society treats women unfairly. Sylvia Ann Hewlett, vice president for economic studies at the United Nations Association, argues, "Women do encounter discrimination in the workplace." She points out that most top executives in American companies are men and men hold most of the highest-paying jobs. Women tend to hold positions in what Hewlett and others call the "pink-collar ghetto"—jobs traditionally held by women, such as teaching, nursing, and clerical work, for which the salaries have remained low. These critics conclude that women's lower earnings are proof of discrimination.

Others disagree that the difference between men's and women's salaries proves discrimination. Yale economics professor Jennifer Roback argues, "Many of the factors that contribute to the earnings gap are the result of personal choices made by women themselves, not decisions thrust on them by bosses." For example, Roback and others state, women take time off to have children and thus do not establish the seniority and experience male employees do. Also, women are more likely than men to choose part-time work because women often need more off-the-job time to care for their children. Roback is one of many who conclude that the difference in men's and women's earnings is not proof of discrimination.

The authors of the viewpoints in the following chapter debate whether or not society treats women fairly.

"Women cannot make it alone. They cannot work and parent and care for their elderly relatives as well without a caring society."

Society Must Work Harder to Increase Equal Opportunities for Women

Ruth Sidel

Ruth Sidel argues in the following viewpoint that American society must change drastically to give women opportunities in such important and traditionally male-dominated fields as economics, politics, and academia. She maintains that eliminating sexism and destroying race and class barriers would create a more just society. Sidel is a feminist author whose books include *Women and Children Last: The Plight of Poor Women in Affluent America* and *Urban Survival: The World of Working Class Women.* She also teaches sociology at Hunter College in the City University of New York.

As you read, consider the following questions:

1. What policies would help women achieve more power and more equality in society, according to the author?
2. What role have men played in developing the concept of the American dream and why is it inappropriate for women, according to Sidel?
3. How does Sidel define a more caring society?

Ruth Sidel, *On Her Own: Growing Up in the Shadow of the American Dream.* New York: Viking Press, 1990. Excerpted with permission.

It is clear that twenty-five years after the publication of *The Feminine Mystique*, much has changed and much has remained the same. Women are attending college and graduate school in greater numbers than ever before. In the area of work, women have made great strides: the vast increase in the number of women in the labor force; the once unimaginable increase in the number of women in high-status, high-income professions; the growing acceptance, both on the part of women and on the part of many men, that women are competent, committed workers who can get the job done and achieve a considerable amount of their identity through their work roles. In keeping with their greatly increased presence in the world of work, women are often pictured by the media, by the fashion industry, even by politicians as serious, significant members of the labor force.

In recent years women have also gained greater control over their bodies. Largely because of the feminist movement, women have far greater understanding of how their bodies work, more control over their own fertility, and far greater participation in the process of childbirth. As this is being written, some of that control is under siege, particularly the right to abortion; but there have been significant strides nonetheless.

And, perhaps most important, many women recognize that they must make their own way in the world, that they must develop their own identity rather than acquire that identity through a relationship with a man. . . .

Women in the Workplace

Contrary to the expectations of the young women interviewed, female workers still occupy the lowest rungs of most occupations, including the prestigious professions they have recently entered in such large numbers. Women may have entered the labor market in record numbers in recent years, but they are still working predominantly in the lowest-paying jobs within the lowest-paying occupations.

In addition, it has become clear since 1980 that poverty dominates and determines the lives of millions of women in the United States. Today two out of three poor adults are women. Teen mothers, female heads of families, divorced women, many working women, elderly women, the "new poor" as well as those who have grown up in poverty are all at substantial risk of spending a significant part of their lives at or below the poverty line. And, of course, if women are poor, their children are poor. One out of five children under the age of eighteen and one out of four under the age of six live in poverty today. One out of every two young black children is officially poor. Perhaps most disturbing, moreover, are the sharp increases over the past decade in the number of children in families with incomes below the poverty line, a group that has been termed "the poorest of the poor." The vast majority of these families are headed by women.

CAREER OPPORTUNITIES:

MEN

WOMEN

WOMEN WITH CHILDREN

© Thompson/Rothco. Reprinted with permission.

Within this context, within the reality of women's true economic situation, what is surprising in talking with young women from various parts of the country—black women, white women, and Hispanic women; affluent, middle-class, and poor women; women who are headed for Ivy League colleges as well as high school dropouts—is the narrowness of their image of success, the uniformity of their dreams. The affluent life as symbolized by the fancy car, the "house on a hill," the "Bloomingdale's wardrobe," "giving everything to my children," was described yearningly time and time again. As if programmed, the same words, the same dreams tumbled out of the mouths of young women from very different backgrounds and life experiences. Success was seen, overwhelmingly, in terms of what they would be able to purchase, what kind of "life-style" they would have. The ability to consume in an upper-middle-class manner was often the ultimate goal. . . .

Given the reality of the job market for women, what will become of their dreams of affluence? Given the reality of the structure of work and the availability of child care, what will become of their image of mothering? Have these young women,

165

in fact, been sold a false dream? Have young women become encouraged to raise their expectations, only to see those expectations unfulfilled because there has not been comparable change within society? Have the major institutions that influence public opinion—the media, advertising, the fashion industry, as well as the industries that produce consumer goods and parts of the educational establishment—fostered these rising expectations because it suits their purposes and, in some cases, their profits? Has the dream of equal opportunity for women and men, of at least partial redistribution of power both within the family and in the society at large, been co-opted and commodified, turned into a sprint for consumer goods rather than a long march toward a more humane life for all of us?. . .

If our society is to be a caring, humane place to live, to rear our children, and to grow old, we must recognize that some aspects of life—the education of our young people, health care, child care, the texture of community life, the quality of the environment—are more important than profit. We as a nation must determine our priorities and act accordingly. If teaching, the care of young children, providing nursing care, and other human services are essential to the quality of life in the United States, then we must recruit our young people into these fields and pay them what the job is really worth. Only then will we be giving them, particularly our young women, real choices. If we want nurses to care for our sick, we must indicate by decent wages and working conditions that the job is valued by society. We must give nurses and other health workers real authority, a meaningful voice in the health-care system, and then, and only then, will some of our best and brightest and most caring women and men choose to enter nursing. Whatever happened to careers in community organizing, urban planning, Legal Aid, and public-health nursing? Young women and men will be able to consider these options only if they are decently paid, have a future and some degree of security and respect.

Private Affluence, Public Squalor

In this fin de siècle period of U.S. history characterized (in the words of John Kenneth Galbraith) by "private affluence" and "public squalor," it may be difficult to see our way clear to putting significantly larger amounts of money into health care, community organizing, education, or even a meaningful effort to deter young people from drug abuse, but we must recognize that these issues are central to the well-being of families and thus central to the very fabric and structure of American society. While the 1980s have surely been characterized by absorption with personal advancement and well-being (particularly economic and physical well-being), there are many indications that Americans are also concerned about the well-being of the society as a whole. Poll after poll has demonstrated that people *are* concerned about issues such as education and homelessness and *are* willing to make sacrifices to enable the society to deal more effectively with these problems. Furthermore, it is often said that there is no money to truly make this into a "kinder, gentler nation" but we must remember that the United States spends $300 billion annually on arms, the U.S. Congress has approved the Bush administration's savings and loan bailout proposal that will cost nearly $160 billion over the next ten years, and the United States has one of the lowest tax rates, particularly for the wealthy, in the industrialized world. I suggest that the money *is* there. The issue is how we choose to allocate it.

The Struggle for Economic Justice

The narrowing wage gap is clearly something to celebrate, as it heralds steady, if slow, movement toward equality in the workplace. But women's limited overall improvement in real wages, combined with the decreasing access to income from other sources, indicate that there is still a long way to go in the struggle for economic justice for women.

Randy Albelda, *Dollars & Sense,* July/August 1988.

What should our priorities be? Among them, parents must have some time at home with their children. Why can't parents of young children work a shorter day or week and not risk losing their jobs? Why aren't parents at the time of the birth or adoption of a baby guaranteed some paid time together with that infant when virtually every other industrialized country has some statutory maternity or parental leave? The parental leave bill that was killed during the 100th Congress called for unpaid leave for the parents of a newborn or newly adopted child. It would have affected only 5 percent of all businesses and 40 percent of all workers (the firms affected would have been those with fifty or more employees). It was estimated by Senator John H. Chafee, Republican of Rhode Island, that the cost would have been $160 million per year, which averages out to one cent per day for each covered employee. The bill also would have provided unpaid leave for parents with seriously ill children. As Senator Christopher J. Dodd, Democrat of Connecticut, a sponsor of the legislation, stated:

Today fewer than one in ten American families have the luxury of having the mother at home with the children while the father is at work.

In this nation today there are 8.7 million women as the sole providers of their families. They are taking care of 16 million kids who have no father at home. And when that child becomes sick or that employee becomes sick, we ought not to say to that family struggling to make ends meet: "Choose. Choose your child or choose your job."

No, women cannot make it alone. They cannot work and parent and care for their elderly relatives as well without a caring society. They cannot work and care for others without sufficient income, parental leave, real flex time, and a work environment that recognizes and understands that a rewarding private life takes time and energy. . . .

It is ironic that young women, a group outside the cultural mainstream in at least two fundamental ways, age and gender, have internalized that most mainstream of ideologies, the American Dream. After examining the realities of women's lives today, it is clear that the American Dream, at least as conventionally conceived, cannot be the blueprint for the majority of women. The fundamental components of the American Dream—an almost devout reliance on individualism; the notion that American society, particularly at the end of the twentieth century and the beginning of the twenty-first, is fluid enough to permit substantial upward mobility; the belief that hard work will lead to economic rewards, even for women, a group that has always been at the margins of the labor force; and the determined optimism in the face of massive social and economic problems—will not serve women well.

The American Dream Is a Myth

We must recognize that even for most men the American Dream, with its belief in the power of the individual to shape his or her own destiny, was a myth. Men usually did not "make it" alone; they did not, as the image goes, tame the West, develop industrial America, and climb the economic ladder alone—and they certainly did not do it while being the primary caregiver for a couple of preschoolers. Most of those men who "made it" in America, whom we think of when we reaffirm our belief in the American Dream, had women beside them every step of the way—women to iron their shirts, press their pants, mend their socks, cook their meals, bring up their children, and soothe them at the end of a hard day. They did not do it alone. They *still* don't do it alone. How can women do it alone? Who is there to mend and press their clothes, cook their meals, bring up their children, and soothe them at the end of a hard day? How can women possibly make it alone when they earn 65 percent of what men earn, when housing is virtually unaffordable for millions of families, when child care is scarce and all too often second-rate or worse? And where did they get the notion that they *should* be able to make it alone? It may be progress

168

that many young women now realize that they cannot depend on marriage and a man for their identity, their protection, their daily bread; but is it progress or is it illusion for them to believe that they can do the caring and the doing and do it all on their own in a society that has done very little to make women truly independent?. . .

We must have the courage and the wisdom as a society to recognize that we need a new vision of America for the twenty-first century, perhaps even a new American Dream. We need a vision that recognizes that we cannot survive without one another, that families must have supports in order to thrive, that women cannot make it alone any more than men ever have.

Women's Future

We want a future where women can raise their sights beyond the kitchen, the kids, and the struggle to simply survive—a future where women can fully participate in the struggle to get rid of *all oppression* on this planet.

But we can't bring about this future without women being liberated and active in every sphere of the struggle to change society.

Revolutionary Worker, July 10, 1989.

We must provide many more paths toward a gratifying, economically secure life. Traditional male occupations cannot be the only routes to the good life; traditional female work must be restructured so that it too can lead to power, prestige, and a life of plenty. And the traditional male work style must give way, for both women and men, to the recognition that work is merely one aspect of life and that private concerns, family life, leisure activities, and participation in community life help to define who we are and must be seen as important both to the individual and to the society.

We must find ways of opening up American society to those who feel outside the system, to those who feel hopeless and despairing. We must educate all of our young people, not simply the most privileged. We must provide them with adequate housing, health care, nutrition, safe communities in which to grow, and, above all, a meaningful role in society. So many of them feel extraneous because so many of them are treated as extraneous, except, possibly, in their roles as consumers. Moreover, providing decent lives for the millions of young people who are Outsiders will provide decent jobs for millions of other Americans and, even more, the sense that one is participating in a worthwhile way in the life of the nation. But, of course, we will not make the society accessible to those who now consider themselves Outsiders unless power and wealth are distributed far more equitably. It has been said before, it will be said again, but it cannot be said too often: there is a greater gap today between the rich and the poor than at any point since the Bureau of the Census began collecting these data in 1947. In 1987 the wealthiest 40 percent of American families received 67.8 percent of the national family income, the highest percentage ever recorded, while the poorest 40 percent received 15.4 percent, the lowest percentage (along with that of 1986) ever recorded. Until we address these fundamental inequities, we cannot hope to enable our young people to become fully participating members of society. . . .

A New Vision

We must develop a vision that recognizes that caring is as important as doing, that caring indeed *is* doing, and that caregivers, both paid and unpaid, are the foundation of a humane society and must be treasured and honored. We need a vision of America that recognizes that we must reorganize our social institutions—our family life, our schools, our places of work, and our communities—to enable all people to care for one another, to enable all people to work and to participate in the public life of the nation. Our courageous, insightful, persevering, and often wise young women deserve no less. Our young men deserve no less. Future generations deserve no less.

"We are busily unmaking one of the proudest social achievements in the nineteenth century, which was to take married women out of the work force so they could devote themselves to family and children."

Increasing Equal Opportunities for Women Damages Society

George Gilder

In the following viewpoint, George Gilder disputes the contention that women have traditionally been treated unfairly in American society. Gilder argues that injustice against women lies in taking them away from their homes and families and forcing them into the workplace. Encouraging women to abandon their homes and children hurts society at large, Gilder believes, because it disrupts family life. Gilder is a writer and lecturer whose books include *Sexual Suicide, Men and Marriage,* and *Microcosm.*

As you read, consider the following questions:

1. According to Gilder, what must happen to prevent society's further decline?
2. How have working women affected American society, according to the author?
3. What role does Gilder advocate for men?

George Gilder, "The Myth of the Role Revolution," in *Gender Sanity,* Nicholas Davidson, ed. Lanham, MD: University Press of America, 1989. Reprinted by permission of the publisher.

Drastic shifts in sex roles do seem to be sweeping through America. Though allegedly hobbled by sex discrimination, women everywhere seem to exhibit career patterns increasingly like men's. If feminists continue to complain that the movement toward employment equality is painfully slow, sociologists offer endless data to prove that it is inexorable. Even the careful statisticians at the Department of Labor project nearly equal male and female job-force participation and similar performance by 1995.

The evidence mounts, and prophets climb it to declaim new sermons from its heights. Since 1890, work-force involvement by women between the ages of twenty-five and forty-four has soared from 15 percent to 60 percent, with the pace of change tripling after 1950. Since World War II, even married women with children under age six have joined the fray, with the proportion of these young mothers in the work force rising from under 10 percent to over 50 percent by 1983. Peter Drucker, the shrewdest of social analysts, declared, "We are busily unmaking one of the proudest social achievements in the nineteenth century, which was to take married women out of the work force so they could devote themselves to family and children."

Media Tales

At the same time, the portentous media tales will show that women are crowding into nontraditional jobs. Between 1960 and 1986, the female share of professional jobs increased from 38 to over 50 percent and women's share of management jobs doubled from 14 percent to more than one-third. Since 1970, reported sociologist Andrew Hacker in *The New York Times Magazine,* the proportion of female packinghouse butchers rose by one-third; nearly 80 percent of new bartending jobs went to women; the share of women lawyers rose from 2 percent to 15 percent; and the female share of banking and financial-management jobs surged from 9 percent to 38 percent.

Altogether, Hacker and other analysts contend, women are displacing more and more men at work. While female employment soars, male work-force participation plummets. Between 1960 and 1984, the proportion of adult men in the work force dropped from 86 percent to 78 percent. Some 58 percent of all men now retire before age sixty-five compared to 36 percent as recently as 1970. By 1995, the Labor Department projects, only 65 percent of men aged fifty-five to sixty-four will remain in the labor force. Perhaps more significant in the long run is the substantial drop in employment and rise in unemployment among young men, particularly young blacks, which has also paralleled female entry into the work force. . . .

Many pundits contend that the evolving American economy

172

will increasingly favor women throughout the job market, from clerical roles to the highest echelons of management. Not only is male physical strength increasingly irrelevant to most jobs, but male aggressiveness and drive are also alleged to be counterproductive in the age of information and services. The prevailing fashions in business leadership, epitomized by *In Search of Excellence* and the best-selling texts on Japanese management, stress "soft" personal skills, intuitive guidance through communication and consensus, not the rigid hierarchies and controls favored by the macho businessmen of the past. The information and service sectors, according to a popular theory, will offer ever wider opportunities to women as time passes and these industries increasingly dominate the economy. Indeed, some analysts assert, feminine skills will tend to prevail over male aggressiveness in all the major businesses of the future. . . .

A Home-Centered Culture

As the home once again becomes the place where crucial functions of society are carried out, it will regain the esteem it has sadly lost—and with it, women's role will regain status. It is a sociological truth that in cultures where the tasks women do are seen as essential to society and its survival, they enjoy high status; in societies where women's tasks are seen as peripheral, they have low status. Applied to our own culture, it should come as no surprise that as the major social functions came to be carried out in institutions outside the home, women at home lost esteem. If we reverse that trend, women will win the respect they are so desperately seeking—*without* having to sacrifice their family relationships to do it.

Nancy R. Pearcey, *The Human Life Review*, Summer 1987.

Now if you are an ordinary man or woman and the changes are real, the trend looms as a monster indeed, initially titillating perhaps, but finally menacing the future of your children and the settled habits of your own home and marriage. But closer scrutiny shows this "revolution"—for all its statistical weight and anecdotal pervasiveness—is just another shadow in the Loch Ness News. . . .

Much of the statistical change in job patterns cited in the stories of sexual revolution reflects instead the industrial revolution. As recently as eighty years ago, most American families were engaged in agriculture; this proportion has dropped to 3 percent. That is truly a revolution, and it has transformed everything else, including the official statistics of women in the work force. Female entrance into market employment has in fact merely lagged behind women's departure from farms. On farms, moreover, as every farmer knows, women did not restrict themselves to the kitchen and boudoir. Women in agriculture worked very hard beyond the hearth and cribside, commonly performing an array of jobs requiring far more onerous physical labor and longer hours than their current work. . . .

American women perform full-time work chiefly as they always have: when they are forced to, usually by the desertion, divorce, death, or scarce earnings of their husbands. Women also are living some 12 percent longer than men and have a longer potential span in the work force after their children grow up. The influx of women into jobs reflects in part the greater number of divorced and single women and in part the abrupt decline in childbearing after the post-World War II surge of fertility—not any basic change in the motives and roles of men and women. . . .

The Persistence of Traditional Roles

A 1982 Harris poll indicated that 39 percent of women would prefer to work only at home and another 14 percent would prefer to do only volunteer work, making a total of 53 percent who do not want to be in the job market outside the home at all. Since another 32 percent want part-time work only, this survey indicates that just 12 percent of all American women desire full-time employment in the labor force outside their own household.

By the mid-1980s, women in large numbers were using entrepreneurial activity to fulfill their preference for work in the home. From knitting mittens to selling real estate and writing software packages for personal computers, women were increasingly launching small businesses in their homes. Between 1972 and 1982, the percent of self-employed women workers in nonagricultural industries rose from 25.6 percent to 31.8 percent of the total number of self-employed in this category and in 1984 and 1985 women were actually forming sole proprietorships faster than men. Once again, though, the statistics do not suggest any female usurpation of the provider role. The average net income of female-operated businesses in 1980 was $2,200. The average net income of the most common such firm—a retail establishment—was $497. Moreover, the average earnings of all female-run firms were dropping in relation to the earnings of similar male-run companies.

Such figures confirm the persistence of traditional sex roles. Women seek education and credentials chiefly in order to gain more time with their families, while men seek these qualifications in order to earn larger incomes and provide for their wives and children. Female physicians, for example, see 38 percent fewer patients per hour and work 22 percent fewer hours than male physicians; female lawyers see fewer clients than male lawyers; female professors write fewer books and research papers than male professors. In general, women in their prime earning years are by various measures between seven and eleven times more likely to leave the work force voluntarily than men are, and have only half as much experience in their jobs. As has been demonstrated in several econometric studies, such differences in behavior amply explain the difference between male and female earnings without any recourse to claims of discrimination. . . .

Female Employment

Trends in manufacturing, moreover, suggest no major shift in favor of female employment in lower-level jobs. The male mechanical aptitudes that still give men between 95 and 99 percent of all jobs in mechanics, repair, machinery, carpentry, construction, and metal crafts will remain vitally important in the service economy. In addition, these aptitudes are readily convertible into skills in the maintenance of computers and other electronic appliances.

Strong Families

Strong families will mean a strong nation; weak families will make us vulnerable to our enemies. . . .

If an enemy wanted to undermine the family as a way of weakening a country, who better to target than the wife and mother whose gentleness, compassion, intuition, and sensitivity make her the heart of the family unit. Tell her that marriage, motherhood, and homemaking are demeaning and that she needs to be "liberated" from this domestic slavery. Offer her a new "bill of rights" that will guarantee complete equality with men, the right to abortion on demand, and even freedom of sexual preference.

James Drummey, *The New American*, January 15, 1990.

The assembly-line roles currently performed by women in technical manufacturing firms, however, are likely to continue to move overseas or give way to automation and robotics. Similarly, the computer revolution, striking at routine clerical functions, will tend to counteract the sexual revolution in employment in service firms. Although women will continue to play vital roles throughout the economy, nothing in the current direction of technical progress seems likely to give them a substantially greater role outside the home than they have today. In fact, the technology of computers and telecommunications may well accelerate the current return of cottage industries and home offices which allow women to remain near their children. . . .

Most feminist proposals seem designed to establish the working mother as the social norm by making it impossible for most male providers to support their families alone. The feminist attack on the social-security system for giving housewives a right to the husband's benefits after he dies; the subsidies for day care; the affirmative-action quotas for women who pursue careers outside the home—all such measures seek to establish the careerist woman as the national standard and incapacitate the woman who tries to care for her own children.

Allan Carlson has explained how a similar policy worked in Sweden. Until 1965, Swedes spurned a quarter-century of feminist indoctrination and followed a social pattern similar to the U.S. Only a quarter of mothers of children under seven entered the work force and more than half of them held part-time jobs. Over the years, however, the Swedish socialists, under pressure from feminists led by Alva Myrdal, managed slowly to destroy the essential supports of the nuclear family. The entire present agenda of American feminism—from universal day care and family-planning programs to paternity leaves for fathers—was eventually enacted.

Carlson writes: "With the homemaker declared to be 'a dying race,' legal changes removed the special protections afforded women in marriage. Changes in Swedish tax law essentially eliminated the joint return for a married couple, and have left all persons paying the same tax, whether alone, married but childless, or married with children. . . ." Moreover, marginal Swedish income taxes were increased to nearly 100 percent at modest income levels, making it all but impossible to support a family on one income by extra personal effort. "Swedish welfare policy was also altered to discourage maternal care of preschool children. Housing and tax benefits are effectively curtailed if families decide to care for their children and refuse to place them in day care centers [and these parents also lose] benefits such as free children's meals and diapers.". . .

The Obsolescence of Marriage

Nonetheless, the Swedish policy was dramatically successful in several important ways. By 1984 the official "poverty line" for a family of four in Sweden was approximately 40 percent above the average annual wage. Therefore only the rich (chiefly families with sources of funds outside Sweden) could maintain a family on one income. The male role as principal provider was effectively abolished for most of the population. This policy, though, resulted not in more egalitarian marriages, but in the obsolescence of marriage itself.

176

Not only did the rate of illegitimacy rise to over 40 percent of all live births, but the marriage rate fell to the lowest level ever recorded in world demographic data. Despite the world's most ambitious programs of sex education and family planning, despite the widespread issuance of free contraceptives, the abortion rate soared to a 1981 level just below the U.S. rate of 43 percent of all live births. The Swedish people voted against the officially favored egalitarian marriage by mostly not marrying at all. The birthrate fell to a point 40 percent below the replacement rate required to maintain zero population growth. Despite one of the world's best-educated populations and some of the world's most resourceful large companies, the Swedish economy foundered. With the industrial world's highest tax rates came also a governmental deficit in the early 1980s some three times as high as America's huge shortfall as a share of GNP [gross national product]. . . .

The Traditional Woman

The war that feminism wages against the traditional woman is not an aberration; it is the logical extension of constructing a new feminist social order. Though men and women are distinctively designed, permanently unequal in their biology, psychology, and social needs; nevertheless, the feminist agenda—with the help of government, the educational establishment, and media—will go forward.

The cost of this experiment will be a tyranny of continuous government tinkering in the relationship of the sexes; the dissolution of the traditional family; and the emergence of what might be derogatorily called the "mass man"—though, in this case, "mass person" might better fit the ideological bill.

James L. Sauer, *The New American,* January 15, 1990.

The central lesson of the Swedish experience is the profound and irretrievable damage inflicted by a policy of driving mothers of small children out of the home and into the work force. Women in the home are not performing some optional role that can be more efficiently fulfilled by the welfare state. Women in the home are not "wasting" their human resources. The role of the mother is the paramount support of civilized human society. It is essential to the socialization both of men and of children. The maternal love and nurture of small children is an asset that can be replaced, if at all, only at vastly greater cost. Such attention is crucial to raising children into healthy and productive citizens. Moreover, the link of men through marriage to the support of particular children is crucial to male motivation and productivity.

The provider role of men not only gives the society the benefit of a lifetime of hard work oriented toward long-term goals. It also channels and disciplines male energies and aggressions that otherwise turn against that society. By contrast, full-time work by mothers of small children comes at a serious twofold cost: first, the loss of the immeasurable social benefit of the mother's loving care for her child; second, the frequent loss of the husband's full-time concentration on his career. The yield of the mother's job to the economy or the man's help in the home only rarely can offset these costs of her employment. The society will pay the costs one way or another: not only through tremendous outlays for day care but also through economic declines, population loss, juvenile delinquency, crime, mental illness, alcoholism, addiction, and divorce.

Together with the tragic breakdown of the American black family, the Swedish example should disabuse Americans of the illusion that it can't happen here. Family breakdown and demoralization can occur with frightening suddenness when government policy destroys the role of the male provider in the family. The alternative to traditional family roles is not a unisex family; it is sexual suicide.

"In the feminist world of tomorrow . . . all people would have the responsibility to nurture, build trust, enhance life, and to participate in political and community affairs."

Feminist Policies Promote Social Justice

Margarita Papandreou

Margarita Papandreou is the president of the Women's Union of Greece, a socialist-feminist organization that works to end patriarchy and capitalism. She is also the international liaison of Women for a Meaningful Summit, a Washington, D.C.-based international organization that works to end the arms race. In the following viewpoint, Papandreou argues that the feminist movement will enable women to become more powerful in society. Powerful women will make society more just, according to Papandreou, because they will enact policies to establish nonviolence, help children, protect the environment, and improve education.

As you read, consider the following questions:

1. How does the author define feminism?
2. How does the author believe women can become more influential in society?
3. What social changes has the feminist movement accomplished since 1970, according to Papandreou?

Margarita Papandreou, "Feminism and Political Power," in *Women, Power, and Policy*, Ellen Boneparth and Emily Stoper, eds. Oxford: Pergamon Press, 1988. Excerpted with permission.

If we define politics as involvement in the public sphere for social, economic or political purposes, whether for creating change or for preservation of the status quo, then women have been involved in politics informally for many years. Most recently, women have been working for change through the large political movement called women's liberation. All through history, however, they have been excluded from the formal political bodies where they could participate in making decisions in pursuit of their goals.

Only recently, in the past few years, a small number of women have become legislators and heads of state in many countries. Despite this involvement in the public sphere, we observe that the system of every country still reflects almost exclusively the male vision of how the members of its society should function. This can be said without exception because there is no society in the world which is not patriarchal, or male-dominated.

Sex Differences

In tests on sex differences in values and interests (the same basic results are seen in almost all cultures) women score high on scales for esthetic, social, and religious values. Men receive high marks for politics, economics, and technology. These *socially induced* characteristics make a difference in male and female culture. How would society be if it developed a culture that had the *value system* of a women's world—that of non-violence, of caring and nurturing, of non-oppressive personal and institutional relations? The answer is necessarily hypothetical. These values would be most likely the basis for governing by women, and we have not had enough women in positions of power to give us a glimpse of such a society. However, in Scandinavian countries where there is a high feminist consciousness and a commitment to social justice, the priorities on issues are different, less militaristic and more humanistic. These so-called feminine values are sorely needed in giving birth to a new ethos—a new era.

Now I come to a key question for feminists. How do we manage from a position of relative powerlessness to change our societies? To realize this vision of the world? How do we manage to make those changes when we are not in positions of power to do so? And, if we need to get into decision-making centers, how do we do that without compromising our own value systems?

Let me start by making a distinction among three terms: *sisterhood*, the *women's movement* and *feminism*. Worldwide or global *sisterhood* can be defined simply as a universal concern and individual caring for women as a group everywhere—a compassion, an understanding, an empathy. It is a way in which women relate to each other. We offer each other the love and support that we have been socialized to lavish primarily on husband and children. It is a consciousness that in spite of all things that divide women—class, religion, color, cultural traditions—we do share things *in common* as a gender group. We are the least educated, the lowest on the economic pyramid, responsible for child-raising and the household, and we have little political and decision-making power in the public sphere.

A Feminist Perspective

Peace work, as well as a wide range of other political issues, could become areas in which feminism potentially extends its range and influence. After all, the women's movement will not have achieved its goal until women are as effective and influential as men in every area of life. For the remainder of the century, not only peace but basic survival issues are a logical area in which to extend a feminist perspective. . . .

For the U.S. women's movement, a new emphasis on poverty issues would bring a number of benefits. First, it would be a way of reaching out to elderly women and women of color and of laying the basis for much stronger coalitions. It would also be a basis for linkage to unions, liberal churches, civil rights groups, and other organizations that have traditionally been concerned with government policies toward the poor. Finally, it would make possible a much stronger international outreach, both to the third world and to social change groups in Europe and elsewhere.

Ellen Boneparth and Emily Stoper, *Women, Power, and Policy,* 1988.

These similarities are the grounds then for *sisterhood*. The *worldwide women's movement* can be considered the organized arm of sisterhood, a loosely knit federation of women's organizations, working in resistance to humiliation, inequality, and injustice. Developing *strategy* for this women's movement is where *feminism* comes in. Feminism embodies the awareness of the special oppression and exploitation that all women face as a gender group. Feminism is the willingness to organize and fight against women's subjugation in society and for the elimination of *sex-based injustice*. Feminists must decide what exactly is wrong, whose fault it is, and what should be done to make matters right. Difficult decisions have to be made, a political-ideological framework developed, and priorities decided. Above all, *we must have a vision*, an image of the kind of world we would like to live in if we had the power to mold it, with a new social organization that would create a different kind of society.

The reason I make these distinctions is that the support of

women in general under sisterhood does not translate necessarily to the support of all women running for or elected to political office. In the case of politics, it is not sufficient that the candidate be a woman; she must be a woman with feminist goals, demands, and principles. Women in political positions will be deciding issues that concern our lives, our children's lives, and the life of society; their *political orientation* is critical. . . .

Feminism is the most powerful revolutionary force in the world today. And feminism is urgently needed in a world that is not working, is dangerously out of control, and is losing a sense of what it means to be human. In getting at the heart of sex bias, feminism is challenging the social fabric of society, its political orientation, and the decisions of its political authority. And, it is challenging *all* political and social systems.

What *does* feminism have to say about the burning political, economic, social issues of today? How do feminists look at the armaments race, nuclear power, international relations, development in the third world, value of women's work, and the budget allocations of our respective countries? Do we have *a new, a different perspective*? An enlarged vision of the human experience?

Political Power

As far as political power is concerned, I wish to focus on mainstream politics and particularly about those societies where electoral politics are possible, where the individual is free to organize to achieve power. I am also going to discuss the power of a mass movement which may ultimately, if used effectively, be the most important force for change. Already women have accomplished much in terms of global consciousness-raising. The women's movement can be credited with changing laws, eliminating barriers to upward mobility in careers, achieving higher levels of education, breaking into "male" fields, and eliminating some sexual stereotyping.

Yet, significant numbers of women have not yet been able to break into that bastion of male power, the traditional political arena—electoral politics. Nor have they, in fact, in one-party states captured important posts in the party or governmental hierarchy. In order to complete the social revolution begun by women, we must develop a strategy that is concerned with the acquisition of political power. Generally, feminists have a negative reaction to such terms. The word power sounds too male. Power for feminists, however, represents the capacity to change—the individual and the environment—without the use of force. In other words, this is not exploitative power, but power that is mutually strengthening. In addition to the lobbying effort, which must continue, women must achieve positions where they can be an integral part of the decision-making process, to decide equally with men on the direction of their societies and of the world. Obtaining these positions can only be done by a strengthening of the women's movement. . . .

A Saner World

Individual women have pursued active roles in fighting the war machine. Maggie Kuhn organized and leads the Gray Panthers, which takes a forceful stand on peace and military issues. Dorothy Eber, 64-year-old mother of four and grandmother of eleven, was arrested on Holy Thursday 1984 for praying. She was one of seven who held a prayer vigil in the office of a big military contractor. She and six other Midwestern women cut the locks of missile silos in Missouri and planted flowers on the site. . . .

The record is full of stories of women who have worked to improve the environment, to strengthen the chances for peace and to insure a better life for their children. . . .

We can all be thankful that women are using their hearts, their minds, and their energies to make this a saner, more peaceful world.

The Washington Spectator, June 15, 1989.

This must be done if feminist principles are to become a way of life. If the women's movement is to increase its power, both as a lobbying force and an organization backing and electing its spokespersons to traditional political positions, then it must become more of a *mass movement,* more of a *grass-roots movement.* It means not only getting in touch with the average woman, the truly dispossessed woman, the racially discriminated-against woman, the factory worker, but also incorporating *her* into the movement. It means learning from *her* how she perceives changes that would make her oppression less, and her life more decent; and how *she* looks at the struggle for equality—what she likes about it, what she finds threatening about it.

Consciousness-Raising

This would be a second stage of consciousness-raising, but at a more sophisticated level. The first stage created an awareness that women had problems in common. The next stage is to discuss priorities in attacking these problems by letting *those speak who previously had the least opportunity to participate in the struggle for equality.* This involves community organization, which will broaden our concept of "women's issues" and propel us into a social reform platform to suit the needs of more and more women. And, it will bring greater numbers of women into the movement. . . .

183

In order to get our spokespeople into decision-making political positions, we have to have a strong and dynamic movement and an ever-growing organization. That is why I emphasize the Second Phase—the community organization/grass-roots phase. In electoral politics today in most democracies, organizational support is a key factor to victory. Charismatic leadership is another, and money, still another. The importance of *organization* for women is primary—both before an election and after. The women's movement is a means for both achieving political office and raising the *conscience* of those who reach office. This answers the earlier question of how do we not compromise our value system in the struggle for power? A broadly based movement will be our candidates' super-ego. It will give the woman who achieves a position in a male-dominated environment the strength and courage to stick to her feminist agenda. We don't have money, and we are not enchanted by the notion of charismatic personality leadership roles. When I say women don't have money, this is not entirely true; women just are not accustomed to putting that money to political purpose. We have not yet learned to support ourselves, at least on any grand scale. Where are the campaign funds for feminist candidates? Where are the foundations, originated by a woman or women, for furthering women's studies, research on women or scholarships? Where is a feminist strategy board, a think tank or a feminist Institute on Foreign Affairs?

International Meaning

While I have been dwelling on a strategy for action within our countries that seems to be of more immediate domestic concern, all actions of feminist organizations have *international meaning*. Feminists throughout the world watch, study, learn, and get ideas from feminist actions in other countries. On international goals, feminists must work to form coalitions with the peace movement, the ecological movement, the movement against hunger in the world, and others. The peace movement especially is a natural home for feminists. Our history confirms this: the Pankhursts, the Ashtons, the Schwimmers, the Jane Addams's in the past; recently the Greenham Common women of Great Britain, women of the Nordic countries, and women in Greece as well have set the example. The looming threat of nuclear devastation demands our participation in peace activities, activities for survival. The connection between militarism and sexism is of great concern to us. Patriarchy is a system of values of competition, aggression, emotional denial, and violence. These values are *particularly* prevalent in war, in which the competition is through force, and there are victors and victims, losers and winners. It is a *Weltanschauung*, a belief which tries to smother the human capacity to care. We must press the peace movement into asking the question of whether peace is possible in a patriarchal world. This will force peace educators to explore the links between denial of women's rights and the war system, and the dependence that both sexism and militarism have on violence.

Undermining Male Dominance

To argue that male dominance is virtually universal is emphatically not to say that it is inevitable. . . . Feminism has arisen not in a social vacuum but as a response to the changing circumstances and opportunities associated with industrialism.

Forces are at work in society helping to undermine the system of male dominance. But feminists need to accelerate and consolidate their impact by bringing the issue into the public political arena.

Vicky Randall, *Women and Politics*, 1987.

We must understand how and why violence has become so much a part of our lives: violence in the home, muggings, rapes in the streets, terrorism throughout the world, confrontation between nations. We are really a world at war. The huge international arms traffic, the immense budgets of defense departments, the fleets traveling the world through international waters, the 40 or more local wars that are raging now: *we are on a war system*. A new mode of thinking, one that feminism is in the process of developing, is essential to a world where conflict can be solved by non-violent means. Feminists are trying to transcend the dichotomous thinking that has produced the we-they syndrome that divides and factionalizes the world, polarizing the world and feeding the war system. Human beings make distinctions between good and evil: *we* being virtuous and noble, *they* being incapable, unreliable, corrupt. In the feminist world of tomorrow, all people would be looked at alike and all people would have the responsibility to nurture, build trust, enhance life, and to participate in political and community affairs. . . .

The feminist movement has a vision. We understand, first of all, that we have but one earth, shared by one human race. This globe is home to all—all people, all life, all laughter, all love, all music, all art. We will make it a woman's world, not in the sense of control, power, or dominance, but in the sense of the revolutionary vision that we have, a revolution of the human spirit. Those values that we call women-centered values—caring, gentleness, equality, justice, dignity, compassion—will be diffused throughout societies worldwide.

"Feminism is a disaster as a universal philosophy."

Feminist Policies Do Not Promote Social Justice

Nicholas Davidson

In the following viewpoint, Nicholas Davidson contends that the feminist movement will destroy, not enhance, social justice. He argues that feminists have a narrow worldview: they believe all women must work outside the home and all men are oppressors. Such a negative view is not only inaccurate, Davidson states, but also thwarts the effort to establish a more just society based on cooperation between the sexes. Davidson holds degrees in history from the University of Massachusetts at Amherst and the University of Chicago. He is the author of *The Failure of Feminism* and the editor of *Gender Sanity*.

As you read, consider the following questions:

1. Why does the author maintain that feminism replaced the feminine mystique with its own mystique?
2. How does feminism actually hurt women in their relationships with men and with family members, in the author's view?
3. What ideas does Davidson believe would be more helpful than feminist ideas in creating a just world?

Reprinted from Nicholas Davidson's *The Failure of Feminism* with permission of Prometheus Books, Buffalo, New York.

In its best sense, "feminism" signifies a broad concern with the well-being of women. The conditions of women's lives are to be improved through social activism of various sorts. This approach raises serious questions. The improvements in American women's (and men's) lives over the past hundred years are due mostly to economic progress and the consequent emergence of a post-industrial middle class society, not to social activism. All the feminism of the past century has not done as much to increase women's choices as the invention of the washing machine. But it is hard to quibble with the fundamental decency of the social activist impulse, or to deny that it has accomplished significant good in some areas.

Contemporary feminism, though, retains this humane approach only in the imaginations of its more distant supporters. Feminism today is a narrowly ideological movement, the last survivor of sixties leftist politics to retain any major influence in American life. A product of the radical rage of the sixties, it remains mired in the quicksand of that era's unwinnable causes.

It is very tempting to take a positive view of the accomplishments of this feminism, to continue to believe it was the "most humane revolution of all," a pure net gain for all concerned. Can such a view be sustained?

Feminism's Achievements

Feminism has real and significant achievements to its credit. Feminists have played a major role in opening doors to women in employment, education, and sports. Feminism has provided a guiding philosophy to many women in their prolonged and bruising penetration of the corporate and academic worlds. Feminism has provided enough of a supporting framework to sustain many women through a difficult period of complete uncertainty about their sex roles. Feminists formed an important part of the constituency for abortion rights at the start of the seventies. They were responsible for desperately needed attention given to the crime of rape. They have thrown the spotlight on the syndrome of battered women. Feminists have played a highly effective role in the grass roots attempt to introduce humanity and common sense to medical practice in America. They have relentlessly hammered home the inadequacy of all intellectual disciplines that fail to take into account a female point of view. History, anthropology, sociology, psychology, sociobiology, primatology, and literary criticism will never be quite the same. Feminists have destroyed the plausibility of oversimple explanations for our partly arbitrary sex roles. Perhaps above all, feminism has helped to tear open the deceptively uniform surface presented by the mystique of femininity to reveal the cornucopia of needs, talents, and aspirations within. . . .

It would be highly unwise to reject these accomplishments. Indeed, it is probably not possible to do so. Future generations will be in part the children of feminism. Feminism has advanced the cause of humanity in important ways. However, we cannot afford to spend all our time eulogizing past accomplishments. We must also cope with the new problems facing us today, which have been brought about in great measure by feminism's very successes. Beside its real accomplishments we must place the failures of feminism.

Feminism's Failures

The first of these lies in the ambiguous nature of all its successes. When one rereads *The Feminine Mystique* a generation later, one realizes how thoroughly feminism replaced the feminine mystique with its own mystique in all the areas Betty Friedan examined: education, psychology, advertising, journalism, and so forth. Feminism successfully took over the cultural loci that were its main targets. It is now ensconced as the official philosophy of America's leading women's colleges, such as Smith, Radcliffe, and Barnard. Universities, corporations, professional associations, and departments of government are committed to enforcing its worldview. In place of the feminine mystique, it supplied its own warnings against men, marriage, spontaneity in love, and femininity. Young women in the eighties received a message as uncompromising as any the fifties had devised.

The Importance of Family

Feminists do not see the importance of a good marriage, a solid home life, children being reared by a mother and a father. Many who came of high quality families with high quality values for American society believe that has been one of the greatest downfalls. When the feminist movement failed to recognize the importance of marriage, the family, and the home, they missed the greatest asset in building strength in their own organization.

Beverly LaHaye, *The Heritage Lectures*, March 10, 1987.

It was not worth opening the door of the workplace to women at the cost of shutting the door of the home. The message against marriage contributed heavily to the formation of an entire cohort of single women. Statisticians concluded in the middle of the eighties that many of them would be unable to marry unless they drastically lowered their standards for husbands (which, moved by the biological imperative to mate with a dominant male, they were not about to do). No amount of ideological apology can undo the fact that many women were marooned in the public arena, some for years and some forever, and denied the equal or greater fulfillments of home and family. Too, as Germaine Greer had at one point predicted, women were granted "admission to the world of the ulcer and the coronary" as, along with their increased participation in the work force, women's rates of cancer, heart disease, and the other great scourges of male occupational stress rose to rival those of men. The feminist attention to rape does not validate the analysis responsible for that attention, that rape is a political crime, or the destructive model of sexuality from which that analysis arises. Nor can the push to include women's points of view in the social sciences conceal that most of the resulting efforts were dogmatic and unimaginative, resulting in at best a marginal advance to human understanding.

Destroying Good Relations Between the Sexes

As a guiding philosophy for women, feminism makes all relations with men difficult, and good relations virtually impossible. In the words of one disillusioned feminist, a leading exponent of Women's Studies, "For a long time, I thought feminism explained everything. It taught me how to analyze what was going on between me and the men I lived and worked with. But now it's left me out on a limb, feeling angry with nowhere to go and no way to turn back.". . .

Feminism is a failure as an intellectual approach. The feminist perspective imposes a one-dimensional interpretation on all aspects of human life, namely, that the evils of the world can all be traced to men oppressing women. This view forces its scientifically minded acolytes into denying the most obvious facts of human biology and psychology. It generates female chauvinism and the sex-hate mongering seen in *The Color Purple,* in which tearing a newborn baby from its mother's arms is presented as typical, everyday male behavior. Not only is the feminist perspective anti-male, it also devalues female experience by denying the authenticity of women's experience under "patriarchy," that is, before the Feminist Era. After her consciousness is raised, the feminist looks at her mother and sees a victim instead of a person.

Exploiting Women

Feminism exploits women in a particularly insidious way. Many is the feminist mother today who imposes feminist goals on her feminine daughter, who tries to accept them out of deference toward a perceived cultural consensus. Feminist teachers, employers, and counselors all pressure young women to live by their tenets. . . .

The feminist revolution never took into account the fact that millions of American women would continue to choose to be housewives. In consequence, feminist policies ignored or, more often, worked against the needs of these millions of American women. Feminists could not help to stabilize "traditional" marriage while they were calling for its destruction.

A Message of Confusion

Feminism tears down a woman's feeling of self-worth. You cannot have a feeling of self-worth if you harbor and display bitterness and hatred toward the male sex. Feminists may not say they hate men, but their actions speak louder than words. They say that women are superior to men, and yet, that you are handicapped if you are born a woman. Feminism is a message of confusion.

Beverly LaHaye, *The Heritage Lectures,* March 10, 1987.

As a political force, feminism's philosophical reductionism has been reflected in a pattern of self-righteousness and irrealism when faced with the hard realities of electoral politics. This led to a "Midas touch in reverse" which has damaged every cause endorsed by organized political feminism. . . .

The failures of feminism are in proportion to its pretensions. Feminism in the seventies aggressively presented itself as *the* movement to liberate humanity. Instead, it now appears that feminism embraces only a small corner of the human experience, which it addresses with a point of view capable of shedding some light, but at the price of severe limitations, including a characteristic set of distorting effects which it cannot correct by itself. . . .

A Philosophy Based on Resentment

Even the idea of "liberating" women implies that they must be enslaved: enslaved by men and by masculinity in all its pernicious guises. The very words "Women's Liberation" thus represent an assault on the necessary relational bases of human existence. Contemporary feminism is a philosophy based on resentment, and while one certainly wishes the situation were different, the conclusion is inescapable that feminism as it exists is one of the most negative worldviews to have emerged in recent years.

For all these reasons, it is impossible to sustain the 1970s characterization of feminism as a universal philosophy with a messianic mission. A better future will come from men and women, not from women alone; and will come from men and women practicing the traditional virtues of masculinity and femininity, albeit sometimes in new contexts, not from a neutered New

190

Woman and New Man whose gender is limited to their genitals. Feminism is not the end of the road. . . .

There is a widespread belief that feminism was a movement to better the condition of women; that feminist leaders just want to give women a better deal. One looks in vain for this sort of feminist leader. Political activism is of course one aspect of contemporary feminism, but it has never been the central one. Contemporary feminism is also a literary movement, a movement of lesbian advocacy, and, above all, a vast effort of cultural propaganda directed against what are usually viewed as the positive bases of the human condition: family, motherhood, gender, and the love between the sexes. If feminism were primarily the positive attempt to improve women's condition that most Americans think it should be, and that some still imagine it is, it would never have occurred to me to write this. Instead, I would be on the barricades with the feminists. . . .

Feminism Can Take Us No Farther

The real achievements of feminism must be admired and preserved, yet the ideology which has brought us this far can take us no farther. It is equally incapable of serving as a constructive guide to women or to men, to intellectual inquiry, social policy, or individual choice. Feminist ideology in any of its current forms is demonstrably misleading as a guide to the human condition. It is true that men have individually and collectively oppressed women at times, but women have also on their own initiative oppressed men and in any case this is not the central force in the human dynamic. The hallmark of the sexes' relations has always been cooperation more than conflict. The form of society is not and has never been determined by men oppressing women. The problems of the human race consequently cannot be solved by homogenizing sexual temperament or eliminating sex roles. Men and women are equally important to the future of humanity; the feminist hypothesis that masculine values are now obsolete because there are "no bears to kill" is not just vindictive but naive. Feminism is a disaster as a universal philosophy, for even if feminism is able to reform itself to better reflect women's points of view, it will still fail to reflect men's points of view.

Because humanity cannot be understood in terms of either sex alone, even the most enlightened feminism is inherently incapable of providing a balanced understanding of gender issues.

"By raising women's wages, comparable worth would weaken a crucial link in the vicious circle of women's oppression."

Comparable Worth Promotes Social Justice

Teresa Amott and Julie Matthaei

Teresa Amott teaches economics at the University of Massachusetts in Boston and has been active in welfare rights struggles. Julie Matthaei teaches economics at Wellesley College in Wellesley, Massachusetts and is the author of *An Economic History of Women in America.* In the following viewpoint, Amott and Matthaei advocate comparable worth to redress inequalities in prestige and pay between men and women.

As you read, consider the following questions:

1. What are the benefits of comparable worth, according to Amott and Matthaei?
2. According to the authors, why is comparable worth necessary for women and minority groups?
3. How has the women's movement influenced the free-market system, in the authors' view?

Teresa Amott and Julie Matthaei, "The Promise of Comparable Worth," *Socialist Review,* April/June 1988. Reprinted with permission.

Leftists and civil rights activists underestimate the radical potential of comparable worth, a reform which strives to raise women's wages to a level of "worth" relative to that of other work done for the same employer. Liberal advocates defend comparable worth initiatives against conservative criticism by arguing that comparable worth simply extends existing market principles by rewarding job traits as the market does. But if a broad spectrum of progressives fails to enter the comparable worth debate, such claims could become self-fulfilling prophecies. . . .

The Comparable Worth Issue

Although the concept of comparable worth first emerged from discussions within the War Labor Board in 1943, the first comparable worth suit was brought against General Electric and Westinghouse by the United Electrical Workers of America (UE) in 1945. In the suit, UE attacked the companies' job descriptions as thinly veiled attempts to pay different, and divisive, wages to men and women.

Comparable worth did not emerge as a broadly-based strategy for the women's movement until the mid-1970s, at which time the "second wave" of feminism took up the demand and argued it as an issue for women rather than solely an aspect of labor movement solidarity. The second wave of pay equity campaigns arose as women's advocates discovered that the 1973 Equal Pay Act, which prohibited unequal pay only in the case of equal (i.e., identical) work, was of limited applicability to women. Partly because the Act was so weak, the average income for women working full-time remained roughly 60 percent of men's income throughout the 1960s and 1970s.

The constancy of the wage gap in the face of civil rights legislation drew attention to the fact that women and men are rarely found in the same jobs, since women have historically been concentrated in a few occupations and excluded from many others. To this day, most women work in occupations with low pay and few opportunities far advancement. These jobs often center around nurturing and serving others; for example, nursing, secretarial and clerical work, teaching, and food service. Throughout the 1970s, for example, over 40 percent of all women workers were crowded into 10 occupations, most of which were over 70 percent female. Men, especially white men, have more job options and generally earn higher pay. For instance, stock clerks, who are predominantly male, earn more than bank tellers, who are predominantly female. Similarly, registered nurses earn less than mail carriers.

The concept of comparable worth was devised to raise wages in female-dominated occupations up to the level paid in male occupations "of comparable worth." Pay equity advocates argue that this is the best strategy for raising women's pay since the majority of women work in sex-typed jobs with no chance, or in some cases no desire, to enter male occupations. The concept requires that jobs deemed to be of "equal value to the employer" pay the same, regardless of their sex-typing.

In no cases are comparable worth adjustments made by lowering the wages of higher-paid jobs. Generally speaking, equity is achieved by larger percentage increases for lower-paid job categories over a period of time until the inequity is eliminated. . . .

Pay Equity

Pay equity is also called "equal pay for work of equal value" or "comparable worth." Pay equity efforts usually involve a job evaluation system which allows a comparison of jobs with different duties but similar levels of skill, effort, responsibility and working conditions. Although laws requiring equal pay for equal work have helped many women, most women remain in occupations which cannot be directly compared to jobs performed by men. Eighty percent of employed women perform "women's work," such as teaching, nursing, library science, clerical and service work.

"Women's work" continues to be low paid. In 1987, employed women working full-time year-round had average earnings that amounted to only 65 percent of the average earnings for their male counterparts. Studies have shown that differences in education, work experience and other factors account for only about half of the wage gap.

Commission on the Economic Status of Women, *Pay Equity: The Minnesota Experience,* 5th revision, December 1989.

It is commonly believed that women are paid less than men because they are less productive, less skilled, or less able. The notion of comparable worth attacks an essential element of this patriarchal ideology. It does so by identifying and highlighting cases in which women are paid less than men although they are equally productive. By showing the extent to which women are discriminated against in pay, comparable worth supports feminist demands for change.

Comparable worth will also increase women's earnings (up to 25 percent, even if job evaluation studies reward job characteristics as the market presently does), and hence give women more economic power relative to men. If groups commissioning such studies also challenge the masculine bias operating in the established point factor systems, greater pay increases can be achieved. For instance, if skills needed for women's jobs, such as nurturing, guidance, and communication, are recognized and rewarded, the points awarded to traditionally female jobs will be considerably higher.

We can also expect that comparable worth will help reduce occupational segregation by sex. As long as "women's" work is considered socially inferior, and is paid as such, men will continue to shun traditionally female occupations. Higher wages in female-dominated jobs would lessen this stigmatization and attract men into these jobs. This would have the double result both of breaking down their sex-typing, and of bringing greater value to activities which are traditionally feminine. It may also have the indirect result of making male-dominated jobs more accessible to women.

In addition, by raising women's wages, comparable worth would weaken a crucial link in the vicious circle of women's oppression. If women were paid equitably, they would be able to support themselves and their children, and would not depend upon men for their economic survival. Women would face less economic coercion to marry or to remain in exploitative relationships with men, and would be freer to pursue nontraditional relationships and living arrangements, such as staying single, relating to men without living together, or being a lesbian. Men would have to offer women more than just their paychecks to attract them to, and keep them in, subservient roles. . . .

The Division of Labor

Comparable worth will help create a social context which would allow for the breakdown of the sexual division of labor in marriage. In this way, comparable work could erode the patriarchal aspects of marriage, which centers on the sexual division of labor (with a husband/bread-winner and a wife/homemaker/low-paid worker) and gives men economic power over their wives. By raising women's wages and destabilizing this division of labor, comparable worth gives women the economic room to struggle for more symmetrical and equal marriages in which both spouses have labor force and home responsibilities. Socialist feminists engaged in comparable worth campaigns must not be afraid to criticize the patriarchal family as oppressive, and speak to the benefits comparable worth can bring by laying the groundwork for more equal partnerships.

Progressives can use comparable worth to open social debate on the value of different kinds of work. We must make the traditionally feminine work of caring for and cooperating with others socially visible, point out its centrality in social reproduction, and argue that it must be part of the lives of all human beings, not just females. This means challenging the hegemony of masculine domination and competition-centered values in our economy and polity over life-sustaining, feminine activities. To do so requires putting forth alternative visions of social life in which both domination and subordination are replaced by mutuality.

In their struggle to alter the existing wage structure, comparable worth advocates have challenged the free market mythology which is used so successfully to defend the status quo. Comparable worth attacks the traditional supposition that the market pays workers "what they're worth." Are market apologists really willing to claim that parking lot attendants are more productive than registered nurses? Assembly-line workers more productive than secretaries? Accepting the premise that a fair wage structure rewards workers according to their relative contributions to their employers, comparable worth advocates use job evaluation studies to show that the wage structure is far from fair. Once it is shown that there is not a direct link between wages and productivity, the other traditional defense of wage inequality—that the market uses wages to motivate increased effort and productivity—is shattered as well.

In addition to undermining two major free market premises, comparable worth raises broader questions about the way in which wages are determined. If wages are not set fairly and efficiently by the forces of supply and demand, as orthodox free market theorists claim, *what is going on?* Why are some workers and some industries paid more than others? A comparable worth strategy exposes the true nature of the market: it is not an impersonal, fair mediator between individuals, but rather a crucible in which those with power exploit those without it.

According to this socialist-feminist interpretation, the only way workers can be guaranteed a "fair shake" in the market is to insist on their worth. Workers must demand, through union, political, and ideological channels, that their value be recognized. In this time of reaction, then, comparable worth provides a clear mandate for more state intervention and union organizing.

Once the process of wage determination is accepted as being the outcome of power struggles and of an out-dated conception of the ideal family, the way forward is clear. In the short term, those who are not unionized and politically organized must bond together to defend their interests. Indeed, with women providing over half of the new union membership in recent years, comparable worth is gaining support among many unions, as well as bolstering labor's credibility as a truly progressive force for economic justice. . . .

Comparable Worth and Racism

Those who are concerned that the women's movement is too narrowly based in the self-interests of middle-class white women have criticized comparable worth as being "a white women's issue." While we share that concern, we believe that comparable worth efforts can also bring about wage increases for women and men of color.

The numerical dominance of whites in the labor force virtually ensures that whites will constitute the majority of workers in any job category. Nonetheless, most women of color are found in female-dominated jobs. This means that wage increases secured through sex-based pay equity campaigns will be of substantial benefit to women of color. In other words, there is no *economic* reason why pay equity should not be a demand with major relevance for women of color. . . .

Pay equity cases usually single out for scrutiny job categories that are over 70 percent female—clerical work, nursing, elementary schoolteaching, food service, childcare, and health technicians, to name a few. Contrary to popular myths, substantial numbers of women of color are now employed in these job categories. According to 1980 census data, over half of white women are employed in jobs which are over 70 percent female, but the

197

same percentage of black, and just under half of all Native American and Asian women are also found in those job categories.

A Massive Task

Given the degree to which women's work is undervalued, restoring the balance will prove a massive task. And, since it cuts to the heart of existing pay differentials (and not only between men's and women's jobs, either!), it will face huge opposition. Male workers will not abandon readily the advantages they have derived from their higher pay and status; employers will be loth to lose their abundant source of cheap labour.

Anne Phillips, *New Internationalist*, March 1988.

It is true that detailed occupational breakdowns often reveal further race segregation *within* women's jobs. For instance, senior typists might all be white while junior typists might be predominantly women of color. Yet sex-based pay equity studies would still single out a job dominated by black women for pay equity upgrading by comparing it to a comparable male-dominated job (which might be held by a man of any race). Therefore, pay equity has the potential to raise wages for the women of color.

Whether it does so or not depends partly on the character of the comparable worth campaign. Much media attention to the comparable worth issue has been directed at professional women—librarians and registered nurses in particular—but pay equity comparisons between men and women can be made *at all levels of the skills hierarchy.* For example, a pay equity campaign might raise the wages of women who clean an office building at night to the same level as the wages of male janitors who clean a factory for the same employer. Job evaluation studies which encompass all the jobs in a firm or government agency will have a greater effect on women of color than those which are aimed only at professional workers. Most state and local government job evaluation initiatives are across-the-board studies of all sex-stereotyped job categories at all skill levels. . . .

Comparable Worth and Men of Color

Although between 10 and 15 percent of employed men of color work in female-dominated job categories, most men of color would only benefit indirectly from gender-based pay equity. Nearly half of all black men, for instance, are either unemployed or not part of the official labor force. Younger black men are even more marginalized: only 37 percent of black men aged 16 to 24 were employed in 1984, compared to 63 percent of white men. This points to the need to treat pay equity as a component of a broader full employment and affirmative action agenda.

The relevance of comparable worth for men and women of color is heightened by their concentration in the public sector where so many pay equity initiatives are found. Blacks and Native Americans are twice as likely to be employed by federal, state or local governments as are white workers. Thus, people of color are actually more likely than whites to be covered by one of the current pay equity studies. . . .

As with any reform, comparable worth may be economically problematic and politically divisive if it is not pursued as part of a larger program. Conservative economists have warned that comparable worth, by raising the wages for women's work, would create uncontrollable inflation. In fact, the inflationary impact would depend upon the magnitude of the pay equity adjustment in a particular time period, as well as the ability of firms and government to pass on the costs to consumers and taxpayers. To address this concern, workers could propose to utilize wage-price controls if inflationary problems develop.

Others worry that firms and state agencies may respond to the increase in the price of women's labor by initiating labor-saving technical change, eliminating state programs, and moving factories to countries in which women still provide a super-exploitable labor force. In the absence of comparable worth, office automation is already threatening the jobs of clerical workers, and the movement of jobs to the Third World has created massive structural unemployment in the US. In order for comparable worth not to exacerbate these problems, it must be pursued in conjunction with demands for job security, retraining, and plant-closing legislation.

Progressive Struggles

Comparable worth is unlikely to help the millions of people, many of them women heading households, who live in poverty because they are forced to accept seasonal or part-time work, or cannot find work at all. Only a broader agenda which includes the right to a job and adequate income will address the needs of these people.

Nevertheless, comparable worth provides progressives with a unique opportunity to initiate and participate in an open-ended social debate on the values of different kinds of social activity, on the desirability of the market economy and of the traditional family, and on the merits of various schemes of income distribution. This debate will be most fruitful if the issues are placed in the broadest possible context, and if comparable worth advocates continue to work in conjunction with other worker-empowering, feminist, anti-racist and progressive struggles.

199

"Comparable worth, while it may benefit a few women in the short run, serves the middle- and long-run interests of no one."

Comparable Worth Does Not Promote Social Justice

Michael Levin

In the following viewpoint, author Michael Levin argues that comparable worth legislation would hinder social justice, not promote it. Levin contends that since women's work cannot be measured against men's, comparable worth would unjustly discriminate against men. Levin is a professor of philosophy at the City University of New York and the author of *Metaphysics and the Mind-Body Problem*. This viewpoint is excerpted from his book *Feminism and Freedom*.

As you read, consider the following questions:

1. What does comparable worth do, in Levin's opinion?
2. According to the author, how would comparable worth harm women?
3. How would comparable worth policies jeopardize the free-market system, according to Levin?

The feminist critique of the market extends beyond hiring practices to the wages paid to women for the jobs they actually hold. Just as discrimination in hiring is taken to require extraordinary government remedies, so too is wage discrimination. With more than 30 million American women working full time, the scope of this issue is enormous.

The theory that women are underpaid rests on a statistical disparity between the average wages of full-time working women and full-time working men; the former are, on average, 60 percent of the latter. This wage gap had narrowed to 37.5 percent by the early 1980s from 41 percent in the 1970s, but the slogan "59¢ to the dollar" has continued to encapsulate the issue. It must be emphasized that the question being raised is not whether women are receiving the same pay as men for the *same* work, which was settled in 1963 when the Equal Pay Act made it illegal to pay a woman less than a man for the same job. The problem, rather, is that men and women tend to do different jobs, and jobs dominated by men tend to pay more than jobs dominated by women. Feminists are quite explicit about having shifted the issue: "Equal pay for the same work is ineffective when equal work, in practice, means the same work, and most women are not doing the same work as most men," [writes Francis Hutner]. People who profess sympathy for the feminist demand for "equal pay for equal work" are choosing a side that has disbanded.

The Comparable Worth Theory

The comparable worth theory is the contention that male-dominated jobs pay more than female-dominated jobs because the pay for female jobs is not proportional to the "intrinsic value" or worth of what women do. Women's wages would rise if compensation were determined by "real," not market value—if, in short, comparably valuable jobs received identical salaries: "The goal of pay equity is accomplished by raising the wages of predominantly female jobs in a workplace to match the wages of similarly valued male jobs," [according to Joy Ann Grune]. The undervaluation of female jobs is thought to be immediately evident from a group of cases regularly cited in the comparable worth literature, such as the considerably higher wages paid to mostly male tree surgeons than to mostly female librarians and nurses. The National Organization of Office Workers cites a bank offering $745-1,090 per month for general clerks, who must analyze invoices and have "good telephone etiquette," and who are usually female, while offering $1,030-1,100 per month for shipping clerks, who need only write legibly and be able to "lift equipment in excess of 100 lbs," but who are usually male. It is thought obvious that the ability to talk on the telephone entitles one to at least as much money as a strong back.

Jobs Do Not Have Intrinsic Worth

"Equal pay for comparable worth" is an unexceptionable idea. Because everyone supports it, it makes an attractive slogan. The problem is defining the "worth" of a job beyond the willingness of employers and consumers to pay for it. All the characteristics that the feminists claim are important—skill, effort, responsibility, working conditions, experience, educational requirements, and the like—are in fact irrelevant if consumers (or taxpayers) do not want the product at the price required by the "comparable pay."

The ability to build an elegant mechanical adding machine requires more training, skill, experience, and responsibility—and entails work under harsher conditions—than using a word processor or driving a truck. But building a mechanical adding machine is worthless, just as many jobs richly paid today (such as antidiscrimination lawyer) may well be seen as worthless in the future as tastes and technologies change. The idea that jobs have an intrinsic worth of their own is medieval in spirit and would return the world to the stagnant system of feudal guilds.

George Gilder, *Gender Sanity*, 1989.

Diffidence about any unclarities in this theory does not deter its advocates, [Nancy Perlman and Bruce Ennis,] from insisting that the theory be applied:

> Although most policy-makers believe research should inform the development of effective policy, it is more often the case that policy development stimulates new research. The area of pay equity is no exception.

Indeed, the idea of comparable worth is virtually never raised without an accompanying demand that it be made law. The idea first came to broad public notice in strikes by municipal workers, and has been sustained mainly by court action. In *Washington v. Gunther*, a case involving female prison guards of female prisoners who claimed that their work was as valuable as that done by better-paid male guards of male prisoners in higher security prisons, the Supreme Court ruled that litigants could test comparable worth in federal courts under Title VII. *AFSCME* [American Federation of State, County and Municipal Employees] *v. Washington State* tested the theory, and a federal court awarded four years back pay and raises to 15,500 female employees of Washington State. Strictly speaking, *AFSCME* did not find discrimination in the wages Washington paid its work-force, but in the state's failure to implement a previously commissioned comparable-worth study after having resolved to abide by its results. Washington had hesitated because it had estimated the cost of implementation to be nearly $65 million; ironically, the cost imposed by *AFSCME* ran close to $1 billion. *AFSCME* was overturned on appeal but, in exchange for a promise from *AFSCME* not to appeal further, Washington agreed to a settlement costing an initial $482 million and $75 million per year thereafter. Despite the clear warning of *AFSCME* that undertaking a comparable worth study invites adversary litigation and burdensome settlements, dozens of states and hundreds of municipalities have commissioned such studies of their workforces. . . .

Apart from the need to remedy injustice, a consideration cited [by Nancy Barrett] with increasing frequency in the comparable worth literature is the single mother who cannot support her family on the wages paid by the jobs such women typically hold:

> The "pay equity" I am going to talk about is whether or not what somebody makes is adequate to support a family. . . . Twenty-seven percent of all divorced and separated women are on welfare. Half of all black babies, in some urban areas more than half of all black babies, are born out of wedlock. . . . The problem, of course, in the welfare system is that most of these poor women can't get jobs that pay enough to support their families, and welfare is really a better deal financially for them.

This consideration may safely be ignored. The *need* of single mothers for higher wages has nothing to do with the value of the work these women do, which is the gravamen of the comparable worth argument. It may be prudent or compassionate to raise wages for the jobs that single mothers tend to take, but it would be equally prudent and compassionate to raise the wages for the jobs men do, since at least as many men need higher wages to support *their* families. Socialism may be indicated, but language should not be tortured into calling it equity.

Why Do Women Earn Less than Men?

Why do women earn so little if the human capital they embody is so valuable and their work so important? The answers given by comparable worth advocates may be ordered by the degree of conscious malevolence they attribute to employers. At one extreme is the accusation that (male) employers actually conspire against women to reduce labor costs ("to maximize profits" is the preferred equivalent). . . .

The reason that the wage gap cannot be due to conscious discrimination is, simply, that, until recently, nobody ever dreamed that the value of disparate jobs could be compared. It would have been impossible for any employer to have intended to compensate women's jobs less than men's jobs of comparable value when it could never have occurred to him that the jobs were comparable. The idea of comparability, if valid at all, became available only in the last decade with the invention of the statistical techniques used in specifying the comparable worth argument.

The Road to Socialism

In place of a relatively free job market, comparable worth would require a federal bureaucracy to determine the appropriate pay for each job and each set of credentials and qualifications and to enforce the law throughout millions of businesses in the inevitable flux of economic change. Utterly subjective despite a show of scientific pettifoggery and precision, comparable worth evaluations would be open to endless litigation and challenge, and thus to arbitrary power.

George Gilder, *Gender Sanity*, 1989.

Any account of wage discrimination must thus posit unintended mechanisms. Serious comparable worth advocates cite two. The first, already mentioned, is the herding of women into job ghettos, which floods the market for those jobs and depresses their wages, [according to Arthur Young].

An alternative hypothesis places the reason for sex-related pay differentials on the traditional sex-segregation of most jobs. Under this hypothesis, the results of "crowding" of females into the clerical and service occupations is an oversupply of labor in these occupations, with resulting lower wages. Traditional programs of salary administration, and particularly the job evaluations by which wage rates are determined, are seen as maintaining and contributing to this pattern of discrimination.

But this hypothesis rests most uneasily with the charge of discrimination, for it concedes that at bottom female wages are determined by the market forces of supply and demand, which in turn express the decisions of the individuals who constitute the market. If women enter the labor force primarily to supplement family income, they will tend to seek employment like clerical work, which permits periodic withdrawal from the labor force without serious impairment of earning capacity. The more would-be secretaries there are, the less an employer must offer to attract secretarial help, but the same is true of *all* jobs. Secretarial wages are discriminatory, and the supply of secretaries an *over*supply, only if "crowding" is not a metaphor but a literal description of employers forcing women into some jobs and barring them from others—a reversion to conspiracy theory. . . .

204

For the sake of argument, then, let us assume a skill which is objectively difficult, reflects much objectively measurable training on the part of its practitioner, and is dangerous as well; but let us also suppose it is a skill no one is interested in. Consider a person who is adept at throwing arrows high into the air and catching them with his teeth. This is extremely difficult to do, and takes endless practice. Basketball players earning six-figure salaries do nothing so demanding. And our man could hurt himself. Unhappily, nobody wants to hire him to throw and catch arrows. He must eke out a living as a street entertainer. Is he somehow being denied his intrinsic worth by passers-by who flip him quarters? Does a circus scout who offers him a pittance undershoot what the knack entitles him to? The answers would seem to be no. Moral and aesthetic merit aside, the skill is economically worthless—unable to command other goods and services—if no one will pay for it. Only someone willing to trade something for this service can confer economic worth on it.

This crucial point is easy enough to see in connection with material substances. It would be absurd to maintain that copper deserves to cost more than gold because it conducts electricity better; gold and copper, absent people's actual desires for them, would just be stuff in the ground. The point is also reasonably clear in relation to the "just price" of money—that is, permissible interest rates, to which medieval theologians devoted much thought. I suspect that the market determination of wages meets greater resistance only because it puts the value of each of us so squarely in the eyes of our beholders.

Money itself is merely the conventional measure of the capacity of a thing to prompt people to exchange their own goods for it. A thing's price summarizes the ebb and flow of its performance in exchange, and has no independent meaning. And here is the black hole at the center of the comparable worth doctrine: There is no such thing as intrinsic economic value. It is a chimera. And this point rings another variation on a by-now familiar theme. Supplanting the market price of labor means overriding the liberty of exchange, association, and contract this market price reflects. For each comparable worth proposal, the question is only one of determining just where it suppresses freedom. . . .

No Self-Limitations

Overall, the many regulations that control banking, trucking, the airlines, mergers, workplace safety, and the like are industry-specific or activity-specific, and are intended, rightly or wrongly, to preserve the free market against its own excesses. Wage and price controls, when imposed, are usually justified as temporary measures to curb inflation. Even socialism itself was originally conceived as a more efficient way of harnessing the productive capacity generated by capitalism. And because New Deal-type regulations purport to secure specific results, they contain built-in standards against which they may be assessed.

But comparable worth, like affirmative action, contains none of these self-limitations. Its scope includes every job in the work force; since most jobs are sex-segregated, most pay scales would be open to challenge. Nor does comparable worth pretend to facilitate the best tendencies of the free market; it explicitly seeks to bypass the market. It does this, moreover, without clearly specifying what positive goal is to be achieved beyond "justice"; under this loose mantle, the pursuit of comparable worth can ignore any economic havoc it wreaks as irrelevant to its "success" as long as the wage gap is closed. If comparable worth is "a feminist road to socialism," as Penn Kemble has called it, it is socialist planning without a plan.

Endless Government Intervention

Like other feminist goals, comparable worth can never be realized through voluntary agreements. If a firm can get secretaries at a market-clearing wage, so can its competitors. Were it to raise its secretarial wages for ethical reasons, its labor costs would rise without any gain in productivity, its products would cost more than those of its competitors, and it would slide into failure. Comparable worth presents a coordination problem of the sort which tends to get solved by government. In short, whether or not the marketplace offers an appropriate ideal of justice, wages will converge to their market value so long as people retain anything like their accustomed economic liberty. Comparable worth can be implemented only by endless government intervention, in the words of a pre-*Gunther* court, "pregnant with the possibility of disrupting the entire economic system of America. . . .

Comparable worth advocates promise that the wage gap will not be closed by cutting male salaries, and it might appear that the gap could be closed slowly and painlessly by freezing or retarding the growth of men's salaries until women's salaries caught up. This is now the policy of the San Jose municipal government under an agreement reached with *AFSCME*. Surely, however, a man who gets a smaller raise that he otherwise would have gotten has, so far as he is concerned, suffered a pay cut because of comparable worth. The argument that comparable worth assists working women struggling to help their families with a second income once again erroneously portrays men and women as competing groups. It helps no one to hold down a husband's wages so that his wife's can be artificially boosted. Failure to appreciate this leads to the absurdity of urging that "men must face the prospect of lower pay, so their wives can move ahead," [according to Andrew Hacker].

It seems unlikely that men or their unions would tolerate a wide-scale arrangement so costly to them. The likeliest short-term effect of comparable worth would be to boost everyone's wages, flooding the market with new money in the absence of new goods—the standard recipe for inflation. (This might be the occasion for the government to begin coordinating wage policy to assure the proper closure of the wage gap.) The longer-run consequence of inflating female salaries and holding down male salaries in defiance of the market would be a massive disincentive to work. Women would already be getting more without having to work harder, and men would not be permitted to get more even if they did work harder. Why, then, should anyone work harder? Work forces would not become more "integrated," since women would have no incentive to leave traditional female work once it paid as much as less pleasant male work. If anything, men would try to invade the newly well-paid female sphere. And at the same time men were queuing up for the typing pool, there would be no reason for a man to undertake unpleasant jobs like collecting refuse if high wages for it were no longer available as an inducement—so there would almost certainly be critical job shortages. Add to this a quota system which would prevent management from replacing women with possibly more desirable men, and a crisis of considerable proportions would be upon us.

Planning for the Inevitable

The attitude of the business community toward comparable worth is epitomized by the American Compensation Association: "Planning for the inevitable appears to be the appropriate response." Like John Bunzel's classification of comparable worth as part of "the revolution of rising entitlements," the ACA's bemused comment does not come to grips with what is distinctive about the comparable worth campaign. It looks like the agitation of one more pressure group, but it is unique in being a movement without potential beneficiaries. . . . Comparable worth, while it may benefit a few women in the short run, serves the middle- and long-run interests of no one—not the married woman nor the career woman already ensconced in a remunerative "nontraditional" position. At best, it gratifies the sense of justice of a small number of ideologues. In practical terms, this means that these ideologues cannot be restrained by the usual interest-balancing mechanisms. Unlike farmers seeking price supports, say, who will moderate their demands in the face of countervailing threats to their interests, comparable worth advocates have no interests to protect. Having nothing to lose, they have no reason to compromise.

Distinguishing Between Fact and Opinion

This activity is designed to help develop the basic reading and thinking skill of distinguishing between fact and opinion. Consider the following statement as an example: "Between 1960 and 1986, the female share of professional jobs increased from 38 to over 50 percent." This statement is a fact which can be verified by checking the *Statistical Almanac* in the local library. But consider a statement which expresses an opinion about men, women, and work: "The reason few professional women have been promoted to top managers is that the men in power fear and will not promote talented women." This statement is clearly an opinion. The possible explanations for the scarcity of women in top management positions are hotly debated. Many people might disagree with the statement and offer other explanations.

When investigating controversial issues it is important that one be able to distinguish between statements of fact and statements of opinion. It is also important to recognize that not all statements of fact are true. They may appear to be true, but some are based on inaccurate or false information. For this activity, however, we are concerned with understanding the difference between those statements which appear to be factual and those which appear to be based primarily on opinion.

Most of the following statements are taken from the viewpoints in this chapter. Consider each statement carefully. *Mark O for any statement you believe is an opinion. Mark F for any statement you believe is a fact. Mark I for any statement you believe is impossible to judge.*

If you are doing this activity as a member of a class or group, compare your answers with those of other class or group members. Be able to defend your answers. You may discover that others come to different conclusions than you do. Listening to the reasons others present for their answers may give you valuable insights into distinguishing between fact and opinion.

O = opinion
F = fact
I = impossible to judge

1. The feminist movement is plunging many women into a strange state of suspicion and resentment.
2. During the 1960s, 1970s, and 1980s, women joined the work force in increasing numbers.
3. The role of mother is the paramount support of civilized human society.
4. Being able to support their families is crucial to men's motivation and productivity.
5. Society has had to change to adjust to the influx of women into the work force.
6. The number of women completing college and graduate school has increased.
7. Instead of relying on men, women should rely on themselves and their careers for self-esteem.
8. Despite increased prominence in the job field, more women are living beneath the poverty line.
9. The government should allocate its money differently to provide for more and better-quality programs for children in the U.S.
10. Women deserve wages equal to men's for work of comparable value.
11. The first comparable worth suit was brought against General Electric and Westinghouse by the United Electrical Workers of America in 1945.
12. Comparable worth will help break down the sexual division of labor in marriages.
13. Thirty million American women work full time.
14. Women often receive lower wages than men for the same job.
15. Men's wages should be raised because they have families to support.
16. Comparable worth will raise inflation and cause widespread unemployment as well as starting the U.S. on the road to socialism.
17. Feminism developed to help women gain equal standing and respect in society.
18. Bitter women who had been hurt in their marriages started the 1960s feminist movement.
19. More women have become heads of state around the world in the 1980s than ever before.

Periodical Bibliography

The following articles have been selected to supplement the diverse views presented in this chapter.

Barbara Amiel — "Feminism Hits Middle Age," *National Review*, November 24, 1989.

Barbara Ehrenreich — "Feminism's Next Wave," *Utne Reader*, March/April 1988.

Barbara Ehrenreich — "The Wretched of the Hearth," *The New Republic*, April 2, 1990.

Maggie Gallagher — "What Men Really Want," *National Review*, May 12, 1987.

Vivian Gornick — "Who Says We Haven't Made a Revolution?" *The New York Times Magazine*, April 15, 1990.

Virginia A. Heffernan — "The Maternal Mystique," *Crisis*, May 1990.

Anthony Layng — "What Keeps Women 'In Their Place?'" *USA Today*, May 1989.

Linda Lehrer — "More than She Bargained For," *Ms.*, January/February 1989.

Charley Reese — "Women's Liberation Is a Cruel Joke," *Conservative Chronicle*, September 9, 1987. Available from *Conservative Chronicle*, PO Box 11297, Des Moines, IA 50441.

Sheila Rowbotham — "Working Women's Untold Story," *Z Magazine*, April 1990.

Sara Saetre — "Comparable Worth," *Utne Reader*, January/February 1989.

Ann Snitow — "Pages from a Gender Diary," *Dissent*, Spring 1989.

Benjamin J. Stein — "Look Back in Anger," *The American Spectator*, June 1990.

Gloria Steinem — "Is a Feminist Ethic the Answer?" *Ms.*, September 1987.

R. Emmett Tyrrell Jr. — "Beauty and the Beasts," *The American Spectator*, October 1989.

Claudia Wallis — "Onward, Women!" *Time*, December 4, 1989.

Chilton Williamson Jr. — "The Right Books," *National Review*, August 4, 1989.

Dina Wills — "The Feminist Movement and Working-Class Women: A Conflict of Values," *USA Today*, January 1990.

What Policies Can Promote Social Justice?

Social Justice

Chapter Preface

Poverty and inequality are injustices that have always existed. In the past, society looked to churches and private charities to provide shelter for the homeless and food for the hungry. When the Great Depression of the 1930s struck, however, U.S. leaders were faced with the fact that churches and charities alone could not feed and clothe twelve million unemployed Americans. To help the nation's poor, President Franklin Delano Roosevelt set up such social programs as social security and the Works Progress Administration. More government programs, like Head Start and CETA (Comprehensive Employment and Training Act), were subsequently established under President Lyndon Johnson's Great Society. Through these federal programs, the U.S. government became actively involved in assisting the poor.

Many Americans believe that programs such as those started under Roosevelt and Johnson can ease the problems of today's poor. For example, John E. Schwarz, a political science professor at the University of Arizona, argues, "In 1980, one in fifteen Americans faced the desperation of poverty, compared with about one in five Americans just a generation earlier. This was accomplished, almost entirely, by the government." If government programs could cut the poverty rate from about 20 percent to about 7 percent in one generation, Schwarz and others believe, similar programs could help disadvantaged Americans today.

But other people criticize government programs for being inefficient and wasteful. Some agree with Charles Murray, the author of *Losing Ground: American Social Policy 1950-1980,* who maintains that although American taxpayers spent millions of dollars on Johnson's Great Society programs, a higher proportion of Americans were poor in 1980 than at any time since 1967. Murray's view, that bureaucratic government programs the founder of the Student/Sponsor partnership, a New York City charity. He contends, "Government has a lot of money but doesn't know how to take care of people." Flanigan and others argue that because private organizations are in direct contact with the poor, these groups have a better understanding of what the poor need in the way of services.

Whether government programs alone can meet the needs of the poor, or if private organizations must also be involved in easing America's social problems, is debated by the authors in the following chapter. They also discuss the broader issue of how America can promote social justice.

"We must recognize that intensive and sometimes costly preventive care for fragile families and vulnerable youngsters represents a sound allocation of resources."

Government Policies Can Promote Social Justice

Lisbeth B. Schorr with Daniel Schorr

Lisbeth B. Schorr is a lecturer in social medicine and health policy at Harvard University in Cambridge, Massachusetts. She has led national efforts for the Johnson and Carter administrations to assist disadvantaged children. Daniel Schorr is a broadcast journalist with more than fifty years of experience. In the following viewpoint, the Schorrs contend that America's social and economic injustices can be corrected with a broad, national commitment to funding government programs.

As you read, consider the following questions:

1. What is the "inverse care law," according to the authors?
2. What role do the authors feel elected officials should play in helping the disadvantaged?
3. How do Americans feel about government programs to help the disadvantaged, according to the Schorrs?

It lies within our reach, before the end of the twentieth century, dramatically to improve the early lives of several million American children growing up at grave risk. We can substantially improve the odds that they will become healthy, sturdy, and productive adults, participants in a twenty-first-century America whose aspirations they will share. The cycle of disadvantage that has seemed so intractable can be broken.

Recognizing the Problem

A critical mass of research and experience, both about what works and what doesn't work, is now available, with answers to the problems that have recently risen to the top of the American domestic agenda. The crisis of high teenage unemployment and unmarried childbearing, disintegrating families, welfare costs, the underclass, low productivity, and increasing childhood poverty has been recognized. The American Enterprise Institute's *New Consensus on Family and Welfare* says the crisis has reached the point of threatening to "corrode a free society." Sociologist James S. Coleman says that we are faced with a breakdown in American society of "the process of making human beings human." Senator Daniel Patrick Moynihan describes the combination of disintegrating families and rampant childhood poverty as "life-threatening to the great cities of the land."

But greater emphasis on the problem has not been accompanied by corresponding attention to promising solutions. It will take more than reform of the welfare system, more than forging closer relationships between public assistance and work, to arrest the intergenerational transmission of poverty, family disintegration, and despair. It will take more than economic measures alone. It will take more than the expansion of access to traditional services. Some of our helping systems may, in fact, be beyond repair and will require rebuilding. The "inverse care law," which holds that those who need the best services get the worst, must be repealed.

This will not happen without a national commitment of consequence—specific in its objective, broad in its scope, and enduring in its staying power.

Commitment to Action

Every American—as voter and taxpayer, as church, PTA, or hospital board member, as business, labor, political, or professional leader—has a role in translating such a commitment into action.

• At the community level we must encourage schools, clinics, and social agencies to act on the evidence that crucial outcomes among high-risk children can be changed by systematic intervention early in the life cycle. We must encourage them to recognize the importance of offering a broad, flexible, and coherent spectrum of services, of responding to children in the contexts of family and community, and of staff with the skills to work with families in relationships of respect and trust. As we observe and monitor the results of such efforts, we must be constantly alert for difficulties that cannot be solved at the local level, and be prepared to recommend and support necessary changes in financing or administrative arrangements wherever they must be made.

A Social Investment

We will all benefit from a stronger, improved social welfare policy. Each and every one of us has a stake in providing infants and young children with the physical and emotional nurturing they need to get a decent start in life—not only because it is right but because if we don't, the costs of illness, dependency, and crime may burden us for decades. We all have an interest in helping adolescents and young adults make the transition from school to productive jobs. We all have a stake in retraining workers left behind by a changing economy so that they are not condemned to unproductive and dependent lives. We all are reassured by providing protection against impoverishment for the infirm elderly.

The Ford Foundation, *The Common Good: Social Welfare and the American Future*, 1989.

- As taxpayers, administrators, legislators, and concerned citizens, we must recognize that intensive and sometimes costly preventive care for fragile families and vulnerable youngsters represents a sound allocation of resources, particularly in view of the high stake we all have in the favorable outcomes of such interventions.
- As citizens and taxpayers, we must support the allocation by local, state, and federal governments, as well as private funders, of the resources required for large-scale implementation of successful programs and policies. We must support elected officials, other policy makers, and administrators who recognize that opportunities to change outcomes for disadvantaged children require sharp departures from current approaches to social policy based on short-term political considerations. We must help them to remain constantly aware of how their decisions affect later outcomes for disadvantaged children. We must assure that in the design of new ways to fund, furnish, or regulate health or social services, child care or education, high priority is given to opportunities to improve the long-term prospects of disadvantaged children.
- All of us must take every available opportunity to recognize

and reward professional, bureaucratic, and academic efforts aimed at breaking the cycle of disadvantage. Those in a position to do so must encourage talented professionals in health, education, child development, social services, and public administration to work with high-risk children and families, and make sure that those who serve high-risk families receive the training that would equip them to work more effectively with these populations.

Reaching the Hard-to-Reach

Do today's political and budgetary realities make a national commitment of consequence to the nation's disadvantaged children seem visionary? Do the costs of successful programs, in dollars and professional resources, mean that rather than being replicated they will be relegated to some musty Utopian attic? That no authority dependent on electoral majorities can be expected to allocate substantial funds to the needs of such a powerless and relatively small constituency?

As more information about the effectiveness of timely, intensive intervention comes to public attention, more Americans will see the wisdom—indeed the necessity—of investing in help to families at risk in order to obviate the more expensive repairs needed after disintegration has taken place. Reaching out to the hard-to-reach, helping the hard-to-help represent not a visionary idea but a practical solution to an urgent national problem.

It may well be that Americans today are becoming more receptive to proposals for new initiatives, based on solid information, aimed at fundamentally improving children's life chances. Increasingly, Americans recognize that investments to improve the futures of disadvantaged children represent a joining of compassion with long-term self-interest.

Americans Want to Help

Three quarters of Americans, according to a Louis Harris poll, said in 1986 that they are prepared to pay higher taxes to provide more day care and education; 88 percent said they want government to provide more health coverage and day care services for children of the poor. On the strength of his landmark 1986 study of American attitudes toward children, Louis Harris reported, "The times are changing, perhaps more rapidly than might be imagined." He emphasized that "people not only want to help children generally, they want particularly to help the children who are living in poverty." He warned, "Politicians who ignore these pleadings from the American people do so at their own peril. It is a plaintive and poignant demand that simply will not go away."

We are now armed with the knowledge to meet that demand. We know how to organize health programs, family agencies, child care, and schools to strengthen families and to prevent casualties at the transition from childhood to adulthood. We know how to intervene to reduce the rotten outcomes of adolescence and to help break the cycle that reaches into succeeding generations. Unshackled from the myth that nothing works, we can mobilize the political will to reduce the number of children hurt by cruel beginnings. By improving the prospects of the least of us, we can assure a more productive, just, and civil nation for all of us.

"I have no more right to use government to take your money than I do to seize it directly at gunpoint."

Government Policies Cannot Promote Social Justice

Philip Smith

In the following viewpoint, Philip Smith argues that it is neither beneficial nor just for the government to force citizens to help the disadvantaged through taxes or government regulation. Smith contends that using tax money to help the underprivileged is robbery, with the taxpayers as the victims. He contends that government programs are unjust, and that private charities are the best and only fair way to help the disadvantaged. A freelance writer, Smith has contributed articles to *The Freeman* and *Reason* magazine.

As you read, consider the following questions:

1. Why does Smith believe that forcing employers to provide child care is unnecessary and unjust?
2. What are the benefits of using charities, according to the author?
3. Why does Smith believe that government social programs are unjust?

Philip Smith, "At Whose Expense?" *The Freeman,* May 1989. Reprinted with permission.

A question often overlooked in public policy debates is deceptively simple: "At whose expense?" Let us reflect for a moment on this question and see if, by answering it, we can clarify some current issues.

Take, for example, child care benefits. When described by child care advocates, the issue seems rather innocuous. "Shouldn't working mothers," they ask, "have a right to adequate child care at reasonable cost?" The answer to such a question would seem to be yes, since parents have a right to seek adequate child care wherever and at whatever cost they choose.

But these advocates often go a step further. They maintain that a parent's right to *seek* child care somehow places a burden on a second party to *provide* it. This second party is usually thought to be the parent's employer, or perhaps the taxpayers. This second party, then, is the answer to the question, "At whose expense?" Immediately another question then comes to mind—why?

Employers Are People

Why should an employer be forced to provide child care? Some will argue that unless force is invoked, there won't be enough child care facilities. This is doubtful, since as a general rule the free market works to meet consumer demands. A demand for child care will be met by profit-seeking entrepreneurs, if the market is free from government interference. However, if child care providers are burdened with too many regulations, laws, and taxes, they may not find it worthwhile to stay in business. Furthermore, if entrepreneurs must compete with government-subsidized providers, they may be driven out of business, thereby reducing the options available to parents.

Most important, however, is the fact that employers are people too—and they have a primary right to do as they choose with their own earnings and property. This includes the right to decide whether to offer employee child care. This is truly an "inalienable" right, and takes precedence over other so-called "rights," such as the parent's "right" to child care at the expense of an unwilling second party.

Likewise, imposing the financial burden on the taxpayers still amounts to forcing the individual taxpayer to purchase child care for someone else. Why should you be forced to pay for my child's care? I have no more right to use government to take your money than I do to seize it directly at gunpoint. The only just system is one in which child care is paid for without the threat of coercion. Any other scheme, regardless of the noble intentions of its designers, plunders one person to provide care for someone else's child.

As another example, let's consider catastrophic health care for the elderly. We might agree that this is a noble and desirable thing—but again we must ask the question: "At whose expense?" And it is here that the arguments for mandatory health care benefits collapse on ethical grounds. For, as with child care, we discover that the burden of financing catastrophic health care is to be placed on an unwilling second party—taxpayers. By what right?

Chuck Asay, by permission of the *Colorado Springs Gazette Telegraph.*

Logically, all people should be free to seek out health insurance from those willing to provide it. As long as the purchasers of a plan give their money willingly, no ethical problems arise. But when one person is forced to fund an insurance plan for another, that person's rights have been violated.

Consider someone who has purchased health insurance for himself and his family. By what right should he be forced to also buy health care for strangers? The answer, of course, is that no one has the right to demand this of him.

The Homeless

As a third example, consider the plight of the homeless. It is a sad but unchanging fact that some people cannot and will not be able to afford a home. Some concerned citizens think the solution is to build housing for the homeless, and perhaps provide food and social services. But once again the question arises: "At whose expense?"

The usual answer is the government. But who pays the government's bills? Clearly you and I do, through taxes taken from us by force. It is the individual taxpayer who finances any such "charity." Advocates of such programs believe themselves empowered to force us to give to their cause, not by persuading us, but by threat of imprisonment under the tax laws.

But what if I have my own favorite charities or causes, and already give to them all that I can? Or what if my neighbor simply doesn't believe he is obligated to build a house for a stranger? By what right can he be forced to give up his money simply because someone else doesn't have enough of his own? The answer, again, is that no such thing should be demanded of him.

But what a cruel state of affairs, some will say. What about those too poor to buy insurance, or child care, or a home? How will they survive?

Charities Solved the Problem

The answer is simple: private, voluntary charity. Human compassion runs deep, resulting in thousands of charitable organizations that exist solely to help the less fortunate, and which get no government funding. These organizations, unlike the government, are limited to peaceful means of persuasion. They cannot take from us by force; they must convince us that their cause is worthy and their goals are in line with our own. When we ask of their work, "At whose expense?" the answer is: willing donors.

A distinction, then, becomes clear. With the help of the handy litmus question, "At whose expense?" we quickly skip to the core of matters which otherwise might seem a confusing mix of merits and drawbacks.

The answer to the question will be either *willing buyers* or *unwilling victims*. In the first case, those who benefit from a good or service are those who pay for it, or for whom a charity has paid the bill; in the second case an agent, usually government, is employed to rob from some to provide for others in the name of "justice" or "compassion." But America was founded on the principle that ends don't justify means. Justice and compassion are never served by violating the rights of free human beings, even for the noblest causes.

3

"In a search for the most powerful tool for social change in the world, the most effective lever available might just turn out to be business."

Corporations Can Promote Social Justice

Marjorie Kelly

In the following viewpoint, Marjorie Kelly argues that many U.S. corporations are working to combat such social problems as poverty and illiteracy. Kelly believes that corporations' abundance of power, resources, and people will enable them to reduce some of America's social problems. Kelly is the editor and publisher of *Business Ethics,* a bimonthly magazine concerned with social responsibility in business.

As you read, consider the following questions:

1. What new kind of corporate ethic does Kelly believe is emerging?
2. How is the relationship between profit-making businesses and nonprofit organizations changing, according to the author?
3. How does Kelly think employees, corporations, and communities will be affected by the changes in business?

Marjorie Kelly, "Revolution in the Marketplace," *Utne Reader,* January/February 1989. Reprinted with permission.

The names come like a litany: Bhopal, the Dalkon Shield, Ivan Boesky, Three Mile Island. It is a litany of the tragedy of business in our time, the tragedy of ruined lives and a tainted earth. And not only in our time, but throughout modern history. The trail of industrialization has been a trail of bloody footprints: stripping native Americans of their homeland, raping the earth, polluting the rivers and the skies and the soil. The history of business is a tale of child labor, robber barons, snake oil salesmen, and sweat shops. In the future, our history will tell of plant closings, nuclear accidents, toxic waste, and ozone depletion.

Business is destroying the earth: If that seems to you an inescapable conclusion, it is with good reason. But there are some today who suggest a surprising sequel to this tale of destruction. There are some who say business might be the last best hope of humanity.

If business has the power to destroy the earth, might it also have the power to heal it? If business has the ability to ruin human lives, might it also have the ability to save them?

From Inhuman to Human

The answer may be yes. From many sectors—inside and outside the corporation, among academics, activists, and New Age thinkers—there are signs that a new life-affirming paradigm is emerging for business. Just as physics is shifting paradigms of the physical world from matter to energy, and as medicine is shifting paradigms of health care from treatment to prevention, so too is a shift under way in business. It is a shift from the inhuman to the human or, in consultant Michael Ducey's phrase, "from jungle to community."

The new paradigm has to do with respect for the human resources in business, and the acknowledgment that workers aren't obedient automatons but team players. It concerns employees demanding jobs with substance and meaning, and with corporations beginning to offer flextime, day care, and worker ownership. The new paradigm has corporations taking a role in helping the schools, reducing pollution, or fighting illiteracy. And it means tougher community standards, with public outcry against animal testing, nuclear power, and business in South Africa. The new paradigm has to do, in short, with making a better world—and using business as a tool.

No, the millennium has not arrived. But there are signs that the way we think about business—and the way business thinks about itself—are beginning to change. . . .

It's respectable these days to be a good corporate citizen. When *Fortune* magazine ranks America's Most Admired Corporations each year, it uses a list of "Eight Key Attributes of Reputation." Right up there alongside "Financial Soundness" is "Community and Environmental Responsibility."

Even conservative *Forbes* shows a few signs of change. In its May 1988 cover story on "The 800 Most Powerful People in Corporate America," it used a headline that could have come straight from a New Age workshop: "Not power but empower." *Forbes* told readers, "The most efficient way to wield power is to democratize it." Describing its talks with powerful corporate leaders, the magazine reported: "These executives reached reflexively for words like 'participatory management,' 'collegiality,' and 'consensus-building' to describe what they do."

Remaking the World

Business in all its manifestations offers us as rich and important a way to improve ourselves and the world around us as does any institution. We go into business not merely to become rich, but to become who we are. We are not trying to make money, but we are attempting a much more important task: to remake our world. If we choose to do it in small, incremental, seemingly inconsequential ways, let us have the grace to know that that is how lasting change is effected.

Paul Hawken, Speech before the Commonwealth Club of California, October 23, 1987.

A more humane vocabulary seems to be entering the management lexicon. According to *Business Week's* April 1988 article on "Management for the 1990s," leadership today calls for "a new ingredient, caring." The magazine quoted one corporate chairman as saying, "The more you want people to have creative ideas and solve difficult problems, the less you can afford to manage them with terror.". . .

From inhuman to human. From jungle to community. A new corporate ethic may be gradually emerging—and it has to do with external as well as internal constituencies. Indeed, the very idea of a corporate "constituency" is being broadened to include the local community, the nation, even the earth itself.

"The terms of the contract between business and society are changing," Henry Ford II observed. "Now we are being asked to serve a wider range of human values and to accept an obligation to members of the public with whom we have no commercial transactions."

CFCs and Toy Guns

Du Pont seems to have been acting in that spirit, responding to its global constituency, when it decided to phase out the production of chlorofluorocarbons (CFCs), which destroy ozone. Similarly responsive moves were made by McDonald's, when it decided to eliminate styrofoam cartons made with CFCs, and by Toys "R" Us, when it decided to stop selling realistic toy guns. If operating from a jungle mentality—as many corporations still do—these companies might have dug in and refused to change, leaving society's problems to society. But operating from a community mindset, they realized that society's problems *are* their problems. . . .

The public welfare is increasingly becoming a private concern. We're accustomed to thinking that non-profit institutions do good, while profit-making companies are greedy and uncaring. But as futurist Hazel Henderson says, we're beginning to tear down the wall between the two. Non-profits are developing profit-making businesses to help themselves survive, while corporations are taking a greater hand in community welfare.

One example is the growing role of business in education. General Electric, the nation's largest defense contractor and the target of a national consumers boycott, spends $50,000 a year working with top students at a public school in New York's Spanish Harlem, helping its GE Scholars get into prestigious universities. The well-known Boston Compact—a pledge by Boston businesses to hire 1,000 graduates a year from inner-city schools—has added a new Compact Ventures program, providing remedial education and mentors for high school students in an effort to stem dropout rates.

Another area where public and private interests blend is in pollution cleanup. The public problem of hazardous waste has been solved in an ingenious way by the private company Marine Shale Processors, which turns toxic materials like paint solvent and chemicals into street paving. In a different approach, Detox Industries of Sugarland, Texas, has developed a method that breaks down polychlorinated biphenyls, or PCBs, biologically—using microorganisms. Even more elegantly, the Environmental Concern company restores native wetlands on the Atlantic Coast, building new marshes, reconstructing lost habitat, and planting vegetation.

Animal Testing

Outside of industry, there are further signs of change. Activists have brought nuclear power to a virtual standstill and successfully fought for animal rights. Revlon, Bausch & Lomb, and Clorox are among the companies now supporting research into alternatives to the Draize test, which calls for toxic substances to be tested on the eyes of rabbits. Colgate has reduced animal use 80 percent in six years, while Avon and Procter & Gamble have eliminated animal tests entirely. . . .

In the financial community, the field of socially responsible investing has grown geometrically, from $40 billion in investments in 1985 to 10 times that amount in 1989. It's been called the fastest growing new niche in the investing world—supporting some two dozen funds, a number of specialty newsletters, and a trade association called the Social Investment Forum.

"Beyond the fine starting salary, the job of poet laureate at this corporation also carries with it an excellent medical and dental plan."

Drawing by Ziegler; © 1988 The New Yorker Magazine, Inc.

Academia has shown a burgeoning interest in business ethics, with a growing number of universities offering required courses in the topic, several conferences being offered each year, and three dozen campus centers of ethics enjoying rising popularity. . . .

Tools for Social Change

All this activity on so many fronts adds up to an emerging new paradigm—a new picture of what's expected of business, and what's possible. It's a picture of workplaces that are healthy for employees, of corporate citizens who are powerful yet responsive, of companies that are tools for social change, and of a corporate community that is a humane presence on the earth. . . .

There's no denying that we live in a troubled world, and that the corporate community has had a hand in creating those troubles. With its soiled past and its powerful self-interest, business may never be a wholly reliable force for the public good. But in a search for the most powerful tool for social change in the world, the most effective lever available might just turn out to be business. It may be an unavoidable truth: Business is our last best hope.

4

VIEWPOINT

"Honesty, integrity, sympathy, charity, autonomy, respect for the moral and legal rights of others . . . have no intrinsic values for corporations."

Corporations Cannot Promote Social Justice

Martin Benjamin and Daniel A. Bronstein

Martin Benjamin, a philosophy professor at Michigan State University in East Lansing, is a specialist in ethics and social and political philosophy. Daniel A. Bronstein teaches environmental law and public health law at Michigan State. He is a specialist in government regulation. Corporations cannot promote social justice, Benjamin and Bronstein maintain in the following viewpoint, because profit is their primary goal. Society cannot expect corporations to be honest and charitable, they argue, for while these qualities have intrinsic value to individuals, they have no value to corporations.

As you read, consider the following questions:

1. How do corporate values differ from an individual's values, according to the authors?
2. What do Benjamin and Bronstein see as the only reason a corporation might have honesty as a company policy?
3. Why do the authors believe it is impossible to hold corporations to the same ethical standards that apply to individuals?

"Moral & Criminal Responsibility & Corporate Persons" by Martin Benjamin and Daniel A. Bronstein in *Corporations and Society: Power and Responsibility,* Warren J. Samuels and Arthur S. Miller, eds. (Greenwood Press, an imprint of Greenwood Publishing Group, Inc., Westport, CT, 1987), pp. 277-281. Copyright © 1987 by Warren J. Samuels and Arthur S. Miller. Reproduced with permission.

Although the concepts and categories of ethics may be applied to the conduct of corporations, there are important differences between the values and principles underlying corporate behavior and those underlying the actions of most individuals. Whereas the former are invariably teleological or based on furthering one or another basic overall goal, the latter usually include a number of nonteleological elements. As individuals, we are often concerned with integrity, autonomy, and responsibility even when they cannot be shown to further a basic goal such as overall happiness. We regard them as important and valuable in themselves and not simply as means to some other more basic ends. But a preoccupation with integrity, autonomy, and responsibility for their own sakes is morally questionable when ascribed to corporations or corporate persons.

Circumstances and Ethics

As formal organizations, corporations are "planned units, deliberately structured for the purpose of attaining specific goals," [according to Amitai Etzioni in *Modern Organizations,* 1964]. All activities of such organizations are determined by the extent to which they contribute to the realizations of particular goals. Thus decision making by a member of an organization, qua member, is determined and constrained by the organization's structure and purpose. As John Ladd has put it:

> When the official decides for the organization, his aim is (or should be) to implement the objectives of the organization *impersonally,* as it were. The decisions are made for the organization, with a view to its objectives and not on the basis of the personal interests or convictions of the individual official who makes the decision. This is the theory of organizational decision-making.

Therefore the conduct of a person within an organization is, as member of the organization, constrained by his or her particular role within it. The ethically right thing to do as a member of the organization is what is required by one's role; and one's role will be more or less fully determined by the organization's goals, its structure, and the prevailing circumstances.

As formal organizations, business corporations are distinguished by their particular goals, which include maximization of profits, growth, and survival. Providing goods and services is a means to this end. The following statement from the board of directors of the 3M Company is exemplary in this regard: "The objective of the 3M Company is to produce quality goods and services that are useful and needed by the public, acceptable to the public, and in the best interests of the global economy—and thereby to earn a profit which is essential to the perpetuation of the useful role of the company." These goals provide the raison d'être and ultimate ethical values of the 3M Company. Other things have ethical value only insofar as they are instrumental in furthering the ultimate goals. It is thus that honesty and keeping one's word in one's dealing with other members of the organization takes on considerable importance. Without them, overall efficiency and the realization of overall goals would be severely compromised.

Other People's Money

I am not impressed by corporate charity and cultural benefaction, which amount to executives playing Medici with other people's money. You wouldn't know, from the lavish parties corporate officers throw for themselves whenever they fund an art exhibit or a PBS [Public Broadcasting System] series, that it's not costing them a penny. The shareholders, who aren't invited, pick up the tab for the parties, too. There's a Catch-22 logic behind corporate charity. . . . It's good for the corporate image to be thought charitable; a good image is good for profits . . . therefore corporate charity is a justifiable expenditure of shareholders' money. But if it's actually a hard-nosed business decision, why give the corporation credit for generosity? In which case the syllogism unravels.

Michael Kinsley, *The Wall Street Journal*, February 19, 1987.

But to one inside an organization, honesty and keeping one's word in one's dealings with outsiders will be important only if they come under the heading of what Ladd calls "limiting operating conditions":

These are conditions that set the upper limits to an organization's operations, e.g., the scarcity of resources, of equipment, of trained personnel, legal restrictions, factors involving employee morale. Such conditions must be taken into account *as data,* so to speak, in organizational decision-making and planning. In this respect information about them is on a par logically with other information and planning utilized in decision-making, e.g., cost-benefit computations.

If, for example, a number of individuals (outsiders or even insiders) believe that a company's aggressively marketing infant formula in third world countries is morally wrong, the company is unlikely to be moved by moral arguments alone as long as what it is doing remains profitable. But if those opposed to the company's practice organize a highly effective boycott of the company's products, their moral views will soon enter into the company's deliberations indirectly as limiting operating conditions. They can, at this point, no more be ignored than a prohibitive increase in the costs of certain raw materials. They are acknowledged not as normative conditions but rather as factual constraints on the realization of the company's goals.

Similarly, if dishonesty with customers is likely to drive them away, a company's representatives ought to be honest—but not because honesty is of intrinsic value or importance. Rather it will be that honesty is the best policy for achieving the overall goal. "It is," as Ladd has pointed out, "fatuous to expect an industrial organization to go out of its way to avoid polluting the atmosphere or to refrain from making napalm bombs or to desist from wire-tapping on purely [noninstrumental] moral grounds. Such actions would be [from the standpoint of the logic of organizational behavior] irrational."

Thus honesty, integrity, sympathy, charity, autonomy, respect for the moral and legal rights of others, and so on, which are often valued for their own sake by individuals as individuals, have no intrinsic values for corporations or other formal organizations. And insofar as they remain true to their organizational roles, bureaucrats and "organization men [and women]" will take notice of these notions only as limiting operating conditions. Moral or legal considerations will be given serious consideration only insofar as it is necessary to do so to further the organization's basic goals. Unenforced or unenforceable legal rights, for example, will carry no weight with a corporation as such, but actual or threatened legal coercion cannot, from an organizational standpoint, rationally be ignored.

The basic principle of the criminal common law is that of *malum in se*, things that are "wrong in and of themselves," [from *Black's Law Dictionary*, 5th edition, 1983]. This immediately demonstrates a fundamental conflict. If corporations are by their nature end- or goal-directed legal persons, how can they acknowledge acts as wrong in and of themselves? If corporations are incapable of recognizing *malum in se*, is it possible to hold one criminally responsible for acts that if performed by a human person would result in criminal liability?

Responsibility for Illegal Acts

For a long time, the law has avoided this problem by the simple expedient of not attempting to hold corporations liable for *malum in se* crimes but only for *malum prohibitum* crimes. *Malum prohibitum* crimes are acts that are "wrong because they are forbidden," [from *Black's Law Dictionary*, 5th edition, 1983]. There is no difficulty in holding corporations responsible for such acts, since the dictates of a legal code are among the considerations (limiting operating conditions) that goal-directed entities must consider in attempting to achieve their aims.

Violations of the antitrust laws are the classic types of criminal cases for corporations. Other types of criminal violations that have been traditionally charged against corporations are violating governmentally mandated standards of workplace safety, antidiscrimination requirements, or environmental protection regulations; bribery of public officials; fraud; and misappropriation of property. . . .

A Corporation's Proper Role

The proper social role of the corporation is to produce the best peanut butter at the lowest price, leaving to individuals and to the political system such matters as support for the arts and how much we spend on defense. There's a lot to be said, even from a left-wing viewpoint, for the idea that corporations should keep to their own sphere and not attempt to become all-embracing social-service agencies.

Michael Kinsley, *The Wall Street Journal*, February 19, 1987.

The classic *malum in se* crimes are those specified in the Ten Commandments. Merely stating this should illustrate the problem. Can a corporation, as such, violate the Ten Commandments? Of particular interest in the light of some recent attempts to prosecute corporations for homicide is the question of the Fifth Commandment, "Thou shalt not kill." It would be very difficult, after all, to picture a corporation being prosecuted for, say, adultery.

The Ford Pinto

The first case of this type to achieve widespread public attention was the attempt to prosecute the Ford Motor Company for manslaughter as the result of alleged negligent or reckless decision making concerning the safety engineering of the Pinto vehicle. Although the defendant corporation and its officers were found innocent after trial, the case can serve as an exemplar for our purposes. In essence, the prosecution in this case attempted to show that the corporation had produced and distributed a vehicle that was known to be defective at the time of production and sale and that even after a great deal of additional information accumulated regarding the nature of the problems, the corporation took no action to correct them. The obvious noncorporate analogy would be the prosecution of a person who was driving a car with brakes known to be faulty, who does not have them repaired because it would cost too much, and who kills someone when the brakes eventually fail and the car does not stop in time. Such cases involving individuals are prosecuted and won regularly.

If, as we have argued, corporations have no concept of inherent right and wrong because they are exclusively goal-directed legal persons, can they be convicted in cases of this type, and what purpose would be served by such a conviction? Remember that we are talking only about the corporate entity itself—not its managers, agents, and owners who, as human persons, can be held to interpersonal standards of moral and legal responsibility. It is very difficult to argue for holding goal-directed entities to interpersonal standards; in fact, we do not believe it can be done.

Perhaps we can make a utilitarian argument for convicting corporations of such crimes. The argument would be that of deterrence; conviction and punishment would deter other corporations from taking similar actions under similar circumstances. An individual convicted of homicide for knowingly driving with faulty brakes could be sentenced to jail or fined. What, however, could have been done to Ford Motor Company had it been found guilty in the Pinto case? By the very nature of corporations, it could only have been fined; one cannot incarcerate a corporation. Were the charge a capital one, punishable by death, it would be possible to impose a similar penalty on a corporation; it could have its charter revoked so that it ceased to exist. There appears to be no middle ground for corporations; they can only be fined or "executed." Thus even on utilitarian grounds, there is a clear distinction between legal and human persons.

Penalties Are Ineffective

Moreover, there appears to be considerable evidence that deterrence does not work on corporations, even if, arguably, it works on individuals (a currently controversial subject). The newspapers regularly report on corporations being convicted of *malum prohibitum* crimes and fined in consequence. The penalties imposed do not appear to discourage other corporations from engaging in similar acts. The possibility of being discovered and the potential magnitude of the fine merely become more data to be included in the analysis of limiting conditions. The dispute about the deterrent effect of the death penalty on human persons is bitter and complicated; the potential deterrent effect of a death penalty for legal persons raises even more unresolved issues.

The fact is that corporations cannot be treated as persons under the criminal law despite the concept of legal personhood. Corporations are entirely goal directed in their nature and outlook; persons in ordinary morality and the criminal law are not.

"Schools should 'emphasize . . . the importance of truthfulness, temperance, purity, public spirit, and respect for honest labor of every kind.'"

Teaching Morality in Schools Can Promote Social Justice

Kathleen Kennedy Townsend

In the following viewpoint, Kathleen Kennedy Townsend argues that America is suffering because public schools are not teaching moral values. She contends that children are growing up without any desire to help the needy or to volunteer in their communities. Efforts at teaching morals have proven effective in the past, she contends, and can help to promote justice if implemented today. Townsend is the director of the Maryland Student Service Alliance, a state program designed to get students involved in community service.

As you read, consider the following questions:

1. Why does Townsend believe public schools have neglected to teach values?
2. How did New York City reduce its crime rate in the mid-1800s, according to Townsend?
3. What values did the California State Assembly consider unacceptable for teaching in the classroom, according to the author?

Kathleen Kennedy Townsend, "Not Just Read and Write, but Right and Wrong," *The Washington Monthly*, January 1990. Reprinted with permission from *The Washington Monthly*. Copyright by The Washington Monthly Company, 1611 Connecticut Ave. NW, Washington, DC 20009. (202) 462-0128.

In a suburban high school's crowded classroom, a group of juniors explained to me why drugs are difficult to control. "You see, Mrs. Townsend, what if you want a new pair of Reeboks? You could sell drugs and make $250 in an afternoon. It's a lot easier and quicker than working at McDonald's. You'd have to work there a whole week."

In my work helping teachers, I've walked into countless high schools where I could have filled a garbage bag with the trash in the halls. Yet I rarely hear teachers asking students to pick up the garbage—or telling them not to litter in the first place.

Of course, many students obey the law, stay away from drugs, and perform selfless acts: they tutor, work with the elderly, or run antidrug campaigns. But too many lack a sense of duty to a larger community.

A survey conducted for People for the American Way asked just over 1,000 Americans between 15 and 24 what goals they considered important. Three times as many selected career success as chose community service—which finished dead last. Only one-third said they could countenance joining the military or working on a political campaign. During one focus group interview for the study, some young people were asked to name qualities that make this country special. There was a long silence until one young man came up with an answer: "Cable TV."

The study concluded, "Young people have learned only half of America's story. . .[they] reveal notions of America's unique character that emphasize freedom and license almost to the complete exclusion of service or participation. . .they fail to perceive a need to reciprocate by exercising the duties and responsibilities of good citizenship."

Failure of Schools

While it is easy enough to blame this problem on the "me-ism" of the Reagan years, it's time to recognize that *it's also the result of deliberate educational policy*. One principal I know speaks for too many others. "Schools," she says, "cannot impose duties on the students. Students come from different backgrounds. They have different standards."

Twice since 1982 the Maryland Department of Education has sent our questionnaires to local education departments soliciting opinions about values education. The answers are typical of those found across the United States. Many respondents were indifferent, simply stating that values education is "inherent" in teaching. Other answers were more hostile: "Specific training in values is a new development which we do not consider essential," and "A special effort would cause trouble."

The consensus of the high school teachers and administrators participating in a curriculum workshop I ran last summer said it all: "Values—we can't get into that."

Schools across America have simply refused to take responsibility for the character of their students. They wash their hands of the teaching of virtue, doing little to create an environment that teaches children the importance of self-discipline, obligation, and civic participation. As one teacher training text says, "There is no right or wrong answer to any question of value."

Teaching What Is Right

Moral education *does* mean that students should be concerned not just about what will *work,* but about what is *right.* It means teaching them to ask: "Is it good?" Moral education also seeks to help students develop a responsible way of thinking, believing, *and* acting. It involves application, instead of mere information. It teaches living, not just by concepts, but by conscience.

Ernest L. Boyer, *Christianity Today,* September 22, 1989.

Is it any surprise that students tend to agree? These days it seems they're all relativists. A collection of high school interviews quotes one 11th-grader as saying, "What one person thinks is bad or wrong, another person might think that it is good or right. I don't think morals should be taught because it would cause more conflicts and mess up the student's mind." One of her classmates adds, "Moral values cannot be taught and people must learn what works for them. In other words, 'Whatever gets you through the night, it's alright.'"

Sensitivity Needed

Now, it's obvious that the public schools are a ticklish arena for instilling values. Our pluralistic society is justly worried about party lines of any kind. That means that teaching values in the schools—whether as an integral part of the traditional classes or as a separate course—requires subtle skills and real sensitivity to student and community needs. Of course, families and churches should play a part, but neither are as strong or effective as they were a generation ago. Only the schools are guaranteed to get a shot at kids. That's why their current fumbling of anything smacking of right and wrong is so disastrous.

The importance of teaching values in the schools was barely mentioned at the education summit presided over by George Bush at the University of Virginia. The meeting was dominated by talk of federal funding and drug education. The underlying valuelessness of American education—an obstacle to the intelligent use of scarce resources and a root cause of drug problems—really didn't come up.

Such a curious oversight at Thomas Jefferson's school!

Jefferson fought for public education because he believed that the citizen's virtue is the foundation of democracy. Only virtuous citizens, he knew, would resist private gain for the public good. And to know the public good, you have to study literature, philosophy, history, and religion.

For many years, Jefferson's wisdom about education prevailed. James Q. Wilson attributes America's low level of crime during the 19th century to the efforts of educators to instill self-discipline. "In the 1830s," he explains, "crime began to rise rapidly. New York had more murders than London, even though New York was only a tiny fraction of the size of London. However, rather than relying on police forces or other government programs, the citizens concentrated on education.

"Sunday schools were started. It was an all-day effort to provide education in morality, education in punctuality, in decency, in following rules, and accepting responsibility, in being generous, in being kind.

"The process was so successful that in the second half of the 19th century, despite urbanization, despite the enormous influx into this country of immigrants from foreign countries all over Europe, despite the widening class cleavages, despite the beginning of an industrial proletariat, despite all those things which textbooks today teach us cause crime to go up, crime went down. And it went down insofar as I, or any historian, can tell because this effort to substitute the ethic of self-control for what appeared to be the emerging ethic of self-expression succeeded." In 1830 the average American drank 10 gallons of distilled liquor a year. By 1850, it was down to two.

Basic Values

The flavor of this 19th-century approach to education is preserved today in many state constitutions. North Dakota's is typical in declaring that public schools should "emphasize all branches of knowledge that tend to impress upon the mind the importance of truthfulness, temperance, purity, public spirit, and respect for honest labor of every kind." In current educational jargon, this approach is called "values inculcation.". . .

In 1981 the California State Assembly considered a bill that spelled out values that should be included in public school instructional materials. Among those values were: honesty, acceptance of responsibility, respect for the individuality of others, respect for the responsibility inherent in being a parent or in a position of authority, the role of the work ethic in achieving personal goals, universal values of right and wrong, respect for property, the importance of the family unit, and the importance of respect for the law.

The bill was defeated.

How have we reached the point where a list of basic values like that is considered unsuitable for schools?. . .

The major criticism of not teaching values is very simple: There are some values that teachers should affirm. Not all values are the same. My daughter is the only girl on her soccer team, and recently some of the boys on the team spit at her. The coach shouldn't have the boys *justify* their actions. He should have them *stop*. He should make sure they know they were wrong. That's what he should do. What he actually did tells you a lot about the schools today. He did nothing.

"Abstract knowledge of right and wrong no more contributes to character than knowledge of physics contributes to bicycling."

Teaching Morality in Schools Cannot Promote Social Justice

Michael Levin

Michael Levin is a professor of philosophy at City College in New York City. In the following viewpoint, Levin contends that teaching morality in schools would be ineffective in fighting social injustice. Children learn values by living them, he argues, not by reading about them. Levin believes that teaching ethics is not only a waste of time, but also potentially harmful, since students could be confused by some of the moral dilemmas presented in the classroom.

As you read, consider the following questions:

1. Why do some Americans want students to study ethics, according to Levin?
2. According to the author, how can one make a child naturally honest?
3. What does Levin feel is the difficult part of doing good?

Let a stockbroker be arrested for shady dealing or a new medical procedure pose unanticipated dilemmas, and there arises a demand for a course in ethics. Law schools, medical schools, business schools—even high schools—are urged to stem a supposed flood immorality by instituting the study of right and wrong. Unfortunately, however, these ethics courses are an utterly pointless exercise.

The idea behind them is that anyone can be taught to distinguish right from wrong in much the way medical students are taught to distinguish the pancreas from the liver.

Case Studies Emphasized

In the typical course, the center of pedagogic gravity is the case study. May a poor man steal medicine for his ailing wife? Should the young mother of three or the productive scientist get the only dialysis machine? Having mastered moral distinctions from this regimen, the graduate is then supposed able to recognize (and resist) a dubious deal or an improper request from a superior.

But this whole exercise rests on a mistake about what makes people good. Moral behavior is the product of training, not reflection. As Aristotle stressed thousands of years ago, you get a good adult by habituating a good child to do the right thing. Praise for truth-telling and sanctions for fibbing will, in time, make him "naturally" honest.

Indeed, abstract knowledge of right and wrong no more contributes to character than knowledge of physics contributes to bicycling. The idea in both cases is to build the proper responses into nerve and sinew: Bicyclists don't have to think about which way to lean and honest men don't have to think how to answer under oath.

There is certainly a place for philosophical reflection on the existence and nature of values. But its practical significance is nil. Telling right from wrong in everyday life is not that hard; the hard part is overcoming laziness and cowardice to do what one perfectly well knows one should. As every parent learns, only good examples and apt incentives can induce that strength.

Pleasing the Parents

Psychologists have laboriously rediscovered the common sense observation that children first conceive morality as rules for pleasing their parents—only with the fullness of time comes a grasp of the idea of conscientious choice.

For this very reason, conscience cannot be hurried into being by exposing children to hard, unclear examples for which they are unready. Honesty may not always be the best policy, but telling a child as much only confuses him. To stick, morality must be taught as if absolute; life will supply the qualifications.

So ethics education carries more disquieting implications than merely the waste of everyone's time. The hard cases meant to shatter student complacency invariably involve conflict between conventional principles, such as property rights and life-saving in the case of the sick wife. Dwelling on these conflicts strongly suggests that conventional morality is incoherent and, consequently, not rationally binding. Ethics education thereby provides one more excuse for shirking one's plain duties.

Teacher Objections to Moral Education

Polls show that most teachers object to the concept of morality education on philosophical or practical grounds; many fear that such programs will stir up controversy in classrooms where diverse student bodies already cause plenty of headaches. Even districts that have printed values curricula and issued teaching materials at great expense find that such items often gather dust on teachers' shelves. . . .

Because of educators' opposition, New Hampshire has delayed implementing a values-education program. The Concord school board also has vowed to keep values education out of its schools. "This wipes out diversity and separation of church and state," Barbara Kuhlman Brown, vice president of the Concord school board, says. "It negates everything public schools stand for."

Using a hypothetical example, Ms. Brown says teachers worry how to respond if a student asks whether her father is a thief for bringing home pens from the office—and then another tells how his father, who loves him dearly and can't afford a bicycle, picked one up on the street for him. To what degree, she also asks, should teachers emphasize courage if a child wonders about rushing into a burning building to save someone?

Mark Beauvais, superintendent of the Concord district, adds, "It would be dangerous, sad and boring to have one view of morality imposed on our people."

Sonia L. Nazario, *The Wall Street Journal*, April 6, 1990.

Second, the examples typical of ethics education courses divert attention from the content of morality proper. Moral character does not require any particular stance on any public issue, be it pollution or apartheid. Honesty, industry and respect for others form the gyroscope that stabilizes an individual on his journey through life, not an itinerary of policy positions.

Yet ethics education, inspired as it is by public events, tends to focus on public action: How should profit be weighed against pollution? When may a government official blow the whistle?

These are interesting and difficult questions but are not likely to be faced by many people.

Less intriguing but cumulatively more important for the character of society are each day's micro-challenges, such as deciding whether to save a Christmas bonus or go on a spree.

A complex world does present special moral puzzles. But ethics educators risk being so many Poloniuses, adding nothing to the subjects they address while discrediting counsel itself.

> *"Volunteers see not only a moral challenge but also a tactical one: to do as much as possible with as little as possible, and then share the idea."*

Volunteers Can Promote Social Justice

Nancy Gibbs

In the following viewpoint, Nancy Gibbs contends that volunteers can often be more effective than government and corporations in promoting social justice. She describes many volunteers who have worked to alleviate the problems of the poor and the sick. Americans are more willing to volunteer than ever before, she claims, and this new spirit of compassion will help make the U.S. a better nation. Gibbs is a staff writer for *Time*, a weekly newsmagazine.

As you read, consider the following questions:

1. Why do poor families give more of their income to charity than rich families, according to Gibbs?
2. Why does the author believe so many Americans feel it is necessary for them to volunteer?
3. What impact does Gibbs think volunteers will have on the image of the 1980s as a decade during which Americans were self-centered?

Kenny spent his first two Christmases in the Harlem hospital where his mother abandoned him, in a roomful of babies with AIDS. His third Christmas he spent in an Albany children's home. There he had the luck to meet his first angel.

Gertrude Lewis spent her days driving a city bus and, every other Saturday, volunteering at the Albany home. "I saw this boy with these beautiful eyes," she recalls, "just looking up and smiling." She was 47 years old, had never married, never had a family of her own. She decided then and there she would become a foster mother.

Now Kenny lies in his crib upstairs in her home, in a house she shares on a tree-lined street, where her heart prepared him room. This nursery is merry with orange walls and pictures and 27 watchful stuffed animals. "It's going to be hard to lose him," says Gertrude.

What are we to make of a woman willing to take to heart a baby she knows is likely to die? Surely, she confounds all descriptions of the roaring '80s as a morally chintzy stretch of history, where such problems as Kenny's are greeted with more petulance than pity. In an age of toxic cynicism, Gertrude is a Samaritan: a woman who, in the spacious privacy of her life, went out of her way to help a child who needed her. She is not running for office, not running charity balls and not running away. Perhaps she seems a rare heroine at an end of a decade when the rich got greedier, the poor got needier and everyone else tended to his own shiny self-interest.

But the redeeming truth, to our own surprise, is that Gertrude is in vast company. Independent Sector, a Washington research and lobbying group, commissioned a Gallup poll to plumb the depths of our charity: What do we give, and why, and who does the giving, and how much? It turns out that almost half of all American adults offer their time to a cause, an astounding figure even allowing for the number of people who lie to pollsters. And most are giving more time than ever. These are commitments, not gestures. The average volunteer offers nearly five hours a week, for a total of 19.5 billion hours in 1987—the equal, roughly, of 10 million full-time employees. There is something infectious about mercy.

And so it is that George Bush looks out over the nation and raptly muses about a thousand points of light, savoring the phrase, if not quite understanding it. He did not add that the lights are shining into corners that have grown bleak and dim in the past eight years. And he got the numbers wrong. Out of sight of the Rose Garden, something like 80 million individuals are doing whatever they can to address the problems that politicians are fleeing.

243

Try to draw a profile of the typical do-gooder, and the only thing certain is that it is probably wrong. Volunteer work is not the sole province of the housewives holding Christmas fairs, the idle rich sponsoring benefits and the young selling cookies. The aggressive, entrepreneurial cast of much modern charity reflects the fact that the largest number of volunteers, according to a J.C. Penney survey, are between the ages of 35 and 49.

A Thousand Points of Light

I've spoken of a thousand points of light—of all the community organizations that are spread like stars throughout the nation doing good. We will work hand in hand, encouraging, sometimes leading, sometimes being led, rewarding. We will work on this in the White House, in the Cabinet agencies. I will go to the people and the programs that are the brighter points of light, and I'll ask every member of my Government to become involved. The old ideas are new again because they're not old, they are timeless: duty, sacrifice, commitment, and a patriotism that finds its expression in taking part and pitching in.

George Bush, *Inaugural Address*, January 20, 1989.

Certainly the most eager and conspicuous new recruits are the yuppies. Since they absorb much of the blame for the moral defoliation of the '80s, they deserve some recognition for their redemption. "We're trying to break the cycle of you get up, you go to work, step over a homeless person on the way to the subway, go to the gym, go to the sushi bar, go home and fall asleep," says Kenneth Adams, executive director of New York Cares, a sort of charitable clearinghouse for yuppies that has recruited 600 young volunteers to tutor dropouts, serve in soup kitchens, renovate housing and visit the elderly. "The Me generation is dying," says Adams, "and New York Cares is one example of how it's being put to rest." Call it yuppie love.

But even that is not the whole story. For all the flood of new professionals into charity work, more than a quarter of all volunteers still come from households with incomes of $20,000 or less. Families earning less than $10,000 a year give more of their income to charity than individuals earning more than $100,000. Since the less rich families in this country rub more intimately against its sores, they are often the first to offer their money and time. "You feel the pain, you feel the hurt," says Wilfred Schill, a North Dakota farmer who with his wife counsels couples who fear foreclosure. "It gives you the greatest incentive to do something like this."

Gallup's evidence defies our low expectations. We are, per-

244

haps, a little better than we think, though maybe not as good as we'd like. If 80 million adults are volunteering, then there may be 80 million impulses for doing so—whether political, professional, spiritual or personal. The precise mixture is measured from needs within and needs without. In the end, the decision to volunteer usually occurs at a crossroads, where moral indignation and moral responsibility meet.

In both the cities and the farmlands, the indignation of the moment is palpable. The Reagan Administration did not invent the poor, but it has largely ignored them. "We've dug deep pits in this country in the past eight years," says Tanya Tull, a Los Angeles housewife who founded Para Los Niños, a family-service facility on Skid Row. "People are falling into them—and we've taken away the ladders too." Reagan's policies, argues Marian Wright Edelman of the Children's Defense Fund, have "created a set of social problems that simply were not there in 1980. We're going to be paying for them for a long time."

Hence the sheer volume of volunteers: an overwhelming majority of Americans believe that charities are needed more now than they were just five or ten years ago. In New York City there are about 35,000 people living on the streets, compared with 500 a decade ago. AIDS, which alone has pulled thousands of people into action, did not exist. Crack, which has perhaps done more to ruin children than any other drug, did not exist. "Volunteerism is as old as the nation," says Winifred Brown, executive director of New York City's Voluntary Action Center, "and it's as new as today's headlines."

But it is not just that the needs are greater. In the minds of many Americans, the weight of moral responsibility shifted, publicly and dramatically, somewhere between Jimmy Carter's "malaise" days in 1979 and the Hands Across America hoopla of 1986. "Government has a lot of money but doesn't know how to take care of people," says banker Peter Flanigan, founder of the Student/Sponsor Partnership, which helps shepherd poor kids through Catholic schools in New York City. "That revives the latent feeling in people that they should do it themselves."

Democracy does demand shared responsibility, not only for our governance but for our welfare as well. Yet each generation weaves its own mythology of philanthropy. Ours in the '80s owes most to the lessons of the 1960s and the heady afternoons of the Great Society. For a time it looked as though Washington would take care of everything: it was government as governess. Caseworkers trooped through the ghettos and housing projects promising advocacy, access and opportunity for the dispossessed. For many, it was a dream that came true. But too often the army hunkered down into an occupying, rather than a liberating, force.

The lasting accomplishments of the Great Society have been challenged by some who believed in it deeply. But beginning in 1981, the very premises of activist government came under attack as Reagan lashed the "welfare queen" and extolled "neighborliness." By the time Charles Murray published *Losing Ground* in 1984, his argument that the War on Poverty had wounded more people than it had saved was poised to become conventional wisdom. "Whatever our political persuasion," says Independent Sector president Brian O'Connell, "we all understand the practical limitations of Big Government, and very often that means setting up alternative organizations."

The Age of Altruism

If the '80s were the Age of Avarice, then the '90s are shaping up as the Age of Altruism. From the White House on down, the message is clear: Get Involved.

Barbara Kantrowitz, *Newsweek*, July 10, 1989.

In place of a waning welfare state, Reagan promised that enterprise freed would bring prosperity for all. A surging economy with low inflation and high employment would do more to help the poor than a raft of welfare programs. As for solving the particular problems of the poor, that was best left to states and towns and, above all, individuals who knew better. This transfer of responsibility camouflaged the neglect of vital programs, particularly subsidized housing and programs for children. "When voluntary action is translated to national policy, it assumes that communities have the ability to pull themselves up by the bootstraps," observes Barry Checkoway, professor of social work at the University of Michigan. "Some of them don't even have boots."

One reason Reagan got away with the cuts was that he so cannily persuaded people that they could do it better themselves. And indeed, individuals began to step in the minute government backed off. "My personal motivation," says Talmage Newton III, 44, a St. Louis advertising executive who chairs Operation Food Search, an organization to distribute food to the poor, "was a belief that any citizens' group can perform any function better than any government, with the exception of national defense."

Reagan's vision of America not only altered what Americans expect of government; it also played deftly on what we expect from ourselves. We are all to some extent tending to our character, trying to turn efforts of will into habits of mind in the hope that generosity will one day come easily. People of all faiths find in charity a chance for thanks, praise and obedience. "What doth the Lord require of thee," asks Micah, "but to do justly, and to love mercy, and to walk humbly with thy God?" To borrow from the Quakers, many volunteers believe that when the worship is over, the service begins.

To be sure, there are also plenty of self-serving reasons to serve: glamour seeking, résumé padding and networking. "There is usually an opening in your life when you decide to volunteer," says Core Trowbridge, 26, volunteer coordinator for TreePeople in Los Angeles. "Young people come here, treating this as a singles' scene. Old people who've retired but not run out of energy come." But when researchers inquire further into motives, the most common reason cited is a desire to do something useful. To comfort a child, succor a patient, rescue a school or salvage a neighborhood gives volunteers a sense of success that few jobs can match. The chance to create and control a daring solution is irresistible and restorative. Attorney Tom Petersen is on leave from the Dade County state attorney's office to establish, among other community programs, Teen Cuisine, which teaches culinary skills to teenage mothers. "We discovered almost by accident," he says, "that creative economic incentives can be much more effective in changing the girls' behavior than traditional counseling."

That sparkle of individual ingenuity sets many new volunteer efforts apart from the huge corporate rescue missions that define much American charity. While the United Way, the American Red Cross and the American Cancer Society serve vast needs and do great good, they are to charity what GM is to industry. Charity too needs its entrepreneurs, dreaming on a different scale, and perhaps genius ripens most fruitfully in a free and private space. That may explain why 105,000 new service organizations were born between 1982 and 1987. "Volunteers are now expected to *solve* problems," says Jerri Spoehel of the Volunteer Center of San Fernando Valley, Calif., "not just stuff envelopes."

When, as now, there is hope ready for harvesting, excellent ideas become especially fertile. The examples of some national heroes—Candy Lightner, founder of Mothers Against Drunk Driving . . . and Eugene Lang, whose I Have a Dream program has spawned innumerable imitations—all proved what extraordinary good can be reaped from one person's crusade. Faced with a desperate need, many new volunteers see not only a moral challenge but also a tactical one: to do as much as possible with as little as possible, and then share the idea, to allow it to spread.

Take Chris Renner, 26, who helped create Food Partnership Inc. outside Los Angeles. It troubled him that food banks were spending a fortune in transport fees to collect donations. With the help of the California Trucking Association and United Way, he worked out a method for trucks to transport food between donors and food banks when they were returning empty from a long haul. So far, the program has carried nearly 4 million lbs. of food and saved the food banks $55,000 in trucking fees.

Or Pedro José Greer, a Miami physician who found his calling not only in hospitals but also under bridges and highways, where many of the city's homeless live. Four years ago, "Dr. Joe," 32, opened a clinic next to a shelter called Camillus House. He now has 130 volunteer doctors and medical personnel working on 40 patients a day. "There is so much talent among the poor, we must help them no matter what," he says. "We lose so much when we lose the people from the inner cities." At the University of Miami medical school, where he is a fellow in hepatology, there is a three-month waiting list for the "homeless elective" for medical students.

Or Suzanne Firtko, an architectural historian in New York City who invented the Street Sheet, instructions that direct homeless people to the nearest soup kitchens and clothes banks. She persuaded Du Pont to donate waterproof, tear-resistant paper, and designed the sheets with easy-to-understand graphics so the disoriented and illiterate could use them. The entire operation that first year cost $1,800. "Projects like mine become very expensive when they're done by established agencies," she says. "It's very cheap when you're doing it at your kitchen table."

The efforts of American Samaritans, in short, reflect a new frame of mind in which sympathy complements competence but does not replace it: wide-eyed but hard-nosed. Private charity cannot and should not replace public policy. It can, however, set standards, set priorities and set an example for the best use of resources. Throwing money at a problem may be just the easiest way to attack it, not the wisest. The more effective forces, it seems, are harder to marshal: vision, tenacity, patience and courage.

In the Bible, Samaritans were viewed with contempt until Jesus' tale of how one of their community showed great mercy to a stranger redeemed them for history. Perhaps the generation that closes the millennium will find the same vindication. The unheralded gestures of gracious individuals may in the end outlast and belie the labels hung on the Me generation. And government, in the meantime, could take some lessons from the most creative of these very private enterprises. Good ideas need money and leadership as well as light and oxygen to brighten and spread. In the process, we might even discover that this is already a kinder, gentler nation than we ever imagined.

Understanding Words in Context

Readers occasionally come across words they do not recognize. And frequently, because they do not know a word or words, they will not fully understand the passage being read. Obviously, the reader can look up an unfamiliar word in a dictionary. By carefully examining the word in the context in which it is used, however, the word's meaning can often be determined. A careful reader may find clues to the meaning of the word in surrounding words, ideas, and attitudes.

Below are excerpts from the viewpoints in this chapter. In each excerpt, one of the words is printed in italics. Try to determine the meaning of each word by reading the excerpt. Under each excerpt you will find four definitions for the italicized word. Choose the one that is closest to your understanding of the word.

Finally, use a dictionary to see how well you have understood the words in context. It will be helpful to discuss with others the clues that helped you decide on each word's meaning.

1. Disintegrating families and *RAMPANT* childhood poverty are destroying the U.S. To remain a world leader, the U.S. must combat these growing problems.

   RAMPANT means:

   a) widespread   b) minimal
   c) restrained   d) false

2. State and federal governments try to *ALLOCATE* tax money fairly so all social service programs receive an adequate share.

   ALLOCATE means:

   a) collect   b) distribute
   c) steal   d) refuse

3. When child-care advocates describe it, the issue of child-care benefits appears *INNOCUOUS*. Child-care benefits, however, could speed the breakdown of the American family.

INNOCUOUS means:

a) painful   b) important
c) harmless   d) tiresome

4. In both the cities and the farmlands, the *INDIGNATION* is obvious. The American people are upset about social problems created by the selfish policies of the previous administration.

INDIGNATION means:

a) joy   b) tolerance
c) surprise   d) anger

5. To prevent the public from recognizing that welfare programs were being cut, the federal government made private groups responsible for taking care of the poor. This *CAMOUFLAGED* the problem of growing poverty as well as the governments' cuts in social service.

CAMOUFLAGED means:

a) exposed   b) helped
c) concealed   d) understood

6. Only one-third of surveyed high school students said they could *COUNTENANCE* joining the military or working on a political campaign. The other two-thirds would not accept jobs in the military or politics.

COUNTENANCE means:

a) tolerate   b) advocate
c) deplore   d) enjoy

7. A child who is *HABITUATED* to do what is right will grow up to be a good adult. Praise for truth-telling and punishment for lying will, in time, make the child naturally honest.

HABITUATED means:

a) bribed   b) stimulated
c) accustomed   d) ordered

8. Students' comfortable and unquestioned assumptions may prevent them from fully understanding issues. Teens' *COMPLACENCY* can be shattered by making them confront hard ethical dilemmas.

COMPLACENCY means:

a) ignorance   b) interest
c) carefulness   d) self-satisfaction

Periodical Bibliography

The following articles have been selected to supplement the diverse views presented in this chapter.

Trevor Armbrister
"When Companies Care," *Reader's Digest,* April 1989.

Ernest L. Boyer
"The Third Wave of School Reform," *Christianity Today,* September 22, 1989.

Joseph Duffy
"Reconstituting America Through National Service," *Vital Speeches of the Day,* July 19, 1989.

Clark Kent Ervin
"Volunteerism: A Grass Roots Alternative to the Welfare State," *The Heritage Lectures,* no. 260, June 28, 1989. Available from The Heritage Foundation, 214 Massachusetts Ave. NE, Washington, DC 20002.

Richard D. Hylton
"Social Ventures," *Mother Jones,* July/August 1989.

Jack Kemp
"An Inquiry into the Nature and Causes of Poverty in America and How to Combat It," *The Heritage Lectures,* no. 263, June 6, 1990. Available from The Heritage Foundation, 214 Massachusetts Ave. NE, Washington, DC 20002.

Michael Kinsley
"Companies as Citizens: Should They Have a Conscience?" *The Wall Street Journal,* February 19, 1987.

Robert Kuttner
"U.S. Business Isn't About to Be Society's Savior," *Business Week,* November 6, 1989.

Frances Moore Lappé, interviewed by Bob Blanchard and Susan Watrous
"Interview with Frances Moore Lappé," *The Progressive,* February 1990.

Nicholas Lemann
"The Unfinished War," *The Atlantic Monthly,* Part I, December 1988; Part II, January 1989.

Thomas Lickona
"How Parents and Schools Can Work Together to Raise Moral Children," *Educational Leadership,* May 1988.

Anne Matthews
"The Thoughts That Count," *Forbes,* February 20, 1989.

Ralph Nader and Mark Green
"Passing On the Legacy of Shame," *The Nation,* April 2, 1990.

Sonia L. Nazario
"Schoolteachers Say It's Wrongheaded to Try to Teach Students What's Right," *The Wall Street Journal,* April 6, 1990.

Organizations to Contact

The editors have compiled the following list of organizations that are concerned with the issues debated in this book. All of them have publications or information available for interested readers. The descriptions are derived from materials provided by the organizations. This list was compiled upon the date of publication. Names and phone numbers of organizations are subject to change.

American Association for Affirmative Action (AAAA)
Emory University
101 Administration Building
Atlanta, GA 30307
(404) 329-6017

The AAAA is a group of equal opportunity and affirmative action officers. The Association serves as a liaison with federal, state, and local agencies involved with ensuring that businesses comply with equal opportunity laws. The organization publishes a quarterly newsletter, the *American Association for Affirmative Action Newsletter.*

American Bar Association (ABA)
750 N. Lake Shore Drive
Chicago, IL 60611
(312) 988-5000

The ABA, the foremost legal organization in the U.S., works to improve the civil and criminal justice systems. It also seeks to improve public access to legal services. The ABA conducts research and educational programs. It publishes the *ABA Newsletter* and *American Bar Association Journal.*

American Civil Liberties Union (ACLU)
132 W. 43rd St.
New York, NY 10036
(212) 944-9800

The ACLU champions the human rights set forth in the U.S. Declaration of Independence and the Constitution. It works for minority, poor, and women's rights. It publishes a variety of newsletters, including *Civil Liberties Report*, and research papers.

The American Enterprise Institute for Public Policy Research (AEI)
1150 17th St. NW
Washington, DC 20036
(202) 862-5800

AEI is a conservative think tank that analyzes national and international economic, political, and social issues. It publishes the monthly *AEI Economist* and the bimonthly *Public Opinion*, as well as numerous papers and books.

American Judicature Society
25 E. Washington St., Suite 1600
Chicago, IL 60602
(312) 558-6900

The Society is a group of lawyers, judges, law teachers, and government officials that promotes effective justice and combats court delays. The Society conducts research, offers a consulting service, and publishes the magazine *Judicature.*

The Brookings Institution
1775 Massachusetts Ave. NW
Washington, DC 20036
(202) 797-6000

The Institution, founded in 1927, is a liberal think tank that conducts research and education on economics and government issues. It publishes *The Brookings Review,* quarterly, and the *Brookings Papers on Economic Activities,* twice a year.

Catalyst
250 Park Ave. S
New York, NY 10002-1459
(212) 777-8900

Catalyst is a national research and advisory organization that helps corporations foster the careers and leadership capabilities of women. It publishes a wide variety of reference materials, including *Beyond the Transition: The Two-Gender Work Force and Corporate Policy* and *New Roles for Men and Women.* It also publishes a *Career Series* for women who are searching for their first jobs, and a monthly newsletter, *Perspective.*

Cato Institute
224 Second St. SE
Washington, DC 20003
(202) 546-0200

The Institute sponsors programs designed to help scholars and laypersons analyze public policy questions. It works to extend the social and economic freedoms of the capitalist system and conducts research on poverty, immigration, and economics. In addition to the monthly publications *Policy Report* and the *Cato Journal,* the Institute publishes books, including *Gender and Equity,* which debates the issue of comparable worth.

Center for the American Woman and Politics (CAWP)
Eagleton Institute of Politics
Rutgers University
New Brunswick, NJ 08901
(201) 828-2210

CAWP is a clearinghouse for women in politics and government. It disseminates information about the backgrounds, status, and impact of women legislators; holds conferences and seminars about women in American politics; underwrites grants for specific, related projects; and takes surveys on women's issues. Members of the organization have published books, monographs, and reports, including *Women as Candidates in American Politics, In the Running: The New Woman Candidate, Women Make a Difference,* and *Woman's Routes to Elective Office: A Comparison with Men's.*

Center of Concern
3700 13th St. SE
Washington, DC 20017
(202) 635-2757

The Center analyzes social and public policy. It works to promote peace and justice through education and discussion. The Center holds consultative status with the United Nations and has participated in UN conferences on international social policy, population, food, women's rights, trade, the environment, unemployment, and international debt. The Center publishes a monthly newsletter, *Center Focus*, as well as books like *Social Analysis: Linking Faith and Justice*, videotapes, and educational material.

Center for Women Policy Studies
2000 P St. NW, Suite 508
Washington, DC 20036
(202) 872-1770

The Center was founded in 1972 and was the first national policy institute focused on women's rights. The organization fights for equal education and job training for women and for reproductive rights laws. The Center publishes papers, including *The SAT Gender Gap: Identifying the Causes*, and *Legal Help for Battered Women*.

Congress of Racial Equality (CORE)
1457 Flatbush Ave.
Brooklyn, NY 11210
(718) 434-3580

The Congress on Racial Equality works to promote civil liberties and social justice. CORE is a human rights organization that seeks to establish true equality and self-determination for all people regardless of race, creed, sex, age, disability, religious or ethnic background. CORE publishes pamphlets and press releases; its national chairperson publishes a column in the *New York Voice*; and the organization publishes a yearly magazine, *CORE Magazine*.

Disability Rights Education and Defense Fund
1616 P St. NW, Suite 100
Washington, DC 20036
(202) 328-5185

The Fund is a national law and policy center devoted to furthering the civil rights of people with disabilities. It promotes the full integration of disabled people into the mainstream of American society. To further that end, the organization provides information about disability-rights laws and policies. It also provides legal advocacy to parents of children with disabilities, including AIDS, to help them find acceptable schools. The Fund publishes *Disability Rights*, a monthly newsletter.

Eagle Forum
PO Box 618
Alton, IL 62002
(618) 462-5415

Eagle Forum is dedicated to preserving traditional family values based on Scripture. It opposes all anti-family, anti-morality, and anti-life programs. It publishes the *Phyllis Schlafly Report*.

Family Research Council
601 Pennsylvania Ave. NW
Washington, DC 20004
(202) 393-2100

The Council is a division of the organization Focus on the Family. It is a conservative social policy research, lobbying, and educational organization. The Council supports pro-family government policies that keep mothers at home with their children. It publishes a monthly newsletter, *Washington Watch*.

Focus on the Family
Pomona, CA 91799
(714) 620-8500

Focus on the Family believes the family is the most important social unit. It believes that homelessness, teen sexuality and pregnancy, and drug abuse are linked to the dissolution of families in the U.S. This group maintains that reestablishing the traditional two-parent family will end many social problems. The organization conducts research and education programs. It publishes *Focus on the Family Citizen, Clubhouse, Breakaway, Family Policy,* and *Research Developments*.

The Heritage Foundation
214 Massachusetts Ave. NE
Washington, DC 20002
(202) 546-4400

The Foundation is a public policy research institute. It supports competitive free enterprise as the basis for a viable world economy. The organization publishes papers on social policy, recent legislation, affirmative action, and comparable worth. It publishes the quarterly journal *Policy Review*, the periodic *Backgrounder,* and the periodic *Heritage Lectures*.

Leadership Conference Education Fund (LCEF)
2027 Massachusetts Ave. NW
Washington, DC 20036
(202) 667-6243

The Fund is a research and education organization that works to strengthen civil rights in the U.S. LCEF publishes a quarterly newsletter, *Civil Rights Monitor*.

The Lincoln Institute for Research and Education
1001 Connecticut Ave. NW
Washington, DC 20036
(202) 223-5110

The Lincoln Institute is an organization that studies public policy issues that affect the lives of black Americans. It maintains that a free-market economy and minimal government interference will improve the lives of blacks most effectively. The Institute sponsors conferences and publishes the *Lincoln Review*.

Male Liberation Foundation (MLF)
701 NE 67th St.
Miami, FL 33138
(305) 756-6249

MLF is a men's liberation organization that works to counteract feminist influence. The Foundation attempts to stop the escalating divorce rate, to make men aware that women now hold more power and money than men, to motivate young men to achieve the career success that young women have, and to support women who are housewives. MLF also opposes all affirmative action legislation. The Foundation publishes a newsletter and a book titled *The First Book on Male Liberation and Sex Equality*.

Minority Rights Group (MRG)
35 Claremont Ave., Box 4S
New York, NY 10027
(212) 864-7986

MRG, based in London, has chapters in ten countries throughout the world. The Group is dedicated to reducing human rights violations and to securing justice for minority groups. MRG fights for refugees, migrant workers, oppressed women and children, and for an end to destructive ethnic and religious conflicts. It has published many reports on minority problems, including reports on racism, the treatment of refugees, and Native Americans in the U.S. MRG publishes the *Newsletter*, bimonthly, as well as reports.

National Association for the Advancement of Colored People (NAACP)
4805 Mt. Hope Drive
Baltimore, MD 21215
(301) 358-8900

The NAACP's purpose is to achieve equal rights for all and to end racial prejudice by removing discrimination in housing, employment, voting, schools, and the courts. The Association publishes a variety of newsletters, books, and pamphlets, and the monthly magazine, *Crisis*.

National Association for the Advancement of White People (NAAWP)
Box 10655
New Orleans, LA 70181

The NAAWP strives to promote equal rights for all, including white people, and special favor for none. The Association aims to end affirmative action programs, busing and forced integration, and anti-white racism. It works to limit immigration, reform welfare programs, and preserve the heritage of whites. The Association frequently publishes the newsletters *NAAWP News* and *NAAWP Program*.

National Center for Neighborhood Enterprise
1367 Connecticut Ave. NW
Washington, DC 20036
(202) 331-1103

The National Center for Neighborhood Enterprise attempts to advance the economic self-sufficiency of black Americans. It works to reverse the dependence of many blacks on government programs and advocates strategies based on a spirit of free enterprise and individual initiative. The Center publishes books, including *On the Road to Economic Freedom* and *Entrepreneur Enclaves*.

National Committee on Pay Equity (NCPE)
1201 16th St. NW, Suite 420
Washington, DC 20036
(202) 822-7304

NCPE members are labor, civil rights, and women's organizations, as well as religious, professional, education, and legal associations. The Committee works to eliminate wage discrimination. The organization sponsors research and conducts polls. It publishes the position papers *The Wage Gap* and *Pay Equity: An Issue of Race, Ethnicity, and Sex*, and a newsletter, *Newsnotes*.

National Council for Research on Women
Sara Delano Roosevelt Memorial House
47-49 E. 65th St.
New York, NY 10021

The Council is a network of organizations representing the academic community, policymakers, and others interested in women's issues. It conducts research and education programs, and acts as a clearinghouse. It publishes reports and an annually updated compilation called *Opportunities for Research and Study*. The organization also publishes a quarterly newsletter, *Women's Research Network News*, in addition to books and reports, including *Women in Academe: Progress and Prospects*.

National Lawyers Guild (NLG)
55 Avenue of the Americas, Third Floor
New York, NY 10013
(212) 966-5000

The NLG is a group of lawyers, law students, and legal professionals that works for economic justice and social equality. It publishes the *National Lawyers Guild Bulletin, Guild Notes*, and the *Guild Practitioner*.

Rockford Institute
934 N. Main St.
Rockford, IL 61103-7061
(815) 964-5053

The Institute works to return America to Judeo-Christian values and supports traditional roles for men and women. It maintains that mothers who work or place their children in child care harm their children. It publishes a newsletter, *Main Street Memorandum;* a monthly periodical, *The Family in America;* and a supplement, *New Research*.

Socialist Party, USA
516 W. 25th St., #404
New York, NY 10001
(212) 691-0776

The Socialist Party, USA is an alternative political party that advocates a socialist economy and a democratic government. The party promotes equal opportunities for women, lesbians and gay men, and ethnic minorities. The organization publishes pamphlets about the party as well as a monthly magazine, *The Socialist*.

VERA Institute of Justice
377 Broadway
New York, NY 10013
(212) 334-1300

VERA advocates a more effective and fairer criminal justice system. It conducts a variety of research projects and publishes the books *Further Work in Criminal Justice* and *Felony Arrests: Their Prosecution and Disposition*.

Young America's Foundation
11800 Sunrise Valley Drive, Suite 808
Reston, VA 22091
(703) 620-5270

The Foundation is a youth organization that supports free enterprise and a strong national defense. The organization maintains that programs designed to help minorities actually harm them. It publishes papers and pamphlets on economics, the Constitution, and minority issues, including *The State Against Blacks*.

Bibliography of Books

Teresa Amott and Julie Matthaei — *Race, Gender, and Work: A Multi-Cultural Economic History of Women in the United States.* Boston: South End Press, 1990.

David L. Bazelon — *Questioning Authority.* New York: Alfred A. Knopf, 1988.

Mary Frances Berry — *Why ERA Failed.* Bloomington: Indiana University Press, 1986.

Roger Betsworth — *Social Ethics: An Examination of American Moral Tradition.* Louisville, KY: Westminster/John Knox Press, 1990.

Ellen Boneparth and Emily Stoper, eds. — *Women, Power, and Policy.* New York: Pergamon Press, 1988.

Stuart Butler and Anna Kondratas — *Out of the Poverty Trap.* New York: Free Press, 1987.

Janet Saltzman Chafetz — *Gender Equity.* Newbury Park, CA: Sage Publications, 1990.

Harold W. Cruse — *Plural but Equal: Blacks & Minorities in America's Plural Society.* New York: William Morrow, 1987.

Nicholas Davidson — *The Failure of Feminism.* Buffalo, NY: Prometheus Books, 1988.

Nicholas Davidson — *Gender Sanity.* Lanham, MD: University Press of America, 1989.

John R. Edwards — *Positive Discrimination, Social Justice, and Social Policy.* New York: Tavistock, 1987.

David Ellwood — *Poor Support: Poverty in the American Family.* New York: Basic Books, 1988.

Sara M. Evans and Barbara J. Nelson — *Wage Justice: Comparable Worth and the Paradox of Technocratic Reform.* Chicago: University of Chicago Press, 1988.

James Fallows — *More Like Us.* Boston: Houghton Mifflin, 1989.

Victor R. Fuchs — *Women's Quest.* Cambridge, MA: Harvard University Press, 1988.

Maggie Gallagher — *Enemies of Eros.* Chicago: Bonus Books, 1989.

Nathan Glazer — *The Limits of Social Policy.* Cambridge, MA: Harvard University Press, 1988.

Robert A. Goldwin — *Why Blacks, Women, and Jews Are Not Mentioned in the Constitution, and Other Unorthodox Views.* Washington, DC: American Enterprise Institute, 1990.

258

Robert A. Goldwin and Art Kaufman, eds.	*Slavery and Its Consequences: The Constitution, Equality, and Race.* Washington, DC: American Enterprise Institute, 1988.
Robert A. Goldwin and William A. Schambra, eds.	*The Constitution, the Courts, and the Quest for Justice.* Washington, DC: American Enterprise Institute, 1989.
Cynthia Harrison	*On Account of Sex.* Berkeley: University of California Press, 1988.
Robert H. Haveman	*Starting Even: An Equal Opportunity Program to Combat the Nation's New Poverty.* New York: Simon & Schuster, 1988.
Virginia Held	*Rights and Goods: Justifying Social Action.* Chicago: University of Chicago Press, 1989.
Sylvia Ann Hewlett	*A Lesser Life: The Myth of Women's Liberation.* New York: William Morrow, 1986.
Kenneth Karst	*Belonging to America: Equal Citizenship and the Constitution.* New Haven, CT: Yale University Press, 1989.
Michael B. Katz	*The Undeserving Poor.* New York: Pantheon Books, 1989.
Mel King	*Chain of Change: Struggles for Black Community Development.* Boston: South End Press, 1990.
Israel Kirzner	*Discovery, Capitalism, and Distributive Justice.* Cambridge, MA: Basil Blackwell, 1989.
Frances Moore Lappé	*Rediscovering America's Values.* New York: Ballantine Books, 1989.
Michael Levin	*Feminism and Freedom.* New Brunswick, NJ: Transaction Books, 1987.
Charles Lockhart	*Gaining Ground: Tailoring Social Programs to American Values.* Berkeley: University of California Press, 1989.
Catharine A. MacKinnon	*Toward a Feminist Theory of the State.* Cambridge, MA: Harvard University Press, 1989.
Manning Marable	*How Capitalism Underdeveloped Black America.* Boston: South End Press, 1990.
Charles Murray	*In Pursuit: Of Happiness and Good Government.* New York: Simon & Schuster, 1989.
John Naisbitt and Patricia Aburdene	*Megatrends 2000.* New York: William Morrow, 1990.
Susan Moller Okin	*Justice, Gender, and the Family.* New York: Basic Books, 1989.
Marvin Olasky	*Freedom, Justice, and Hope: Toward a Strategy for the Poor and the Oppressed.* Westchester, IL: Crossway Books, 1987.

Michael Novak	*The Limits of Social Policy.* Cambridge, MA: Harvard University Press, 1989.
Ellen Frankel Paul	*Equal Opportunity.* New York: Basil Blackwell, 1987.
Vicky Randall	*Women and Politics: An International Perspective.* Chicago: University of Chicago Press, 1987.
Deborah Rhode	*Justice and Gender: Sex Discrimination and the Law.* Cambridge, MA: Harvard University Press, 1989.
David R. Riemer	*The Prisoners of Welfare: Liberating America's Poor from Unemployment and Low Wages.* New York: Praeger Publishers, 1988.
Warren J. Samuels and Arthur S. Miller	*Corporations and Society.* Westport, CT: Greenwood Press, 1987.
Lisbeth Schorr with Daniel Schorr	*Within Our Reach: Breaking the Cycle of Disadvantage.* New York: Anchor/Doubleday, 1988.
Anita Shreve	*Women Together, Women Alone.* New York: Viking Press, 1989.
Ruth Sidel	*On Her Own: Growing Up in the Shadow of the American Dream.* New York: Viking Press, 1990.
John Silbur	*Straight Shooting: What's Wrong with America and How to Fix It.* New York: Harper & Row, 1989.
Gerry Spence	*With Justice for None: Destroying an American Myth.* New York: Times Books, 1989.
T.M. Thomas and Jesse Levitt	*Justice: Interdisciplinary and Global Perspectives.* Lanham, MD: University Press of America, 1988.
Marilyn Waring	*If Women Counted.* New York: Harper & Row, 1988.
Ronald C. White Jr.	*Liberty and Justice for All.* New York: Harper & Row, 1990.
Walter E. Williams	*All It Takes Is Guts: A Minority View.* Washington, DC: Regnery Gateway, 1987.
William Julius Wilson	*The Truly Disadvantaged: The Inner City, the Underclass, and Public Policy.* Chicago: University of Chicago Press, 1987.
Bruce Wright	*Black Robes, White Justice.* Secaucus, NJ: Lyle Stuart Inc., 1987.

Index